WRITE YOURSELF

Creative Writing and Personal Development

Gillie Bolton

Foreword by Nicholas F. Mazza

Jessica Kingsley *Publishers*
London and Philadelphia

First published in 2011
by Jessica Kingsley Publishers
116 Pentonville Road
London N1 9JB, UK
and
400 Market Street, Suite 400
Philadelphia, PA 19106, USA

www.jkp.com

Copyright © Gillie Bolton 2011
Foreword copyright © Nicholas F. Mazza 2011

Library of Congress Cataloging in Publication Data
A CIP catalog record for this book is available from the Library of Congress

British Library Cataloguing in Publication Data
A CIP catalogue record for this book is available from the British Library

ISBN 978 1 84905 110 1

Printed and bound in Great Britain by the MPG Books Group

Contents

Part Three: How to Run Groups; Conclusion

Foreword

Sometimes we write to survive, perhaps to gain some sense of control during turbulent times. Sometimes we write to remember, perhaps to cope with life transitions that always involve loss. Sometimes we write for discovery, perhaps inspired by person or place and seeking to grow. Sometimes we just write. In this remarkable book, through selected research, practitioner/scholar contributions, vignettes and compelling exercises, the reader has the opportunity to prevail in affirming what matters most, the human connection to person, place and spirit.

The place of writing in therapeutic, educational and personal growth capacities has received significant attention in the expressive arts therapies, most notably poetry therapy, which focuses on language, symbol and story. Creative and focused writing has also received attention as a therapeutic agent in a number of clinical theories, particularly narrative, humanistic and cognitive-behavioural approaches to practice. Beyond professional capacities, survivors of community tragedies have often turned to writing and art as an emotional release, a way of connecting with each other, and honouring the memory of deceased loved ones.

Gillie Bolton, drawing upon her more than 25 years of experience in developing reflective and therapeutic writing, has demonstrated a keen understanding of the process and power of creative and expressive writing to effect growth and healing. Other scholars in the allied helping and educational professions have provided qualitative and quantitative evidence on the health aspects (as well as the dangers) of expressive writing. Building on selected sources of support in the literature,

Bolton's primary focus is on the applied (practical) aspects of writing for personal development. Identifying and discussing multiple writing forms (e.g. poetry, fiction, blogs, autobiography), this book covers a wide range of client concerns, settings and practice modalities (individual, group, community). The practical elements and theoretical/philosophical discussion provided in this book serve to advance the reader's continued learning and growth. For those involved in research, the precise exercises and practice descriptions can be subjected to disciplined investigation. For the therapist and educator, the many methods and guidelines add to his or her professional repertoire and serve as a reminder of the importance of critical and creative thinking. For the writer/poet, all of the above and more.

This book by Gillie Bolton is a celebration and call to the place of writing (both personally and professionally) in our life journey. *Gratefully Unfinished* is the common element in creative writing, therapy, education and community development. A special thanks to Gillie Bolton for providing another compelling reminder to keep on responding to and creating literature. We keep on facing life changes. We keep on learning. It's a poetic approach to life. We keep on... Don't try to absorb this book at one time. Go back and keep on...

Nicholas F. Mazza
Dean and Patricia V. Vance Professor of Social Work
College of Social Work, The Florida State University

Acknowledgements

Writing *Write Yourself* has been like creating a multidimensional jigsaw. Some of the pieces have been long on my desk, waiting for their fellows. Others have been a joy of discovery – aha, blue sky! Finally the last piece keyed in, and here's the coherent picture: the result of 12 years of research and practice.

So many people have contributed, or helped me learn and understand, giving *Write Yourself* the glow of life. Patients, clients and professionals have generously given written signed permission to quote their writing. I thank David Hart, Vicky Field, Penelope Shuttle, Alicia Stubbersfield, John Latham, Joan Poulson, Andrew Rudd, Chris Woods, Jeannie Wright, Jackie Brown, Paul Brown, David Hannay, David Gelipter, Peter Nelson, Moira Brimacombe, Jo Cannon, Charles Heatley, Jane Searle, Caroline Walton, Rosie Welch, Shirley Brierley, Clare Connolly, Maggie Eisner, Seth Jenkinson, Sheena McMain, Mark Purvis, Becky Ship, Mike Leuty, Angela Stoner, Colin Ludlow, Anne Bonner, Marge Craig, Kath Gains, Nazrul Islam, Derek Snaith, Mandy Whitfield, Carol Willis, Liz Burns, Bronte Bedford Payne, Elaine Brunswick, Mary Dicker, David and Joan Ellison, Carol Gardiner, Heather Hawkins, Rosemary Hoggett, Ann Jacob, Vivienne Phillips, Dorothy Reynolds, Pamela Russell, Rosemary Willet, Linda Garbutt, Monica Suswin, Lucy Henshall, Jonathan Knight, Sarah Salway, Lydia Fulleylove, River Wolton, Kate Anthony, Fiona Friend, Sheila Hayman, Bill Noble, Tricia McAdoo, Massimo Park, Emily Wills, Judy Clinton, Julie Sanders, Najwa Mounla, John Engel, Nick Mazza, Gwyneth Lewis and Juhani Ihanus.

Staff and patients of organisations which supported my research deserve much thanks: University College Hospital London Myerstein Institute of Oncology and Teenage Cancer Trust Unit, Camden Palliative

Care Unit, King's College London Arts and Medicine Unit (English Department), Sheffield University Institute of General Practice, Sheffield University Department of Palliative Medicine, Arts Council England, The Wilkes Fellowship, The Economic Social Research Council and Royal College of General Practitioners.

Elusive bright elements have been given by Kate Billingham, Berlie Doherty, Robert Hamberger and Michele Petrone. Jessica Kingsley and Claire Cooper have been perfect, caring, critical editors. I could not have even realised there was a lovely picture to be found, let alone create the jigsaw, without Dan and Alice Rowland. And, finally, Stephen Rowland's pianist's fingers have made music of *Write Yourself*.

Preface

Write Yourself is both a resource for introducing and supporting other people in writing, and an inspiration to you, my reader, for your own personal writing. Both are vital. This writing is a creative joy and personal resource-well of immeasurable depth. Doing ourselves whatever we help others to do means we are more likely to understand what they go through. Inspiring and encouraging others is a joy; sharing their writing is a privilege. This work brings us into close contact with others and their honesty and willingness to push courageously at the boundaries of their own experience and knowledge.

Write Yourself is an introduction to explorative and expressive writing, its practices and principles, and its difference from creative writing for publication. It showcases and explains how writing can be valuable for children, therapy or counselling clients, very sick people, those suffering from depression, anxiety or mental health problems, people trying to recover from substance or alcohol abuse, victims of torture, refugees and asylum seekers, and professionals seeking an effective form of reflection upon their practice. Last but not least are two chapters on running groups, covering a range of size, duration and number of sessions. Elements such as fiction, story and metaphor are introduced early on, and developed throughout, as relevant to each chapter theme (the very sick, for example).

The chapters of *Write Yourself* can be read in any order. Chapters 1–3 and 12–14 are of value to all readers as they are introductory to working with any client group. Chapters which seem less relevant to you might well be very useful. This work is with people and writing, rather than specific problems, so processes and exercises used are very similar whatever the perceived need or want. You might never work with children, yet find just the right approach or exercise in that chapter for your own group.

Write Yourself contains many writing exercises: descriptions within each chapter, and more at each chapter end. Most of these activities are appropriate for most client groups, perhaps needing imaginative adapting for your group. For this reason the Appendix lists exercises by theme and not by appropriateness to particular client groups. Chapters 1–3 and 12–13, explaining how to start and ways of working with individuals and groups, will be invaluable to making best use of these activities. My method for thinking of new exercises, which you might also try, is working out what might have set other writers off; I used the poetry anthologies *Staying Alive* and *Being Alive* (Astley 2002, 2004), and novels and stories from my shelves. *The Therapeutic Potential of Creative Writing* (Bolton 1999a), *Writing Works* (Bolton, Field and Thompson 2006), *Writing Routes* (Bolton, Field and Thompson 2010) and *Reflective Practice Writing and Professional Development* (Bolton 2010) contain a wealth of further exercises and advice. You will of course develop your own ways of doing things, and your own exercises. Please let me know some of these, to help extend and disseminate knowledge, skills and experience.

During 25 years of working with writing I've come closer to understanding what happens when we write. Some of it, I accept, is a mystery. Whatever research is done on the chemistry and neural pathways of the brain and its connection with our bodies, we'll never understand creativity fully. Poetry has seemed a route to gaining some grasp; one attempt is in *Writing Works*, another the dedication to *The Therapeutic Potential of Creative Writing*. My journals and files are full of other attempts. Here is another, not entirely to my satisfaction, as I think poetry is much more subtle and gentle than surgery. If you would like to have a go yourself, please do send it to me (www.gilliebolton.com).

Poetry

Sometimes surgery probes no further than skin,
smoothing out the bumps and wrinkles of experience.

To cure, the knife cuts deep through fat and muscle
excising hurt from gut, breast or heart.

The needle reconnects veins, arteries, sinews,
tucks away raw edges.

Leaving a jagged scar:
the signature of healing.

PART ONE

Creative Personal Writing – What, Why, How, Who, When, Where

CHAPTER 1

Becoming Our Own Shaman: Introduction to Therapeutic Creative Writing

'Would you tell me, please, which way I ought to go from
here?'

'That depends a good deal on where you want to get to,'
said the Cheshire Cat.

'I don't much care where —' said Alice.

'Then it doesn't matter which way you go,' said the Cat.

'So long as I get *somewhere*,' Alice added as an explanation.

Lewis Carroll 1954 (1865), p. 54

Art has the power to help people understand themselves, each other and
their world better, to *reach that depth, make sense of my life* (all italicised
quotes are by very sick or terminally ill writers). Art, creative use of the
imagination, is a magical quality which marks us out as different from
most other creatures. Creativity is a process of learning; it can deeply
affect self- and world-views because it is attained through experience,
exploration and expression rather than instruction. 'Knowledge is
limited. Imagination encircles the world' (Einstein 2002 [1929]).
Writing uses subtle, deeply human modes of communication such as
narrative, detailed accurate description, experimenting with point of
view, image (particularly metaphor) and, particularly in the case of

poetry, rhythm and repetition. Breaking the skin of lifegiving clear well-water, creative explorative and expressive writing can communicate psychological, social, cultural and spiritual truths. This insight can be achieved appropriately and gently when people give themselves permission to explore experience and express feelings, memories and knowledge through writing. Effective learning is like growing wheat, a staple fundamental food. Its seeds need patience, sunshine, well-prepared ground, and appropriate moisture and nutrients.

> Art allows a safe revisiting of that place of revulsion. It has been compared to a rollercoaster ride. We ride a rollercoaster in order to be terrified, and yet none of us would willingly step on a rollercoaster knowing it to be unsafe.
>
> But art, writing, music…allows us to revisit painful times whilst knowing that the seatbelt is secure around us, rigorous safety checks have been passed, and we are going to walk away from the memory intact. (Teenage Cancer Trust Unit [TCTU] patient)

Apollo is god of both poetry and healing. Writers have probably always known the deeply healing power of writing, certainly since the ancient Greek poet Sappho. But they have kept the secret until recently. Now it is increasingly used in mainstream and complementary healthcare, medicine and therapy. Writing is powerful communication: perhaps even more so than speech, as it does not disappear on the breath. Every utterance is communication between interlocutors. But no one initially listens to writing except the quiet accepting page, which creates a record. The etymological roots of the word 'record' are 're', meaning again, and 'cord', meaning heart (*Oxford English Dictionary*). Recording is getting closer to what is in the heart. The writer is their own first reader, their own primary interlocutor. So writing, in the first instance, is a private communication with the heart of the self. Strenuous but not thought-engaging exercise such as digging or solitary walking can induce a similar mental state. It can't be chance that poet S. T. Coleridge walked and climbed strenuously for miles and miles, and then wrote on mountain tops (Holmes 1989).

Expressive and explorative writing is really a process of deep listening, attending to some of the many aspects of the self habitually blanketed during waking lives. Some of these aspects we ignore at our peril. People who write for the first time with a trusted facilitator say things like 'it unlocked something I didn't know was there' (participant in a family medicine project) (Opher and Wills 2004). And 'Hell, did I write that? Was that really me? You can't pick something safe with writing, like you can with role-play. I suppose it's because you're not listening to yourself as you write. Writing takes you out of control' (Bolton 1999a, 2001).

'You're not listening to yourself *as* you write.' No, while writing, the page offers no judgment at all. But there *is* a future interlocutor: writing with a white pen on white paper would not have the same effect. You listen to yourself *after* you write, rereading. Writing creates tangible footprints which can, and probably will, be followed, but it postpones interlocution. There is no immediate reaction of head-nodding, smiling, frowning or grimacing, no immediate response of questions, affirmation, shouts or screams. The process of gaining insight is three-staged: first the dash onto the page, then rereading to the self, then the sometimes emotional reading and sharing with a carefully chosen other (or others). Writers have authority: nobody else is in control, though it takes some a long time, or even never, to realise this.

Writing can help achieve increased communication, self-understanding and well-being (NHS Estates 2002; Staricoff 2004; White 2004), alleviate stress and anxiety (Anderson and MacCurdy 2000), dramatically support positive self image (Tasker 2005), and can have significant therapeutic effects (Help the Hospices 2005). The *British Medical Journal* editor recommended that an NHS budget percentage should go to the arts (Smith 2002). This is nothing new: healing at the ancient Greek Temple Hospice of Asklepios was based on dream images and watching poetic plays which communicated deep psychological, cultural and political insight. The tradition continues. John Kani, South African co-author of *Siswe Bansi is Dead*, said 'theatre is a weapon of change' (Kani 2007). Writing his play about apartheid, *Nothing But the Truth*, enabled him to forgive himself for hating his brother's murderers. His daughter only understood about the fight against apartheid when she saw the play. Marion Steel (2010) created a profound reflection on death, love and loss using a mixture of poetry, fiction, autobiography and philosophical musing to examine and deal with her complex bereavement reaction to a patient's death.

All this sounds so purposive, yet to work both as writing and therapeutically it has to be undertaken in a pure spirit of enquiry. Explorative enquiry is process- rather than product-based: seeking answers to perceived problems or *to get published* will not create useful or communicative texts. Attempting therapeutic writing purposively would be as much use as therapists knowing what clients were to explore. Alice throughout her adventures underground accepted that it didn't 'matter which way you go', but she insisted she did want to 'get *somewhere*' (Carroll 1954 [1865]). She certainly always got 'somewhere' dynamic. Shakespeare's sonnets were perhaps a 'way of working out what he's thinking, not […] a means of reporting what he thought' (Paterson 2010, p. 3).

Writers have used images to describe their art, and what it offers them. Poet Seamus Heaney's bucket reached pure essential well-water:

> Usually you begin [writing] by dropping the bucket half way down the shaft and winding up a taking of air. You are missing the real thing until one day the chain draws unexpectedly tight and you have dipped into water that will continue to entice you back. You'll have broken the skin of the pool of yourself.
>
> *Seamus Heaney 1980a, p. 47*

Helene Cixous (1991) filched jewels from the jewelry box of her unconscious. Ted Hughes' (1967) intensity of experience was like a dog fox's stench and presence. Keats (2000 [1817]) thought it had to come naturally like leaves on a tree, and Heaney (1980b) elsewhere dug with his pen. All describe intense, personally worthwhile discovery and creation in writing.

Cry Baby
Only once did I ever
see my father cry.
I caught him wiping an eye
dragged under for a moment
by the sinking in his heart.
It was Paul Robson singing
Sometimes I Feel
Like a Motherless Child.

Now,
alone in the empty silence of the night,
I understand. (Member of Families and Friends of Drug Misusers, Anthology ed. Mike Hoy undated)

What is therapeutic writing?

Therapeutic creative writing offers personal, explorative and expressive processes, similar to creative writing's first stages. Patients, clients, tutees and students are offered guidance and inspiration by a clinician, facilitator or creative writer, and support in choosing a subject and form. Each writer works according to their own interests, concerns, wants and needs. Authority and control always reside with writers, to reread, share with appropriate others or not, store unread, or possibly destroy therapeutically.

The emphasis is on a process of satisfaction and interest to writers, and possibly a few close individuals. Whereas literary writing is oriented towards products of as high a quality as possible (e.g. poetry, fiction, drama), theapeutic writing is generally aimed at an unknown readership (see Chapter 2).

Therapeutic writing can help people understand themselves better, and deal with depression, distress, anxiety, addiction, fear of disease, treatment and life changes and losses such as illness, job loss, marital breakdown and bereavement. Ten or so solitary writing minutes daily can be significant. Special materials are unnecessary: paper today has unwanted typing on the back and a chunk torn from one corner.

Who writes?

Some fall naturally into reflective creative mode: *I'm going to write a book about my life!* Others want to experiment with approaches, work at allowing themselves not to achieve a product, or be open to admitting fears, anxieties and problematic memories as well as hopes and happiness. There is no 'type' who can or can't write. Some respond well to encouragement, specific exercises and positive response; others get more out of singing, acting, painting or talking; some do not want to engage in an art at all.

Write Yourself explains and demonstrates writing's usefulness to depression, anxiety and specific problems, and its appropriateness to groups and individuals, via email and web, to children and adults. Those in distress respond positively to writing, rather than fearing disclosure or appearing foolish. The need for help being too great for such self-protective delaying reactions, many, after initial hesitation, grasp paper and pen as an interested, patient, understanding audience. Some, however, feel safer and more self-respectful hugging anxious thoughts or painful memories to the end. All we can do is offer the process with sincerity and openness: if they're ready they'll take it; if not we've done our best.

Why it works

Writing provides simple, quiet, private, focused, recorded forms of reflection, of paying proper attention to one's own self. We know, remember and feel far more than we realise: humans are fabulously complex beings. Yet much of this is stored inaccessibly, especially at times of great need. Writing can encourage our closed internal doors to slip ajar. Material on the other side of these doors is sensitive and vulnerable: care is needed over appropriate ethical boundaries and principles. *Write Yourself* examines these in detail, with regard to a wide range of people and situations.

Any issue can potentially be shared relatively fearlessly with a piece of paper because it will never get bored, angry, distressed or shocked, and its potential impeccable memory is impersonal. I say 'potential' as writing can be ripped up, burned, flushed away: creating it will have helped without rereading. Writing can be read and reflected upon, perhaps developed, redrafted, perhaps later shared with a trusted confidential other, or group. Writing's privacy makes it qualitatively different from conversation, which will be remembered idiosyncratically: interlocutors cannot be asked to forget what they have heard.

Thinking is also private, but it's hard to focus, and even harder to remember reliably. Recording by tape or CD or electronically has to be associated with hearing one's own voice, which many dislike, and requires mediating technology.

Writing can be a private communication first with paper and then with the self: *these pieces are not really for anyone else other than yourself; it's a way of talking to the universe.* This privacy can enable exploration of areas unknown prior to writing (examination of troublesome emotions, memories or sticky issues perhaps): *the darkest depths and enlightening peaks.* People write often with no planning, forethought or real clarity about what is landing on the paper: a controlled *moment of madness.* The process is physical: the body writes, sometimes as if without the cognisance of the mind. Not so strange when you recall the 'word was made flesh', not speech. Allowing words to fall onto the page and then seeing what's there can feel like playing around (Winnicott 1971).

Different writing strategies are helpful; Ted Hughes called them games to outwit the controlling inner policeman (1982). *Write Yourself* explains and gives examples, including free-flow (e.g. personal journal), reminiscence (my illness story), logical cogent thinking (listing and weighing pros and cons), symbolic image exploration (metaphor, dreams), fictional communication with a significant other (unsent letters), communicating with different aspects of the self (dialogues with cancer, my frightened self), fictional stories (A little boy had cancer, and...) and catharsis (shouting anger with a scarlet pen): *catharsis is expression to an (imagined) listener who understands.*

Initial understandings are reached on reading silently to the self, and perhaps redrafting: sometimes emotional and cathartic. Then sharing with a carefully chosen other can be *someone objective to talk simmering and difficult emotions through with, helping me deal with the issues writing raised.* Reading aloud to this other can encourage writers to recognise and own what they have written about. Reading the actual words, rather than paraphrasing, is important: writing is different from speech and the point is to express the written. People find this writing and discussion can help them talk to others: *I do find it easier to talk about it now.*

Writing remains unchanged until revisited. Writers reread their material to see what they've written: an intense listening and responding. Sometimes they are not ready: *I can re-experience or destroy.* Storing writings unread can give essential waiting time. Sealing writing into an envelope can have further power: research has shown that descriptions of regretted decisions, sealed thus, decreased negative feelings about the decision. Controls showed unsealed envelopes and descriptions of insignificant events to be less effective (Burkeman 2010).

Writing, like all arts, can aid healing because people who understand their wants and needs, or hopes and fears, better are less likely to become ill, experience less severe symptoms when they do, and tend to recover more quickly, or are more at peace with chronic or terminal illness. Two overviews of research (Pennebaker and Chung 2007; Stuckey and Nobel 2010) (mostly randomised controlled laboratory studies) show how writing helped people overcome physical symptoms and addictions as well as communicate and sleep better. A leading medical journal editorial commenting on J. M. Smyth's (1999) research stated:

> Were the authors to have provided similar outcome evidence
> about a new drug, it likely would be in widespread use within

a short time. Why? We would think we understood the 'mechanism' (whether we did or not) and there would be a mediating industry to promote its use. Manufacturers of paper and pencils are not likely to push journalling as a treatment... (Spiegel 1999, p. 1329)

Overcoming blocks

We multi-task, rush from care to concern, sit through mediated entertainment, suffer being limited to the checkable and accountable by quality control. Our minds and bodies, however, can be unshackled from the *to do* lists, from the desperate need to be seen to achieve and produce.

Some, new to writing, feel nervous or inadequate due to old associations with being a writer or student. Yet this is not like writing for publication, or academic assessment. There is no teacher with a stern correcting pen, and no requirements of proper structure, form or grammar. And it can be done in different places with different materials and at any time of day or night. Gilly Pugh reflected how an exercise was 'incredibly freeing... Suddenly I don't have to be clever, I just have to tell a story' (see Bolton *et al.* 2010).

Rosalind Adams, who works with children and elderly people, struggled to learn this authority and ownership of her own writing: 'By far the most precious thing I've learned about writing is the skill to open my heart to my notebook. It's a simple skill but it took a series of workshops to enable me to get the full benefit of this sort of writing. I can now write what I truly feel and I regularly surprise myself with what appears on the page' (Adams 2011).

We can only open our hearts to those we utterly trust, such as the accepting page. Giving this trust might not come easily, and might take 'a series of workshops', but it's worth struggling for. Some, however, distrust family, friends or colleagues, fearing the wrong person might read their writing. One nurse took her journal with her everywhere, such was her anxiety. Two novelist friends arranged for their personal journals to be destroyed unread if they died suddenly, though they were not worried enough to stop writing. Strategies for the storage of writing can help. I think no one would want to decode my handwriting; my scribble would probably be rather boring to anyone else.

The *Write Yourself* process is simple, but the memories, thoughts and feelings raised are complex, and can be uncomfortable or even painful.

It can be likened to a search for treasure where fearful rivers need to be crossed and dragons slain, or an intense and wonderful romance laced with quarrels and misunderstandings. People do cry at their writing. Handled well and sensitively, these are healing tears.

And despite being not-for-publication, explorative writings are often clear, powerful expressions of deep human experience. Reading such material with writers, sharing their journey, is a privilege, and can often be enlightening to a facilitator or professional.

> The freedom to express myself more fully in writing, came to me in an unexpected way. We had been asked to take along a favourite poem to read aloud, but I rejected the one I had chosen, as too emotive for me to share. It's called 'At School' and paints a picture of a boy who tries to explain and then draw and paint 'about the things inside that needed saying'... Eventually the feelings he had been bursting to share, died; and he did not care any more.
>
> Suddenly I realised the significance of the poem for me, and why I find it so upsetting... By having the courage to go on a creative writing course, where I would find support, I had made a vital step towards freedom from the past. I felt a feeling of release and the words came tumbling out. During that week, it no longer mattered particularly what anyone else might think about my writing. More importantly it did not surprise me what I was expressing: I was so conscious of 'where the words come from' and of the 'freedom to be' – me. (Sorrell 1996, p. 36)

Write Yourself contains a wide range of exercises for approaching personal issues from side angles, for example image exploration. Not tackling painful issues head on can provide potential avenues towards otherwise unapproachable areas. New understandings can be generated by new relationships between the thing and the image, for example.

Writing materials

These can make a difference. Children like coloured paper and pens (healthcare and medical professionals do too); everyone likes nice paper, notebooks, sharp pencils and bright pens. Good materials are a pleasure and indicate respect. Peter Nelson spent time buying a leather folder and

fountain pen (see Chapter 6), a nurse found a shocking pink book and
pen, one patient a cerise leather notebook.

Here is a partially sighted writer:

> I used a personal shorthand, consisting of abbreviations, some
> actual Pitman shorthand and what, I think, is a bit like the
> text messaging method – missing out vowels and using, for
> example, u for you. All this was in capital letters.
>
> I think now I might use my laptop, with earphones so no
> one else could hear the screen reader. The wonderful thing
> about this would be that I could then use speakers and the
> computer would read out to everyone what I had written.
> When it comes to rereading my writing later, I have found
> listening and transcribing my reflections an additional force
> in the creative/therapeutic process. *Hearing* what I am writing
> as I type it, seems to add another dimension to the process:
> about acknowledging two different and equally valid forms of
> writing, I think. (Linda Garbutt)

For people with mobility, where they write might make a difference:
Peter Nelson drove miles to a country park and did amazingly different
writing on a lake-side bench than at his computer (see Chapter 6). And
when to write: the middle of the night or first thing in the morning can
be great.

For those confined to bed, I sat with them, sometimes also scribbling
to keep them company. Sometimes they'd write for a few minutes and
get stuck. We read it through together and I'd perhaps ask them to tell
me a bit more, or how they felt about an issue: *sometimes like I didn't know
what to write about really, I got stuck for things to write about and she gave me
suggestions.* Some preferred me to return when they'd written on their
own. Most wanted me to read it with them, occasionally they didn't.

A story

A TCTU patient where I researched therapeutic writing (see Chapter 4
and 5) wanted to write a children's story. I was surprised; young people
can be sensitive about being perceived as mature. Sick people need a
great deal of reassurance about who they are, what they are, and where
they belong: that their self is not disintegrating along with their body. Ill
people often regress to needing reassurance and care they had grown out

of when well. A sick adult will read children's fiction or poetry or adults' equivalent: straightforward tales in familiar surroundings with happy endings. Children will revert to younger literature. Children's stories offer a secure familiar base to adventure into the big frightening world, and to return to (see Chapter 4). With little more than encouragement, he wrote:

THE DRAGON'S EGG

It was two weeks into the summer holidays. The sun was shining and the birds were singing. It was a lovely Saturday afternoon in the park. Where we find Timmy. Timmy is 13 years old, and is playing in the park with his friends. On his way home Timmy finds an odd looking ball.

'What is it?' Timmy says to himself. 'It's not a football.' It looks more like a giant egg. It's white with green spots all over it. Timmy walks over to get a better look, he reaches out to touch it and it starts to shake. Timmy has no idea what it could be but he picks it up and takes it home with him.

When Timmy gets home he runs up to his room and puts the egg on his bed. He starts walking round the room looking at the egg trying to think about what he's going to do with it. Suddenly it shakes a bit and then a bit more and then it cracked around the top of the egg. Timmy's not sure if he should stay or run. Suddenly the top of the egg pops off.

Out from the top of the egg a small pointed head peeped out with bright yellow eyes and staring at what ever it was. The creature wiggled around and the rest of the egg broke away.

'WOW', Timmy said in amazement 'you're a dragon'. That's what it had to be. It had two wings and a long tail. It was fire red and scaly. The dragon looked at Timmy. Timmy looked at the dragon. Then the dragon started to move, moving towards Timmy. Timmy took a step back, not knowing what was going to happen next. And then the dragon spoke. 'Mum Ma'. In shock Timmy said 'You can talk'. 'Mum Ma' the dragon replied. 'Oh No,' Timmy said, 'I'd better get you something to eat.'

Timmy checked the landing and the stairs for signs of Mum and Dad. It looks like no-one's home. So Timmy takes the dragon downstairs to the kitchen and tries to find something to feed the dragon. But the dragon starts sniffing around the cupboards and the fridge and once he opens them, he eats everything in sight.

Timmy has no idea how he is going to tell his mum about the mess his new pet has made. Timmy thinks now he has a pet dragon, it needs a name, 'I think I'm going to call you Ding.' So Timmy takes Ding out into the garden hoping Ding won't make any more mess. Ding starts running, hopping and jumping around the garden, laughing away. Timmy is finding Ding's dancing very funny.

Ding stops in the middle of the garden and looks at his wings. He gives them a flap and then he starts flapping harder and begins to leave the ground. Ding then comes down, lands, runs toward Timmy, scoops him up on to his back, then turns round. Ding starts to run and flap, run and flap, and then Woosh! up into the sky. 'WOW! Weee!' shouts Timmy, 'We're flying, we're flying' he cried. The pair of them zoom through the clouds, around the tall building in town. 'Higher, faster', Timmy shouts. They whiz through the sky and zoom towards the ground and then they shoot back up into the sky.

They fly over the park and come down to land. Timmy jumps off. 'Ding that was great. I had so much fun, but I think we'd better be getting home because it's getting late', says Timmy.

But then Timmy hears a thumping sound, soon he can feel it in the ground. He looks round 'Oh my', says Timmy. Walking towards him and Ding is a Big Mummy Dragon. She must have lost her egg, and now she has come to find her Baby. Timmy starts feeling sad because he knows what he has to do. He has to let Ding go back with his mother.

Ding walks over to his mother and sniffs her a bit, and then crys 'Mum Ma'. Ding moves up against his mother, he turns round to Timmy and sees and sounds upset. He walks over to Timmy and brushes up against him. Ding looks at Timmy and says 'Bye Bye Timmy'.

Timmy says back 'yer Bye Ding. I'll miss you, I hope I'll see you soon.' Ding licks Timmy's cheek, Timmy throws his arms around Ding. Then Ding turns and goes with his mum as they fly off into the sky.

But Ding flys by one last time to say goodbye. Waving, Timmy shouts 'Bye Ding take care, see you soon.' Timmy starts to make his way home trying to think about what he was going to say to his mum about the mess in the kitchen. 'Oh well', he says.

Adam's story is of love and loss. But the loss is to freedom and joy in flight. A story of parenting, it depicts real care. The little hero learns to love and fly, then letting go for the sake of the loved one. He learns mature sadness and loss tinged with satisfaction and joy: it is better to have loved and lost than not have loved at all. The big world out there isn't as scary as he feared; monsters are friendly and can offer joyful adventures, and have loving mothers. And if flight was perhaps an unconscious image for death, it is a positive image: though, tragically, Adam did 'not go gentle into that good night, [and he] rage[d], rage[d] against the dying of the light' (Thomas 2003, p. 46). He did, though, write this story, and 'it's under the mask of fiction that you can tell the truth' (Gao 2009, p. 11).

Adam wished to continue by writing the same story from the point of view of the baby dragon. I encouraged him in this. But he did not have long enough to live.

Conclusion

The shaman bravely travels to other psychological lands to bring back healing. A writer travels wherever their pen takes them: alone, nearly in silence, and for themselves. Not knowing where, and what they want to bring back, is vital, just as Alice found with her explorations in Wonderland (Carroll 1954 [1865]). As T. S. Eliot pointed out (1936), we all come back to where we started: me, here and now.

It's not easy work, but I think we need not be afraid to listen, and to extend a supportive encouraging hand to those who are listening to themselves by writing. Poetry and healing have gone hand in hand for millennia: we can continue this powerful relationship. Therapeutic creative writing has been introduced as a straightforward process which can reach through to areas needing exploration and expression. This might be enjoyable and exciting. It can, however, seem alarming, necessitating clear ethical boundaries and skilful focused support. Chapter 2 gives methods for facilitating starting to write, and ways of supporting writers' journeys.

Write!

After writing, reread silently to yourself with care (or store it, or you might even want to destroy it). Then share it with a carefully chosen other or group, if appropriate.

1. Write about any or all of these; it might come out as a story, or a reminiscence:

   ○ a toy or game you remember from your childhood (e.g. my teddy…)

   ○ a pet or other animal

   ○ a piece of clothing, either yours or belonging to a relative, or perhaps a doll

   ○ footwear, either yours or someone else's, or that you wanted and couldn't have

   ○ a bag, basket, box or other container and what it contained

   ○ a piece of jewelry which belonged to your mother/aunt/other close adult

   ○ a tool which belonged to someone close to you (spanner, penknife, pen).

2. Think of an animal or creature you've met briefly at any time of your life: in a building, out in the woods, fields or street (we watched a family of mice under the London tube railway tracks…).

   ○ Write about that encounter, including any feelings or memories it raises.

3. You find something valuable inside an object or garment you buy in the charity/thrift shop:

   ○ What?

   ○ What does this lead to?

   ○ Write your thoughts, or the story.

   One of your treasured possessions ends up being sold.

   ○ Write the thoughts of its new owner about you (whom they never knew) once it's settled into their own home and life.

CHAPTER 2

'A Story of Gaining Understanding and Insight': How to Begin

'Speech is silver; silence is golden.'
Proverb

How do I write? One word at a time. The first sentence feels like the tip of a thread. I pull it very gently. Another sentence. And again I try, teasing out phrase after phrase and hoping that the thread will not break. It is as if before me there is an invisible garment of which only one thread can be seen. Each day I draw it out a little further.

Niall Williams 2008, p. 75

Writing uses words, our everyday communicating medium. Requiring only basic literacy skills, paper and pencil, writing is simple and cheap. A stumbling block can be negative memories of spelling, grammar and construction taught with an authoritarian confidence-destroying red pen. *Write Yourself* contains many ways to extinguish these fears, and begin to enjoy the freedom of writing without performance anxieties. Explorative and expressive writing is private, to be read initially by the writer alone, then possibly shared with one or two carefully chosen others. All that is needed is willingness to:

- have a go at open exploration and expression, alone in creative golden silence

- let go of previous inhibitions about *rules*; if grammatical accuracy is needed, redrafting is straightforward

- trust the process and respect both writer and reader: oneself

- give yourself the gift of the small amount of time and energy required

- be willing to face some uncomfortable feelings and memories, knowing that writing is gentle and paced and will only present the manageable, and anyway can be stopped at any time and when the right person to talk to is found.

Starting to write is enjoyable, with initial unassuming steps. We write one word at a time, seeing where it leads, as Williams (2008) points out. Some immediately want to write their illness's full story (teenage cancer patient), or their life (80+ year old). Many find lists or letters a good opener. Encouragement and support are helpful, especially initially, as is empathetic interest combined with lack of surprise, shock or untoward interest at anything written or divulged. Even writing nothing is not a failure, but an indication that the time is not right, or that writing is not for them.

Key to success is perceiving it as flexible, versatile, straightforward, enjoyable and private. And with no purpose other than personal exploration and expression. To help people feel *I love writing*, I tell them this before starting:

- you can choose what and how to write

- everything you write will be right: because it's an expression of your own experience, knowledge and memories, and you can't get such things about yourself wrong

- the writing belongs to you; you need only share what YOU wish to share

- it's yours!: you are in charge of where it's kept, and who reads it or doesn't

- no one will talk about it without your permission

- grammar, spelling, etc. DO NOT MATTER: they even get in the way and can be sorted out later if wished

- it needs no special form or structure
- you will be helped with what to write and how.

Sickness, anxiety or bereavement can make it hard to voice problems and fears. Many, conversely, need to express ups and downs far more than friends, relatives or staff have time or patience for. Paper and pen are endlessly patient, present, and never make a comment. A teenage cancer patient wrote: 'The more I think about these little things that make me happy the more determined I get not to let this illness take these things away from me.'

Permission to express and explore openly, and assurance of ownership and confidentiality, are more powerful than specific exercises. Writing can then be paced and a trustworthy exploration and expression of memories, thoughts, feelings, inspirations: *it's something I have done myself. No one can correct me. It's mine.* Some might be uncomfortable or painful; writers can always stop and talk to someone they trust, or do something completely different and comforting until it feels safe enough to continue. Some topics which seem too painful to approach one day might present themselves in writing in a different, and OK, way later. Anyone displaying personal instability or imbalance, with psychiatric diagnoses, however, needs professional (e.g. clinical or therapeutic) support as well as a writer, writing therapist, tutor or facilitator.

What to write

Six minutes' free writing

This opening strategy is a beginning for every creative or therapeutic writing session. It gets the pen or pencil moving over that space frightening to every writer: a blank page. It can note and temporarily store safely some of the muddle of thoughts which can otherwise dominate. It can capture insights or inspirations which seem to spring from nowhere; these can then be developed in the ensuing writing.

Put the pen on the page and write with no forethought or planning and certainly no awareness of grammar or form. A list might come out, or seemingly jumbled odds and ends; our minds often jump about before we find a path through. Whatever it is it will be right. It need never be shared, and need never be reread: it's completely private. Writers can then fruitfully move on to any of the following.

Lists

Lists seem undemanding, everyday, very useful with new writers. No sentences, no paragraphs, and the form is all middle with no beginning and end. Try writing a word, any word, at the top of the page, and list whatever comes underneath. Or write the word in the middle of the page and allow all words and phrases to cluster over the page from this central word. If you can't think of a word, open a book at random: cookery, novel, poetry, text book or work related.

Lists such as *What I fear about going into hospice, Things I miss about home*. A hospice psychotherapist said 'I shall use them with bereaved relatives, ask them to write positive and negative feelings'. There can be as many subjects as writers: gentle chatting with an individual or group finds them. A simple list can resemble cogent poetry of sincere opinion and feeling.

> TCTU is a very good place. I list the things that they do:
> They work for cancer patients
> They give treatment against disease
> The place is very good
> They have good staff and cleaners
> …
> Being a cancer patient, it has changed my life.
> But it is the treatment given to me which has changed my life.
> (Teenage Cancer Trust Unit [TCTU] patient)

Description

Describing accurately helps focus attention on detail and nuance, a cornerstone of living writing. Exactly why something is liked, the quality of the cat's purr and just how she curls on my lap can be supportively enjoyable. An accurate description of home when in hospital can be calming and soothing. Describing the ward can help focus on concerns and good aspects.

> Pumps bleeping all the time
> The bleeping of the red lights on the ceiling at night
> The coldness in the night
> The quiet at night, though sometimes it's noisy
> people chatting
> a lot of visitors coming in and chatting

The light through the windows – sometimes bright
The smell of the food when they bring in the food is disgusting
it smells like school dinner...
The doctors are a bit annoying sometimes
they ask you the same questions all the time, like:
'Are you feeling sick?'
'Have you got a cold?'
'Have you got a temperature?'
'Have you had any ulcers?'
'Have you got any breathing problems?'
...
I don't like coming here. (TCTU patient)

Narrative

Humans are narrative-making creatures; creating stories is our way of making sense of things. Illness, bereavement and loss can disrupt understanding of life, its hitherto habitual story. People naturally wish to recount personal troubles, doing so with little encouragement. Writing can get this off the chest to a reliable audience. People seem to gain benefit from writing the exact story of their illness and its repercussions.

Reminiscence can also increase quality of life. It can enhance jewel memories, reconnect elders to their vibrant former selves, remind them of good times and key relationships, leave a record for family and friends, and help deal with hidden traumatic memories, even at this late stage. A palliative care patient's life story began: 'I was about five years old when I realised I had a very caring Dad that loved me very much.'

Family medicine patients were introduced to reminiscence poetry writing by poet Emily Wills (for her collection see Wills 2008). Sally Hayward, who 'finds writing helps her come to terms with difficult life events', wrote: 'It's time to go home now / Keep those good memories alive in one's mind forever' (Opher and Wills 2003, p. 59, 4). Emily asked a group to imagine what memory they'd put in a box. Sally Davis wrote: 'In the box is / The September sunlight shining sideways across the garden / And someone practicing the saxophone / With / A nightmare fading into reality and / I'll make some tea' (Opher and Wills 2003, p. 30).

Image and metaphor

A staple of poetry and prose, metaphor focuses upon significance: what things mean to us, remind us of and what they stand for in our own particular universe. The significance of one thing is carried over to another: abstract words like 'anxiety' and 'love' are difficult to grasp; the image of being harried by wolves is not, as in 'anxiety was a wolf pack'. Adrienne Rich spoke of 'the great muscle of metaphor, drawing strength from resemblance in difference' (2006, p. 2). We perceive beyond things, we look and listen inside ourselves to help understand ourselves, situations, pasts, hopes and fears better; to do this we need to perceive through the *thingness, itness* of things, to focus upon metaphorical realities; what wolves are really like is immaterial here. Puns also create powerful images; see Jackie Brown's play on 'poaching' (1993, p. 25; see Chapter 6).

Writers also focus on the *thingness* of things; they can carefully observe and describe a red rose: perfume, velvet petals, shape, form, thorns, intense colour, even taste. Here we want readers to smell, taste, feel and see the rose, and hear the patter of rain on shiny so-green leaves. A writing skill is to perceive depths beyond the real, to switch between perceiving metaphorically and literally: 'all that is real is in constant contact with magic and mystery' (Diaghilev 2010, p. 17).

> What's the 'blockage' in my bowel that started all this off in the first place? What's the lump I couldn't get rid of without surgery? If I'm now having difficulty eating/swallowing, what is it that I'm finding so hard to swallow? (Colin Ludlow)

The responses Colin wrote were 'quite painful to write about'. Here Susannah fruitfully tussles with childhood memories:

My Mother Was...

that giant spider lurking in the dark to entangle the innocent, leaving living shells sucked dry of life force and joy
a trap, huge steel jaws hidden under brambles, waiting to spring on the unwary child seeking juicy blackberries
sulphurous yellow, the green of rottingness
a game designed to prove there are losers in the family, that adults always win
an internet site of child porn, sneaked under the cover of a happy family.
Do I need to write more? You get the picture? (Susannah)

Letters and dialogues

Dialogues or letters never to be sent can be written to and from alive or dead people, injured or hurt body parts (see Bolton 1999a), and aspects of the self (inner child). Direct communication with an internal *you* can enable venting, or discovery of feelings, thoughts or memories. One patient wrote an exercise-book-length 'letter to my cancer' working through anger, fear, hatred, denial, bargaining; another wrote a letter to his injured shoulder (Bolton 1999a). Colin Ludlow wrote a dialogue between his 'Child Me' and his inner 'Mr Policeman'. He also wrote a letter to himself from his 'Spiritual Father', and from his late mother, ending with this:

> Hush, be still. Your 'mother' is still here. Deep inside you, in the love of others round about you. Don't talk. Just feel the warmth and tenderness. You'll soon feel better. Perhaps borne up by my Spiritual Father and Caressing Mother, I have felt calmer and more relaxed over the past couple of months after a pretty bumpy time… (Palliative care patient; for his story of his illness see Ludlow 2008)

Letters or emails to be sent can be practised, before a satisfactory version is created. Here, a relationship breakup is helped by carefully formed emails, as well as journal writing:

My Emails, by Anon

I am experiencing an enormous sense of relief having written about the way my husband and I after a year of separation are communicating through e-mail. I found writing this, during a very tricky turn in how we relate, very useful personally. I laid all the twists and turns of our recent difficult exchange out on my screen and paper in green ink. I like green ink: it is soothing and healing. My intention in my relating to my husband, or indeed anyone, is to come from the best place within myself. This doesn't mean I override my feelings; far from it.

I started with anger and frustration. He was contacting me all the time. Writing several thousand words allowed me to sort out what I felt and thought, and that I wanted to communicate by a really short e-mail. Although intuitively I knew my point of view before I started, the writing backed up, reinforced and explained this in greater detail to myself. Furthermore despite wavering at times, it helped me to stick to it. And I ended up uncovering great sadness.

The writing clarified my position because I wrote freely and easily: without risking derision or misunderstanding but also knowing he experiences the situation differently. I am claiming my own truth fully for myself through writing, not to be right or correct. My shaping of writing is in three steps: first get it down any old how (splurge); second make additions to give body, context; three start to shape in order. Giving myself the categories of: Background/ Incident Out of the Blue/Journal Writing/Unsent Letter in Full/E-mail/& Conclusion pulled my messy, unpleasant and unwelcome experience into pleasing, coherent and complete shape. I had to make a decision where to stop to give a satisfying ending, belying the ongoing conflict-ridden reality. Pulling this writing together makes me feel more distant and secure now in my decision not to have any more dialogue about our difficult relationship.

Writing about it fully engaged me, cleared my mind, as I could inhabit all my roles of separated and 'wronged' wife (although the decision was mutual), writer, and one-time psychotherapist. Explaining my own process here helped more than I might have imagined. Even though I am well familiar with this writing process, it always comes as a refreshing surprise, and emphasises the safety of e-mails for smoothing over exchanges about arrangements.

Here is an extract from an early sent e-mail:

> The reason I am liking the e-mail for 'stuff' stuff is in recognition of your repeated need to say you are separate yet maintain contact. It is my way of cleanly relating without the muddle, disagreements and upset which seem to happen so quickly if we meet and talk. With most people I would not express my feelings through e-mail: it is all too easy to bash away at the keyboard. But with you we know each other too well. So this way I maintain some 'real' contact, expressing some of what I feel without face-to-face talking which triggers bad feelings. Which is why we have needed to separate. Yet we need to be in communication.

Writing gives me a container, a shape like sculpting from a piece of unhewn stone, a place to say this is what happened and what it is like for me and this is what I think and feel, and finally this is what I did, how I managed it: end of story. Life goes on, but the writing has a clear beginning, middle and end. And my approach to our difficulties is now in traditional story form in my mind. Writing this, and my new decision to put a circle around what I am willing to talk about, has created a defined boundary around the shifting and unstable situation.

I felt a freeing up that you Gillie read the 3000 words, although I felt disloyal in sending it to you. You, my trustworthy reader of my stuff, know how I express myself in words therefore you know how I think and feel and the layered quality of how I approach my life dilemmas. Sharing gives a good feeling. It only needs one person.

Forms of writing

All the above methods can be used in journal, story, poetry, blog, zine or autobiographical writing.

Journal

Journals can contain 'splurge', moans and complaints, cathartic outbursts, or any other required form. Entries require no beginning and end. A journal is all middle, and therefore can be picked up and put down at any time or in mid sentence. A palliative care patient wrote about everyday matters for some time, then suddenly changed gear as he gained confidence in me and in writing:

> There's a couple of fairly important bits of my life I haven't touched on... When it comes to friendship it's been a disappointment throughout my life. I always end up being disappointed. You get to the stage when you wonder if it is something you're doing wrong. You don't want to come across too hungry. Too hungry for friendship. (Palliative care patient)

Many creative and therapeutic writers keep personal journals: a completely private space for musing, reflecting, creating, agonising. 'We are talking about something private, about bits of the mind's string too short to use, an indiscriminate and erratic assemblage with meaning only for its maker' (Didion 1968, p. 117). Poet Dannie Abse, after his wife's death, responded to 'the small interior voice that keeps urging me "Physician, heal thyself" and [that] as a result [I'm] committed to this journal, this on-going prescription for self-regeneration' (2007, p. 125). Laitinen and Ettorre found that, by writing diaries, depressed women 'were better able to learn to *feel* their emotions and cope better with their problems…by allowing them to become active subjects in their own healing' (2007, p. 19). A self-therapy journal writer, having rejected counselling because of its imbalance of control and dependency, said journals were 'like…a journey back to myself' (Wright 2009, p. 236). Here is a family medicine patient's poem: 'Diaries are / Important / And let us / Reflect on our thoughts of / Yesterdays' (Sally Hayward in Opher and Wills 2003, p. 4).

Blogs

Many find sharing experiences, thoughts, feelings and anxieties with an unknown public helpful. Some blogs have interactive pages where readers can post responses or similar experiences, writing anonymously.

Zines

Homemade magazines distributed to family and friends, zines give a voice to those who feel under-represented in the media. Offering all the benefits of communicating, of not being alone, they are a tangible product, unlike blogs (Flood 2008), encouraging doodling and cutting and pasting accompanying visual images. Their freedom of expression, and lack of formality and convention, makes them an accessible, varied and anarchic form. Perzines are intensely personal, often written by young women about experiences generally considered taboo. The zine-making process seems grounding and calming, with great satisfaction; 'nothing beats the feeling of a DIY paper zine in your hand. It is a way of creating something that can speak to other people, give marginalized groups a voice and, potentially, start to build communities. And most importantly of all, it is therapy that we can give ourselves' (Flood 2008, p. 14).

Fiction

We undertook a joint story writing venture in the TCTU. Adam knew what he wanted to write and set off writing alone (see Chapter 1). The others didn't, and I took them through a simple character, setting and plot-finding exercise:

1. Think of a young person: What is their name? What are they wearing? Where are they?

2. This person meets someone else; where? What are they doing together?

3. Something unexpected happens; what?

4. They meet someone or something else; who?

5. And so on... I make it up as I go along. If anyone got stuck we talked it through when we read out after each bit, or they gain inspiration from each other.

Here is the ending of a story which involved a sailing adventure, and a tiger:

> When morning came they all waked up and said good bye to each other and they left a nice bright calm morning and returned to their beautiful island. When they returned they saw some strangers coming from their hut. Luana and Tommy took out their spears and ran behind them. But as the strangers turned around it was just their parents. They ran and hug them. They frightened their parents. When everything was settled they sat down and talked about everything they did yesterday and had a nice tropical lunch. (TCTU patient)

Everyone read back their few sentences after each element. Beforehand the room was full of individual people; by the end it was populated by characters, situations and places we'd invented, and patients knew each other much better. This method can be adapted, and used with adults. For another TCTU story, see Chapter 4.

Poetry

Poetry's short lines and succinctness can contain great feeling and it is often written at a time of emotional need; it can be easy to write as grammar, spelling and use of English can be innovative and creative. Another way of defusing anxiety about poetry is to define it as writing which doesn't reach the right-hand page margin.

> Once in a while
> the disguise that I use
> to make you think
> I'm happy – slips.
> My lips are tired of smiling.

And each of the 24 muscles
Required to pull off
this crime – give up.
I just can't live up
to your expectations any more.
So let me go now
Before I cry. (Palliative care patient)

A strict form such as acrostic can seemingly create a poem out of nothing, the letter at the beginning of each line enabling a flow. As with all strict forms, this partial removal of decisions can enable what needs to be written (for another acrostic see Chapter 12):

Does no one here believe me, can none of you see?
Everything this frail old man used to be?
Man of great integrity, man of many skills
Ever giving of his time to those with greater ills
Now you see a fragile mind, a body far from well
Trapped he is, inside a lonely, living hell
In pieces, disassembled, broken up, no longer whole
And I pray the Lord takes care to protect his very soul.

Written 10 November 2006 as my father's health
declined yet further (Dr Lucy Henshall)

'My heart in hiding' (Hopkins 1953, p. 30): Poetry writing to help me find myself

This is an account of a poem I wrote following a period when my personal journal writing had dried up; it felt like losing a best friend. My inner critic (or inner saboteur) nagged when I tried to journal-write, and destroyed my sleep. My unrestful state was deepened by two family anxieties. My block meant writing couldn't help my anxiety and my anxiety fuelled the inner critic and block.

Then a friend gave me a simple exercise. Alicia Stubbersfield, co-member of my poetry group *Off the Page*, suggested I observe my everyday surroundings carefully and precisely, making five lists of things I noticed about:

1. the natural world

2. the built environment

3. a person or people

4. the news or other media

5. an habitual activity: typing an email, cooking…

It suited me, in my uncreative state, to use Alicia's categories like a schoolchild with homework. My lists had to cover my five senses as well as the sixth, I decided. The senses have always been a checklist for my descriptive writing. Sounds, smells and tactile sensations, as well as colour and visual form, can create scenes with few words. Taste can too; though it's not always the first sense to come to mind. I've often found myself transported to somewhere, or completely absorbed in the here and now, by focusing upon one of my non-dominant senses.

I was reminded of Eastern *mindfulness*, paying attention to what we are doing at any one time, cutting out extraneous thoughts or awareness: the opposite of multi-tasking. I try to build this into my life and journal writing, becoming more aware of minute details of my world (natural, built and cultural).

So I was given permission to roam around the early spring garden and scribble about divergent and otherwise insignificant things, some with a paragraph, some only a phrase. The shift of focus between the lists continually re-engaged my attention. Interestingly I wrote nothing about *the built environment*. Here are a few items:

Flowers in too small a vase, falling languidly, generously
The smooth warmth of pearls
A nail paring from your big toe like a great white staple in the carpet
The neighbour's cherry obscuring my view of the tor
My mother's cameo on her bottle green lapel
Lying in bed in the morning stimulates the creative intellect

My list would have remained in my journal, undeveloped. But my friends Alicia and Robert Hamberger (for their poetry see Hamberger 2007; Stubbersfield 2006) encouraged me to look for relationships between items, and make some poetic sense. This creative redrafting was absorbing. What is the relationship between a very cross squirrel, the sound of chiselling, a cold cup of tea, the balm of soft sunshine and wind, a smell turning house into home, and some chance media information? It was fun; moreover it kept my mind off self-blaming treadmills. Neither of my weighty problems wormed their way in. And making something always makes me feel better.

Observe

The squirrel squawks and jibbers, jerks his tail
yet doesn't fall off the branch.

Blonde ringlets of wood drift from the chisel
to float on your cold scummed tea.

The radio murmurs that brown bears,
re-introduced into the Alps, maul climbers.

A thrush sings along to your almost inaudible hum,
repeating it over and over from the oak.

My friend brings tulips, pink like nail varnish,
and the sun wraps an arm around us.

The Lancet, wind-tumbled on the grass,
says energetic sex prevents male heart-attack.

You make the house smell of home
lifting bread from the oven

and lose yourself in harmony with Schubert.
I watch your fingers on the keys.

Autobiography

Andrew Motion's autobiography covering the death of his young mother
reinhabits his childish lack of understanding and anguish:

> At the door, I tell Kit I'll follow in a minute, and turn back
> into the room. A lumpy thought is stuck in my head and I
> can't find space for it: I need a minute alone. I'm thinking
> that for most people childhood ends slowly, so nobody can
> see where one part of life finished and the next bit starts. But
> my childhood has ended suddenly. In a day… I don't want
> to talk about it in the grown up language I haven't learned
> yet. Maybe I don't even want to understand it. I just want
> everything as it was. (Motion 2006, p. 16)

Below a novelist describes tussling with writing personally.

Writing My Own Story, by Sarah Salway

A recent memoir piece about my father's death didn't turn out how I expected it to, but this often happens. In my experience, when I plan my writing too carefully it's normally because I'm scared of what might turn up on the page. It is not for nothing that Patricia Duncker wrote: 'Writers betray themselves. The writing hand can know things that the writing mind would rather not think' (2002, p. 183).

Before my father had gone into hospital for what was supposed to be a routine operation, I had been writing about my own hospital ordeal as a new-born baby. Except what I was actually writing was how it felt to have no feeling about something that changed the course of my life. In retrospect, perhaps this was why I couldn't get into the writing. Because I really had no feeling about it, I wasn't risking anything, or learning anything, through the telling.

But sitting by the side of my father's hospital bed, it was still this story I hoped to write. I listened as my brothers and sister – all older than me – told me their versions of what they remembered, and strangely these didn't always tally with my version. My sister told me that she would never have carried out death dances in the hospital car park – and yet I'd told this story so often it felt as though I had seen her do it myself. My brother said that I was never treated as a sickly baby. He remembers being able to cuddle me straight away – and yet, and yet.

Although I had thought it was my story, I had to honour their versions of their truth. How strange that it should be so difficult to change the story you tell about yourself, even if it's to put a better, happier one in its place. My writing, which I had been struggling with anyway, became even more stuck.

So months later, after my father had died and I started writing about our experience with him in hospital, it seemed natural to weave my old story into his. A birth story, and a death story. I started by writing about scars. Mine from my baby operation, and the scars my father had harvested as they tried one medical intervention after another to keep him alive.

However I'm ashamed to say that even as I was writing it, I was still thinking 'but what about me and my story'. Because have I told you that when I was a baby, in hospital, my sister had…

Oh wait. I keep forgetting that this is no longer a truth I can fall back on.

When I handed an early draft of my memoir to Gillie to read, she asked me what it had felt like to write. Good, was my first reaction, but then I thought some more. What had come out for me in writing my essay was that however much I might try to question my family stories, they are still part of me. In many ways the stories I told in my essay about my father – that he was an outsider, that he never obeyed the rules, that he was somehow unlucky – were all stories that I had applied without thinking to my own situation as a baby who managed to make it against the odds. Was this why I had resisted changing my own story from 'poor little me' – the outsider, the unlucky baby, the rule breaker – to the more robust baby my brother and sister remembered?

Because stories can change, we just need to be able to listen to them properly first. Elizabeth Stone says this about her own family stories:

> What struck me first, how much under my skin they were; second, once my childhood was over, how little deliberate attention I ever paid to them, and third how thoroughly invisible they were to anyone else. (1998, p. 6)

An invisible scar? Or a healing bandage? I can see now that I was finally able to write a piece that mattered to me because of the element of risk involved in bringing these stories out into the open. Onto the operating table, to keep the hospital metaphor going. My father might have died, but his stories, the meaning behind the stories I am still telling about my family, live on. It is up to me to get them out from under my skin so I can keep on questioning them, and more importantly, to understand the new stories I tell better.

'I couldn't ever write my family story,' a friend told me recently. 'I had a happy childhood.'

I felt winded by this. I wanted to tell her that my childhood was relatively happy too. I think, however, she was talking about the myth that Tolstoy was guilty of perpetuating: that only unhappy families are worth writing about. But of course not every happy family *is* the same, and by writing my stories, dissecting them and facing the discomfort of having them questioned, I can do what Seamus Heaney calls breaking 'the skin on the pool of yourself' (1980a, p. 47). If I want to write authentically, then it's important to learn as much as I can about myself and where I come from.

The truth is that I have struggled in the past to write autobiographically. A tutor once told me that although she had never seen a cliché in my fiction, my memoir writing was full of them. In retrospect, these clichés were a form of defence in case I should be seen as destroying my family's 'truth'. John Kotre describes how important this is:

> A family's collective memory says who it is, how it began and what it hopes to be… The stories define our traits, saying that we're a practical lot, or stubborn, or intelligent, or troubled. Our children learn from the stories how the world works and what can be expected from it. (1995, p. 222)

So when I answered Gillie's question about how I felt writing my family with the simple answer, 'Good', I was telling the truth. But this was because I had already faced a number of difficult questions before I had put pen to paper. Would I have to write an unhappy version in order to be interesting? Was I betraying my family by disputing its teachings? Worse, if I told the truth as I actually saw it, would I be expelled from the family – a traditional punishment for community members who question accepted beliefs?

I made the decision to worry about all of those challenges after the piece was written. During the actual writing process, my job was to get the story down as I saw it, and to relish the risks involved because I knew I was learning things. When she describes her own memoir writing, Margaret Forster sums up for me exactly how it feels:

> …so I can stop now, writing in the third person, stop retelling stories I was told about the years before I was born… I am there, at the centre. What a difference it makes, how dangerous it is. (1996, p. 133)

Perhaps, with all this going on, it's not surprising how hard it is to uncover truths about our lives, and to let the 'writing hand' lead us to knowledge we may not want. And perhaps it is no coincidence that the first piece of autobiography I have felt happy with was written side by side with my father, even in a metaphorical fashion. But now, it's time for me to step into the centre and start writing my own authentic life story. One with real feeling this time.

What a difference it makes, how dangerous it is.

What happens next

Redrafting is also therapeutic, as Sarah says. Vital images clarify, as the experience, emotion or memory is captured as accurately as possible in apt, succinct words and images. Neither speech nor thought can be redrafted thus. Redrafting is re-recording, getting closer to what is in the heart all the time. The learning and satisfaction gained from the initial writing is sufficient for many therapeutic writers, however.

Writers sometimes like typed copies to reread and perhaps share with family or carers. A photocopied ward booklet, with a cover designed by a group member, or attractive display on the wall, can be rewarding. Groups like rereading their own and others' contributions, a reminder of important and enjoyable work. Some write *blogs*. Many people prefer to keep writing private: of course much is personal such as a diary or unsent letter.

This chapter has introduced the beginning stages of writing and how to facilitate it so writers are encouraged and supported in encounters with dragons and angels. Chapter 3 outlines essential fundamental values and principles, and gives advice and strategies on setting up and maintaining clear, helpful ethical boundaries. It also describes how therapeutic writing differs from creative writing.

Write!

After your six-minute freewrite (see above), reread silently to yourself with care (store, or even destroy, it). Then share it with a carefully chosen other or group, if appropriate.

1. First:
   - Describe in detail your enjoyment of an aspect of your hobby to someone who has never experienced it (e.g. digging compost into a vegetable bed).

○ Think of something you've never done, but would have liked to (e.g. driven a tractor). Write anything which comes: an account, description, reflective thoughts…

2. Describing one or all of these, tell the story using as many details as possible. There may be a memory of a specific:

   ○ smell, fragrance, odour

   ○ colour, object, environmental feature (e.g. lake)

   ○ piece of music, birdsong, animal noise, mechanical noise, person's voice, natural noise (e.g. wind)

   ○ taste of food, drink or anything else

   ○ physical feeling through fingers, feet, lips, bodily skin – such as texture, warmth/cold

   ○ experience from your sixth sense.

3. Think of a person you know well, and would like to reflect more deeply about.

   ○ Put their name at the top of a page.

   ○ Write, with no pre-thought, a list of phrases about them, as long a list as you can (remember they need never see this).

   ○ Now write another list:

     ▸ if your person were an animal, what animal would they be? (what animal would they BE, not what animal do they particularly like)

     ▸ if your person were a colour, what would they be?

     ▸ if your person were a child's toy, what would they be?

     ▸ if they were a cleaning material, what would they be?

   ○ Now write a letter telling them you are thinking of them and asking a question.

   ○ Write their reply, responding to your question.

CHAPTER 3

'I Got in Touch with Myself':
Values, Principles, Practice

Most of our energy goes into upholding our own importance. This is most obvious in our endless worry about the presentation of the self, about whether or not we are admired or liked or acknowledged... If we are capable of losing some of that importance, two extraordinary things would happen to us. One, we would free our energy from trying to maintain the illusory idea of our grandeur; and, two, we would provide ourselves with enough energy to...catch a glimpse of the actual grandeur of the universe.

Carlos Castenada 1993, p. 37

Our deepest fear is not that we are inadequate. Our deepest fear is that we are powerful beyond measure. It is our light, not our darkness, that most frightens us. We ask ourselves, Who am I to be brilliant, gorgeous, talented, fabulous? Actually, who are you *not* to be?... Your playing small doesn't serve the world... We are all meant to shine... And as we let our own light shine, we unconsciously give other people permission to do the same... Our self perception determines our behaviour. If we think we're magnificent creatures with an infinite abundance of love and power to give, then we tend to behave that way, and the energy we radiate reflects those thoughts no matter what we do.

Marianne Williamson 1996, pp. 190–191, 167

A surgeon once snapped at me: 'How can writing mend a broken leg?' Well of course it can't, but anyone who knows about the relationship of mind, body and spirit knows contented people don't get so ill, experience less severe symptoms when they do, and recover more quickly (research evidence in Chapter 1). And what makes happier people? Understanding what they need, not being terrified of what's inside them, being able to ask for what they want, and accepting where they are in life.

Dannie Abse, poet and physician, said in *The Lancet* medical journal that poems 'profoundly alter the man or woman who wrote them' (1998, p. 362). There is a thirst for this profound altering, for this deepening of self-understanding and expression. The rash of poems that followed Princess Diana's death and 9/11 demonstrate that people have much to express and explore. They need permission for this with their own grief, anxieties or memories, not just for an unknown princess icon. We all need this permission, though writing is not for everyone. But it is for many.

Williamson and Castenada seem to be saying contradictory things. I think they both mean the route to leading fulfilled lives and helping others is via allowing ourselves to be ourselves. Not only to recognise our 'one wild and precious life' (Oliver 1992, p. 54), but to enable ourselves to let it shine without striving either to hide its light, or for artificial brightness.

So often we want, but don't really know what. People who over-eat (or drink) know they want, but don't know what, and so they reach for available comfort: food or alcohol. It isn't what they really want or need, so they carry on over-eating or drinking, in an effort to stop that terrible crying want.

In a gilt frame above me as I write is a William Blake etching of someone climbing a ladder leant against the moon. The caption reads: 'I want! I want!' We all have an innate right to want, not quite the moon, but then the person who feels they want the moon has not had their most basic needs satisfied. We are born and we die wanting. That's OK. What isn't OK is constant denial of want, or re-channelling into something inappropriate or unsatisfactory.

I suspect my framing of this Blake in gilt is unconscious irony. So much guilt is problematically associated with wanting. If we can listen to ourselves coherently, lovingly and without guilt then we can begin to communicate with those desperately wanting selves, as well as our loving and supportive selves. We can then begin to sort out how to relate to the world with a measure of control over our own lives.

Maggie O'Farrell, in her Foreword to *The Yellow Wallpaper* by Charlotte Perkins Gilman, describes it as 'a cry, not so much of defiance, but of demand. A demand to be heard, a demand to be understood, a demand to be acknowledged. You hear echoes of this cry in…Sylvia Plath, in Antonia White' (2009, p. 18).

You are the person who knows you by heart. Yet you are probably quite a stranger to yourself. It's a funny thing: we are the greatest authorities on ourselves, yet we are extraordinarily deaf to the 'still small voices' inside, which offer the keys to understanding. Get to know the person 'who knows you by heart' better.

Values and principles

Expressive, explorative, reflective creative writing needs boldness based on trust in the process, and respect for the writer-self. Writing keeps an accurate record. Writers can, if they choose, reread immediately, or several years later: it will not change, unlike an argument where each party is certain their recollection is accurate. Writing can then be restructured, added to, have material removed or altered, even be rephrased to express an opposite opinion or point of view. Writing is plastic in this way, unlike audio- or video-taped discussion or monologue. Alternatively, destroying writing can have therapeutic benefit.

My journal is for me, or occasionally for a couple of others as well. I can say what I like, when, and how I like. The boldness this sort of writing requires is also based on self-respect. This in turn is based on a generosity to myself: the gift of time, materials and focused solitary attention, and a putting on one side the sense of my own inadequacy. A willingness to believe (or perhaps willingness to suspend my disbelief) that all those different aspects of myself which writing explores say things that are OK for me to hear. They're mine. They're me. The foundations below, one therapeutic writer said, 'helped me consider and appreciate the value and quality of my life and experiences'.

Trust in explorative and expressive writing

This can reduce self-consciousness, allowing writers to tap into their strong, wise, creative sides. Whatever you write will be right for you at that time. Although possibly initially unclear or lacking in understanding, we are the world's best authorities on our own experience and so cannot write wrongly about it. Writers who trust they will not be laughed at, despised, disbelieved or shouted at by the paper enable the expression of experiences, thoughts and feelings difficult or even impossible to share directly with another. Writers can furthermore explore areas about which they are unclear or unaware of before commencing, allowing forgotten memories or unarticulated theories to surface. This writing takes free-rein: in letting go we can find our direction.

Self-respect

Willingness to explore beliefs, actions, values and identity is respect for personal integrity. Writing can give confidence that we have something vital to communicate, and can say it well, enhanced by knowing it is only for us to read, at least initially: there is no teacher-reader waiting to correct. We therefore communicate respectfully with ourselves, tackling inevitable hopes, fears, hesitations. Examining a range of different elements which make up ourselves (e.g. destructive inner critics, and wise internal supervisors) can help personal integration (see below). An unselfconscious integrating certainty gained from respecting ourselves in all our diversity can allow insightful openness and creative uncertainty.

Responsibility

We are fully responsible for everything we write and our response to it, even when facilitated. We have full authority over our writing at every stage, including rereading to ourselves and possibly sharing with confidential, trusted readers. Writing fiction can, for example, offer significant insight (see Munno's 2006 story, Chapter 11). Such authors gain clarity into others' perceptions, or other possibilities. In taking full responsibility for our actions we gain freedom to understand, explore and experiment with inspirational playful creativity. Too often we expect GPs, therapists, insurers and lawyers to take responsibility for our anxieties and problems. Deep, yet tentative, private personal enquiry has gone out of fashion.

Generosity

We willingly give energy, time and commitment to those with whom we work, and to our own personal and professional development in a spirit of enquiry. This giving enables us to gain inspiration and experience from others, and from our own enhanced self-understanding.

Positive regard

We write about family and friends, colleagues and students, clients or patients. Any feeling can be explored within the privacy of writing, both for cathartic release, and in order to understand and discover appropriate ways to act in the future. We can express and explore a range of memories, thoughts and feelings, yet still retain positive regard for these other people. Writing can even enhance positive regard by shedding light on negative experiences.

The relationship of therapeutic writing to creative or literary writing

Bonnie Greer (2009) thinks authors write 'night books' and 'day books'. In a night book

> the reader is a kind of intruder…there is something private happening, something that the writer herself cannot understand, and is learning as she reads, as she writes… The night book puts interiority forward, trusts it, encourages it… The daemon is there and the writer just has to obey. Or not. But since I have acknowledged and named the 'night book' I have found a kind of liberation in myself, in my everyday life. (p. 134)

Therapeutic explorative and expressive writing is Greer's 'night' writing, intended for private rereading; sometimes 'the writer herself cannot understand'. Interestingly Saul Bellow is said to have believed that whatever he got up to write in the middle of the night was the best.

Almost every creative writer does some 'night' or therapeutic writing; such personally beneficial pathways are sometimes apparent in published poetry, fiction or plays. The redrafting stages of literary writing ensure writing is crafted into literary products rather than personal tirades, moans or exposure of pain. Redrafting for publication can involve literary writers taking their own bleeding heart, anguished mind or tortured body off the page: readers of published texts are not interested in writers personally, but in what they have to say. Anne Sexton started writing therapeutically at the suggestion of her psychiatrist, redrafting to create internationally published poems. Her therapist thought she thus staved off her eventual suicide (Lester and Terry 1992; Middlebrook 1992).

Readers of therapeutic writing, on the other hand, are deeply interested in *writers*, in their confidential private expression and personal development: exploring *with* therapeutic writers is a privilege. Reading personal material with no relationship with writers would be boring and probably seem self-indulgent.

Most therapeutic writers don't bother with redrafting and editing or publication. Engaging in these later stages without the goal of publication can be treasure hunts for dealing with deep-seated problems. Redrafting can lead vital images to become sharper and more meaningful, as the experience, emotion or memory is captured as accurately as possible. Though I recommend people with psychiatric diagnoses should be supported by therapeutic, medical or healthcare professionals.

Therapeutic writing need not obey normal writing rules, as a relationship with the writer aids understanding. Literature has rules and forms (the short story), as does everyday writing (syntax; letter writing form), to ensure as effective communication as possible. Blogs and zines (see Chapter 2), which could reach audiences of millions, but probably only a handful of sympathetic people, are usually also written in a personal, non-rule-directed form. The use of strict form, such as the sonnet, can however also be extremely therapeutic (Hamberger in Bolton *et al.* 2004 and 2006).

Here follows a writing workshop with a leaderless poetry group. Such dynamic events are inspiring and revitalising: the sheer pleasure of making something from nothing has tremendous charge, like electricity.

Unbuttoning: Writing and the self

Poetry is essentially primitive – a fundamental requirement of the human spirit…as natural and necessary as breathing.

Andrew Motion 2009, p. 4

The buttons scattered onto the table between us. Willing hands fanned, preventing them rolling away. Six poets used to critiquing our poems, we were now exploring first-draft writing. The large button collection, many antique, were from my grandmothers and other sources. Previous to pouring this multicoloured cascade, we had all written for six minutes with no subject, and no thought of reading out. Each had scribbled furiously whatever was there, with no attention to grammar, punctuation, or even sense: writing for the sake of writing, to spill the contents of the mind onto the page. After examining the buttons, we then chose some for ourselves and each other with no explanation and little talk. There was a childish pleasure in playing with these lovely things, combined with a childlike pleasure of giving and receiving gifts.

Tearing ourselves away from the gleaming colourful heap, we each wrote about our own pile, initially anything about the button experience, for about ten minutes. Then I suggested that some of the buttons might represent someone or something in each of our lives, past or present. We had 20 to 30 minutes for this.

A TIN OF BUTTONS, BY CHRIS WOODS

You empty the bucket over the table top
and waves of buttons break across driftwood.
We choose shells for each other on this beach.

bright and symmetrical or soft and playful.
We give them because we like them.
We give them because we are like them.

They link in helices, then break and reform.
You give me your inheritance of buttons.
We pass buttons between us like messages.

What is this code we use, deciphered through
fingertips? We give a bit of ourselves
to each other, pass it on in sequin sequence.

Going back through generations of buttons
I find the colour of your eyes, that military
 bearing, your mother's playfulness and fun

and my childhood. The last button I choose

for myself is brown and leathery like a conker
or a chestnut roasting in a bonfire of buttons.

BUTTONS, BY ALICIA STUBBERSFIELD

This workshop allowed us to be children again, sorting through
and choosing those which appealed to us. One delightful aspect
was that Gillie suggested that we picked buttons for each other
and these gifts gave an added layer of trust amongst people who
already knew each other well.

The buttons chosen by me and for me became symbolic of
particular times and people in my life. They told a story, albeit
only a glimpse of it, as one small black button with a pink gleam
at its centre suggested.

Change the buttons and you'll get away with it…

Find the pink tin, psychedelic flowers
on the rusting lid. Prise it open.

Buttons run through your fingers,
not-quite-sand on the West Shore,
small, cool pebbles ground by sea.

Imagine the garments, long gone,
made into dusters or given to the rag
and bone man calling down our street.

Pick some out – one a fifties beaded hat
my aunt wore going back to Nashville,
her baby son in her arms.

This the perfect bow my mother tied
into my pin-curled hair, arranging me
for the photograph.

Here is the Art Deco bathroom at our hotel,
black tiles and green bath, basin, toilet.
I was Olivia de Havilland.

Now the ocean beyond our window,
storm-churned, cloud edged by lightning,
mother-of-pearl moon hidden.

This is the pink gleam of a story,

an ammonite uncurling ancient dreams.

We explored different ways of writing 'as natural and necessary as breathing' for ourselves and possibly each other. Vital personal images emerged, allowing access into mental and feeling areas not habitually experienced. Initial explorative stages of poetry, fiction and drama (notes, scribblings, journal entries) all draw upon the self. Writers dialogue with their inner selves, often very deeply in a qualitatively different way to thinking and musing: Bakhtin calls this being multi-voiced or polyphonic (1981; see also Rowan 1990). Personal memories, dreams, reflections, hopes, fears and so on are explored and mined; inner thoughts and experiences not generally expressed are laid open to the scrutiny of others sometimes extremely courageously.

THROWING, BY JOAN POULSON

The handling of the buttons was very pleasurable and, as I touched and turned, I felt increasingly relaxed. Then Gillie suggested that if we saw a button we identified with another member we might pass it to add to their growing heap. This was a joy, no sense of anything but delight in seeing something I felt might make a tiny gift: probably intensified because we had worked together for years and there is a strong sense of trust within the group.

I have mislaid my notes and can't recall how I met with the memory of 'my' button tin, the one I flung at my husband. I think the draft begins to show that the three gestures were enacted over a number of years and that, eventually, I left my marriage.

> There was the flinging of the button tin
> across the kitchen, buttons like metallic,
> colourful bees. Another time, she'd thrown
> a kettle in the kitchen,
> hit the bee-man on his shoulder.
>
> Years later the jug of milk scudding across the table,
> being spontaneous as her therapist advised.
> Three spontaneities in that long marriage.
> Throwing, she hadn't thought of the clearing away. (Joan
> Poulson)

Writers often explore through images. William Carlos Williams expressed this simply: 'No ideas but in things' (1976 [1944] p. 133). The writer does not begin with thoughts and ideas, but observation and images: things. My own experience reinforces the psychological theory that metaphor can give access to buried traumatic memories (Bolton 1991, 2003, 2006; Modell 1997). Metaphor gives a relatively safe non-direct approach to remembered or felt experience. Images can be explored sensitively, leading to far greater understanding than directly addressing the feelings or experiences.

THE BUTTONS EXPERIENCE, BY ROBERT HAMBERGER

Buttons poured out like pebbles on a shore, and a number of us played with this image in our writing. The first part felt playful and child-like, with an adult's sensibility working behind the scenes. Fingering through hundreds of buttons (knowing this one might bring Alicia pleasure; that one felt like an aspect of Joan's character; this one was part of my response towards Gillie or Chris or Andrew) was both a joy and a subtle risk. Can I hand over this button-message; will they like it; how will it be received? Similarly, receiving buttons felt a mixture of pleasure and curiosity about how others might see me.

When Gillie asked us to write the second brief piece about the button experience, it arrived as prose for me, starting with memories of my mother doing out-work, finishing trousers. Even these memories were blurred by questions about myself, how I may be perceived. Here's an extract:

> Of course seeing them I remembered the sewing tin and the little card of buttons. I just assumed mum's out-work happened most evenings. I realised of course it was for money, but it was as unquestioned as the weather. Are these buttons me? Let me be glitter or mother-of-pearl. A button the colour of custard powder; an intricate star; the broken stones. Is that me? Toggles on a duffle-coat for the boys and me as a boy. I was proud of the brown-wool jumper and a camel the colour of custard over my chest. If the years add up to a handful of buttons, sort them, count them: one a golden rose, another a black daisy, another a purple tulip and four diamonds by an opaque heart.

That phrase at the end was picked up and played with when we had a longer time to write. I was particularly interested in a large mother-of-pearl button, but deliberately resisted writing about my mother, since I've been working on poems about her for years. I wanted to explore a freer, less memory-driven way of writing, that played with metaphor around the sound and feel of a mass of buttons. After various false starts and re-drafts this appeared:

> If the years add up to a handful of buttons
> hailstones scatter at my ankles.
>
> Falling moons, mere glass and oysters,
> snail-shells, acorns, mother-of-pearl.
>
> A sheer drop and I'm splintering with them:
> shingle and tide, shingle and tide.

I still don't 'understand' this piece logically, but it felt liberating to free myself from mother-memories, so to speak, to try instead to describe through images what might be happening to me at this point in my life, my fiftieth year. As was probably inevitable, the following day my mother came back powerfully in the first lines of a poem from a workshop led by another group member. Joan guided us sensitively to write about a journey we may take tomorrow, which of course always has to start from today. (Robert Hamberger 2007)

The buttons were like windows into our writing group's inner writing selves. Gaps in walls enable the warmth and illuminative power of sunlight to come through. Windows or openings need to be created (see also Chapter 14).

We used several other space-opening devices that writing weekend: the idea of journeys taken tomorrow; Buddhist meditation techniques; an object chosen with closed eyes from a treasure box full of old toys, length of rope, toddler's shoe, string of beads and so on (if you can possibly imagine what the so-on might be). Not everyone went on a memory journey with the buttons.

Button, by Andrew Rudd

I didn't have any immediate evocations of childhood or memory, but found a Victorian button with an engraved picture of a bowman pointing an arrow down from what appeared to be a bridge. This suggested the buttons as fish, and the reflection came to life at this point. Each button has two 'eyes' and a distinctive shape, and I started to name the 'fish' I had. It is a kind of associative daydream where unfamiliar objects engage with the language, and draw out names – names which are created by combining words and making metaphors. That's the process I may continue with if I decide to develop the poem.

> On the five-arched bridge
> the bowman holds fish
> in the still gaze of his arrow.

> Sliver, Florentine, Mottleglide,
> Twignose, Blueswirl, Button:
> caught in the sun's unbiased
> light.

One group member, John Latham, was abroad. We arranged selected buttons on white paper; Andrew photographed and mailed them to John who sent this a month later.

BUTTON BOX, BY JOHN LATHAM

Don't worry, this is not an attempt at resurrection. Long time though it took, I have let you go. If anything at all it's a haphazard search for some kind of thread, a search through your button box as you called it, though it always was a tin. A thread I may not find amongst these scraps and whorls of cotton, tangled up at random with hundreds of buttons, of every conceivable colour, size, design; made of bone, wood, brass, glass, leather, tin, and materials unknown to modern eyes: almost anything, it seems, that could be fashioned into a thin, strong disc, to slip snugly sideways through a hand-stitched button-hole. Almost anything here, except plastic.

Once consigned to the tin their chance of re-use was negligible. That wasn't the point of them. Penny cards of buttons were the ones used for replacements, garments made at home. The buttons and miscellany of other items in the tin were, it seems to me, the working-class woman's equivalent of the jewelry they would never have, but more powerful in their associations, even when – as decades passed – they became submerged one great river, with only stubs and nubs of rock that could be individually recognised. As the fingers that sifted them changed from smooth to calloused, the tin filled slowly up, not just with buttons, but the history of a life, incomplete of course, illegible in parts, but even so – it seems to me – the kind of history that matters most: not kings and coronets, earthquakes or great wars, but fireside evenings, by candle-light if the shilling had run out, quiet mostly, coals settling, a snatch of chat, the most common movements the turning of a page, a spurt of flame, a needle's elegant trajectory, the raising, lowering of a cup of tea. I'm wrong, it's not a thread I seek, but the potage of a history: of yours.

As a child I often pictured the road leading to Heaven. It was paved with buttons from the tin. A history, a symphony, the music always different, the notes unchanged. I drift my fingers through them, close the lid, knowing I'll be back.

Conclusion

Writing can enable 'a glimpse of the actual grandeur of the universe', and remind us we have an 'abundance of love and power to give', as we have seen (Williamson 1996, p. 167). We learn a lot about ourselves, and the healing is accompanied by laughter and talk as well as tears. Many do not want or need redrafting and editing. There is no boundary between literary and personal development writing in the first exploratory writing stage. Introducing writing to those with no thought of publication takes 'literature off its high horse' (Schneiderman 1995, p. 619). We help people unbutton their own memories and metaphors.

This chapter, and the rest of Part One, gave foundations for working with others with writing. Part Two gives in-depth examples of work with different populations of clients and patients, and information on how to work in a focused yet safe enough way. Chapter 4 explores working with children.

Write!

After your six-minute freewrite (see Chapter 2), reread silently to yourself with care (or store, or even destroy, it). Then share it with a carefully chosen other or group, if appropriate.

1. First:

- Write a list of words about: your work, a primary relationship (e.g. with a life partner, parent or child), your home, your hobby, or something else important to you.

- Now highlight all the abstract nouns (e.g. love, hate, tenderness, support, hilarity).

- Choose two of these; at least one must be positive.

- Now put one at the top of a page (let's say *hope*) and create a list:

  - If *hope* were a creature (animal, insect, fish, etc.), what would it be? (e.g. *hope* is the white butterfly flying through my open office window)

  - If *hope* were a food what would it be?

  - If *hope* were a season or weather what would it be?

  - Think of other categories; add them to your list.

- Read your list through: it might be a poem; it might tell you quite a lot.

- Now, if you like, imagine all or some of these elements are in a picture; describe the picture.

- This picture hangs in a room; describe the room and what it would be like to live or work there.

- Now do the same process with the second word you chose from your original list.

2. Make a list of:

   - an old thing

   - a new thing

   - a borrowed thing

   - a blue thing.

   Describe each carefully.

   Now write a list of

- an old smell or taste

- a new colour or something else you've seen

- a borrowed memory (something a parent or partner told you about perhaps)

- a blue piece of music, picture or building.

Write notes about each, allowing the words to appear on the page.

Now write a list of these, expanding each element as you go along:

- an old emotion

- a new feeling you've never felt, or only felt recently

- an emotion you experienced in another (a child's delight)

- a blue feeling.

Now write a piece mixing and melding elements from these in some way: allow it to happen.

3. *Silence*: 'Words are only / For what can be said; silence / Has a bigger vocabulary' (Fanthorpe 1996, p. 3).

Write about something silent: give it words (e.g. a little child's expression when given her comfort cloth; a wilting flower…).

PART TWO

Writing with Specific Groups

---·•◦•·---

CHAPTER 4

'Secrets Kept Safe and Sound': Children Writing

'You can't depend on your eyes if your imagination is out of focus.'
Mark Twain 2009, p. 16

When he speaks of writing, he gestures like a magician pulling a rope of silk scarves from deep within himself. 'I don't write easily,' he explains. 'Writing is always taking out a piece of yourself; it's a mixture of pain and pleasure…' After such a childhood, Appelfeld insists that he could not have become anything other than a writer. 'The paper became somewhere I found my mother, my father.'

Ahron Appelfeld 2005, p. 15, interviewed by H. Anderson

Education and therapy have a narrow dividing line, both being learning about ourselves, our world, how it works, and how we work in it. A child adapts and relates to the grown-up world, hopefully wielding it to their advantage.

Children naturally construct narratives, and play with words and images; young children *all* the time. Writing (often associated with drawing) can be a straightforward way for children to express thought, feeling, memories, dreams: whether joyfully hopeful or fear- and anxiety-laden. It brings the affirmation of self-expression and creativity. 'The arts help children learn to say what cannot be said…they must reach into their poetic capacities to find the words… The arts are our culture's most powerful means for making life in its particulars vivid. In this way, the arts elevate consciousness' (Eisner 1985, p. 69).

Children can be burdened with inhibitions, perhaps even more than adults, preventing exploration and expression. Teachers and parents can unintentionally inhibit by instructing how to do things *properly* and correcting, rather than working from children's experience, skills, needs and wants; peers can damage by mocking. Once children trust that personal expression is valued, writing content will develop, as well as clarity and expression. Once freed from constraint, children (and adults) write wonderful grammar and form, with great content: because they grasp a desire to learn what they need, when they need it. Lydia Fulleylove describes an intensive writing experience, respectful of child writers and their writing.

THE WRITING SNAKE, BY LYDIA FULLEYLOVE

It's Sunday morning, the second day of a Northcourt cross-arts weekend. The snake is a long piece of white gauze which we have all carried from the house to let it drift across the lawn above the stream. Everyone crawls under, the material draped over each person so we are completely covered. Everyone knows they can opt out at any point but no one does. For twenty minutes all we hear is the sound of the garden and sometimes the scrape of our pencils as we record our immediate responses: feelings, senses, thoughts, memories. One by one, as we are ready, we crawl outside and start to draft our poems.

Northcourt weekends were set up during my spell as Literature Education Development Worker on the Isle of Wight, funded by Arts Council England (ACE) and Isle of Wight Council but now run independently. Northcourt is a private manor house in the fold of the Downs, set in a beautiful garden. Living close by, I saw its potential as a place of retreat and inspiration, and arranged with the owners to hire rooms and use of the garden for writing weekends. The weekends are not residential though the children often say they wish they were!

> Secret place
> private space
> where time stands still,
> no one to shout
> just the sound of nature
> the trickle of a stream. (Rosie)

A place to hide
a private sanctuary.
You can reach out and be comforted
by the warm blanket of air,
somewhere to forget and remember,
you can switch channels on entering
it helps you to understand,
it comforts you. (Joseph)

Within the bounds of Northcourt's warm walled gardens
a white snake stretches and swallows
a couple of dozen children.
Inside its tunnelled intestines they sit
illumined by the white light of writing
or rest, peaceful, whole,
inside the garden,
inside the snake,
inside themselves. (Pat Murgatroyd, adult tutor)

This weekend is following the theme of *inside and outside* which grew from a discussion of whether in our high speed constant communication society, young people have enough time for quiet and solitude, to inhabit that inward space needed for reflection and imagination. In planning the weekend, writer Philip Gross, artist Zelie Gross, and I wanted to balance this with the outward pleasures of working in the house and gardens and of collaboration in the group. Afterwards, many of the young writers named the quiet time when they were inside the snake as their favourite activity. Their writing shows how much they valued this time.

The experience of space and quiet has been a significant part of Northcourt weekends from the start in 1998, though we hadn't before consciously shaped and included it in quite this way. Each weekend has been a new experiment based on the discoveries of the previous one, yet growing from key elements present from the beginning: the opportunity to work in inspiring surroundings *alongside professional writers and artists*, the provision of a *sustained period of time*, away from the distractions of home and school, with those precious spaces for *silence, reflection, solitude*; the development of *collaborative* as well as individual pieces, learning important social, as well as creative, skills; the beginning of the exploration of *cross arts work* with writing, drama and visual art as powerful new means to self-expression and exploration; the offering of *structures and shapes* to help them to discover fresh ideas and new things in themselves through new means of self expression. And although we celebrate with performance and anthologies when appropriate, the weekends are about process not 'end product'. We hope the children will come away with a strong sense of their own potential. As one child writer put it: 'The snake uncoils. His journey's just begun.'

The young people, usually aged between 11 and 14, come from a wide cross-section of backgrounds. Some may be identified as 'gifted and talented', others, as 'underachieving'. They have in common a strong interest in the creative arts. They often flourish in a more relaxed atmosphere where adults work alongside as fellow writers and guides rather than as teachers. For Year 8 students, a Northcourt weekend can be especially significant. It comes at a transition point in their lives between 'middle' and 'high' schools when they let go of the familiar and move on to new schools.

Let's take a look at the experience through the eyes of young writers, who like many, seemed to grow in confidence as the weekend went on. One writer said:

> It was totally different from school. For a start we called the adults by their first names. When it came to writing or drawing, everyone did it, adults working alongside us and they'd share their poems too at the end, though you could always say no. The place was nothing like a classroom, more like something out of a story, grey stone manor house, wild gardens, woods, stream, and panelled drawing room with comfy sofas. It was inspiring just being there. I was really nervous at first but we were put into 'home groups' of eight with an adult. I'd been worried about not knowing anyone as no one else was there from our school but by the end of the weekend, I'd made new friends, including two who were going on to the same high school next year. Lydia said making mistakes was OK, you couldn't be a writer without trying things out and gradually I stopped being worried that I'd get it wrong. Drawing was one of the things I liked best, specially when we had to 'take a line for a walk', just keep looking at the thing we'd chosen all the time we were drawing, no rubbing out! You had to be really still and forget about everything else.

Sometimes we could choose our own quiet place to write. At the end my friend Tallulah wrote this poem called 'A Writer's Paradise'. It showed what I felt too. (Compilation of young writers)

> A towering house and wild gardens,
> A place of song, dance and adventure,
> A place which holds my whispered dreams,
> A place of my secrets kept safe and sound,
> Northcourt holds the memory of me. (Tallulah)

Tallulah's poem also shows the power of place. It can both inspire us and help us to feel safe to express new ideas and feelings.

Crossing the arts

Drawing activities, like the young writer mentions, became an important part of the Northcourt weekends. Children in this age group are often more self-conscious than younger ones, and write in ways which they think will please a teacher, rather than express what they might want to say. Drawing not only encourages observation skills needed for creating satisfying pieces of writing but also offers a means of expression when words will not come. For some children, the focus needed has a visible calming effect. And others who are 'stuck' often open up with a story or poem in response to another child's drawing.

Practical drama work with vigorous physical warm-ups offers a way in for other children. It helps us all switch on, engage with each other immediately, makes us laugh. Fast-moving flow writing also helps shift us from careful 'think before you write': planned writing familiar in schools. Some of the children, particularly the less technically confident writers, can hardly believe their luck; and nervous or worried children begin to relax. When we begin to discuss and create characters with a dilemma, children can explore an experience of their own but at a comfortable distance, or try to put themselves in someone else's place. Often the themes the children choose to explore seem close to their experience: loneliness/ isolation, bullying, a parent leaving, even the death of a parent, unemployment, life threatening illness.

My Dad's got a new girlfriend, Susie. She's a cow! I hate her! Most of all I hate my dad. How could he do this to me? Most of all, how could he do this to Mum? She won't admit it but she really loves him. I used to hear her tell her friends how wonderful dad was. All she says now is, 'How could the cheating scum-bag put us through this?' (Lucy)

Mum is always shouting at me. I wish I could live with my dad. I would give up most of my things to see him. I want to see him so badly. Should I run away? Could I run away? (Kimberley)

Later, the children work in groups of three to write and perform scenes for their characters, a significant learning experience, as we realise the degree of give and take and 'letting go' which are needed in collaborative script-writing. On one weekend, adult writers worked to stitch together a drama from the children's monologues and scenes, which picked up the theme of loneliness, centred on 'Bill', an outsider character. The boy who had created this character moved from his 'on the edge' position at the start of the weekend to becoming totally involved and central to the drama. The creation of the collaborative piece is also important for some young writers' self-esteem: a chance for less confident children to see their writing valued and working effectively in the context of the whole, 'like a real play'. This experience is similar to the collaborative poem making on a poetry/art weekend when the whole group has contributed lines to a poem scribed by an adult writer, who afterwards shapes and orders the ideas and 'gives them back' to the group.

What I've done is simply what I do with my own drafts. Sometimes a less confident child is surprised to find a line of theirs suddenly looks like a 'proper poem' without a word being changed – just bolder use of lines and spaces... The words must not feel *taken* but *borrowed*, that's the test.

Philip Gross 2006, p. 23

Ephemeral sculpture weekends offered children a particularly intense experience. The experience of letting go in writing or art when we cut and re-make or, as here, return our sculptures to nature, was closely and naturally reflected as children explored letting go situations on life.

Spell of the Patchwork Elephant

Look one way, I am the face of a patchwork elephant,
My trunk cascades to the ground, like a waterfall.
Look another and I am a ladle of forest soup,
A broth of petals, spindly twigs, a strange haul.

I'm a long paddle lapping water,
A whale of material substance, I float
I am bleeding, broken bark,
My hull cuts the water, like a powerful boat.

The wash of colour rushes closer,
A whale's head scooping up the sea,
A fast flowing river from a many coloured spring,
A rhythmic rhyme for you and me. (Group poem)

Three young people crouch on the grass beside a 'found' sculpture made from fallen things collected from Northcourt Manor's garden. Beyond them, alongside the stream, leaning against trees, hanging from a branch, whatever fits the site and the materials, are other sculptures and groups of children writing or talking as they write a four line stanza as they visit each piece of art. Their poems grow from sharp observation of each other's sculptures as well as from imagination. These three are now back with their own sculpture, each offering a line and collaborating to produce a final line which rhymes with line two and then cutting, editing and choosing the best order for their set of four line stanzas.

Everyone began by looking at photos of Andy Goldsworthy's work and talking about spirits of place and the idea of ephemeral sculpture, discussing how it might change and disappear. Then we went out to collect 'fallen things': twigs, leaves, bark, flowers, from the garden. This practical activity in small groups took the place of 'warm ups' in previous weekends; the shared task becoming in itself a way of relaxing and getting to know each other as well as an initial collaboration of artists.

The following day begins with a ceremony of 'letting go', part of our undertaking to return the found materials. Each group dismantles their sculpture and walks to the 'end ground' giving it back to the garden in a closing ritual, with any words they choose to say. They have explored the creative skills of making, letting go and re-making.

But there's another dimension. Afterwards, they start to talk about other times of letting go in their lives. The poems about loss, about the death of a grandparent, about moving house or losing a pet, emerge without prompting. Artistic and writerly skills are closely and naturally reflected as the children explore 'real life' letting go.

My Dog
One day I called him but he never came,
I went to feed him but he wasn't there,
When I picked up his lead to take him for a walk,
He wasn't there to take,
He has gone, gone forever,
I miss him now,
I miss his hugs and barks,
I miss the best dog ever. (Pembe)

Creative arts weekends can offer children 'the inspiration, insight and strength which come with intense creation' (Appelfeld 2005, p. 15). Children and adults alike can return to everyday lives with sharpened creative skills. And beyond this, a sense of surprise and delight in what they discovered through their exploration of both the place and themselves.

What will come down the river today,
the wavy meandering river?
Will it be a survivor's raft
Hastily strung together?

What will come down the river today,
The clear, sparkling river?
Will it be a boat made of sunlight,
Glinting like sunken treasure? (Katherine)

Lydia describes an away-from-home/school magical experience for children. Teachers, parents and others who work with or care for children can also help.

Every child has a story to tell of major or minor trauma: bullying, abuse, bereavement. Psychologist Alice Miller says children are good at silence, keeping distress hidden and untold (1987). A child locked in anxiety, fear or stress cannot respond to education. They cannot learn from their senses if their imaginations are out of focus. An ancient story tells of a pupil's consternation at her teacher continuing to pour tea until it flows over the table and floor. 'You are just like this cup,' asserts the teacher, 'too full to take more.' We can help children begin to unclog minds and spirits of fear, anxiety, hurt and, distress, preventing effective thought and development.

Writing can offer self-expression and exploration of material difficult, or even impossible, to say. Journals offer private space, the succinctness and musicality of poetry offers convention-free permission, and metaphor can give safe-enough indirect spaces. A teenage cancer patient told me: 'My mum saw the poem and asked to see it, so she knew how I felt.' He couldn't tell his mum, but he could tell her in poetry.

Why, what, how, when, where?

Writing can be qualitatively different from talking, partly because no one else is listening. This physical, slow, creative act records the thoughts and feelings and inspirations of that moment, faithfully keeping the exact words until wanted, perhaps to be rewritten again and again. A child writer can choose to reread, screw it up unread, or show it to a trusted reader. The success of the Samaritans' email service to young people is no coincidence.

Children gain confidence to write given only pencil, paper, the security to write in privacy, an attentive, caring and confidential reader, lack of constraining writing rules, developing an effective grasp of English constructions when they want and need to use them. Some need building up to this, by for instance talking before writing as in circle-time, or supported relationships with a peer study-buddy. An understanding teacher quickly gains experience in reading and responding, to encourage further exploration and expression.

Children can write in crowded classrooms, yet away in a secure private world of their own, if the teacher engenders a respectful, safe, confidential atmosphere. One young cancer patient I worked with found writing really useful, and then stopped, refusing to see me again. I was mystified until I learned he had written about a dream for a member of staff, who shared it with other colleagues without asking him first. He was deeply hurt. It's important to offer children, as much as adults, total respect and confidentiality.

My young cancer patients wrote what they thought and felt about being ill, about the ward and their treatment, how they envisage their futures, and events from their pasts (see Chapters 1, 4 and 5). Once we went on a magic carpet journey, listing their needs starting with clothes and continuing to the personal and spiritual (Bolton in Bolton *et al.* 2006).

Writing forms for children
Journals
Journals are an age-old method to gain contact with experiences, feelings, knowledge, memories. And to communicate: diaries are being used to bring Jewish and Arab children together in the Middle East. Both individual and class journals are valuable.

Traditionally diaries are private (mine had a lock and key). Individual journals can also be a communication between teacher and child. If children are rewarded for writing thoughts, ideas, feelings and dreams, they will soon want to express and explore vital personal and social issues. Readers need to be aware that sometimes treasures are hidden below seemingly banal surfaces.

Class journals belong to a whole class. One primary school teacher gave children the responsibility to write and draw daily in turns in a freely available book. These young children followed their teacher's lead in taking pride and interest in listening to the voices of others, developing a growing culture of shared experience.

Reflection
Primary class activities can be stopped sensitively and pupils asked to write what they are feeling and thinking at any moment during expressive drama, practical maths, science, physical education and so forth. They'll be surprised initially; but fleeting ideas and images can be captured.

Writer-in-residence River Wolton involved young children in intensive drama and performance poetry about Ancient Egypt. Children began to explore and express feelings about death and dying. The distance of a pharaoh's death enabled them safely to come close to their own feelings about perhaps the death of a grandparent. Such reflective pauses can be introduced into many areas of classroom life. Another teacher took his class to an adjoining graveyard, where they sat in the long grass writing poems.

Stories – with child cancer patients

Narrative making, whether about real or fictional events, comes naturally to children. They'll tell you what they've been doing just as readily as about their imaginary friend. Ask them to describe their picture and they'll tell you its story. Children find story structure natural and perhaps even supportive. A story has a secure beginning, middle and end, and specific predictable characters and places, even if these are fabulous (see Adam's story, Chapter 1; Josephine's magic carpet adventure [Bolton *et al.* 2006, p. 208]). This is unlike events in life which are all muddly middle with little or no discernible beginning, and rarely satisfactory ends. A child's story often ends with comfortingly going to bed, for example. And real people are unpredictable: mum can be loving and caring one minute and turn into a raging witch the next. Have a look at the firm plot structure of Adam's story in Chapter 1: beginning, middle and end, and a safe habitual environment of bedroom, kitchen, garden; and the reliable archetypal nature of the characters. The 13-year-old Teenage Cancer Trust Unit (TCTU) patient's *pop star* below is also an archetype of a wise, powerful adviser (for an adult's wise, powerful inner adviser see Chapter 5).

Children with secure attachments tend to wield narrative to represent and reflect upon complex events. This seems to facilitate the development of secure attachments with others in childhood, and later in adulthood (McCabe, Peterson and Connors 2006; Peterkin and Prettyman 2009). Writing and sharing stories can help children develop narrative abilities and appreciation, thereby possibly helping more secure attachments (Peterkin and Prettyman 2009).

Children's stories can do even more than this. They can use characters to do, say and experience things they cannot themselves. Writing helped the young teenage cancer patients I worked with say things they couldn't speak (see Chapters 4 and 5). They were multicultural, some with English as a second language, some not very able with writing, some very bright. All extremely sick.

A 13-year-old wrote fiction with great earnestness. Here is the final section of his story about a 5-year-old struggling in a ward very like his own. However hard the staff tried (and try they did), an oncology ward is nothing like home.

> The other children that he had made friends with on the ward were very friendly and talkative. They knew each other for about a year

now, and they were ready to do anything for each other because they had gone through so much together, experienced so many pains together.

The next day the organisers introduced a singer who brings the children some presents. He sings pop music, and he's been on Top of the Pops. His songs have been number 1. He also does many charity events, concerts, and he loves children. With him he brings copies of his albums with diskmans – one for everyone. And autographed pictures, and photographs and things like that. All the children are really excited when he sings live for them. He has heard about Ben's sleeping problem and he tells him that everything will be OK. He tells him to listen to his music and that'll help him sleep. He tells him to just think of ideas at night for stories – could be anything – adventure, fantasy, horror – like the story they heard read at night. And he tells him that the ones he wants to remember maybe he can write them in his diary or something the next day. He suggests Ben might write a diary about what's been happening.

Ben is amazed at what the superstar is telling him and he is surprised at how much the guy knows about him and his life. In the common room after hearing the story all the children and the nurses say goodnight to each other with hugs and kisses and retire to their beds.

As Ben wasn't sleepy he reflected back on the words of the superstar. And he decided to write a diary. Firstly he wrote about his parents and his family being there for him all the time. He dedicated a number of pages to his kittens for being there no matter what happened, even when he was in trouble. We wrote about all of his friends, his superstar, all that had happened on the first day. He wrote about the nurses taking care of him well, activities taking place, and what he planned to do ahead. He writes a couple of lines about the surroundings and the countryside.

He thinks he can cope with it now, and people have comforted him and told him of techniques he can use. He came back to the present and dreaded the moments when his parents would leave him. He lifted up his diskman, put the headphones in his ears and slowly closed his eyes. (TCTU patient)

I quote from my research field-notes:

This patient, an extremely polite, serious charming 14-year-old, whose school work was nearly always scientific, wrote this long story on several occasions. His little protagonist bravely tackles fear and isolation (similar to his cancer ward), helped by an authority figure, a pop star. He used Ben's struggles and life successes to say things to himself. Issues can sometimes be expressed and explored fictionally, when they can't be tackled head on. The pop star dispensed wisdom, clearly helpfully satisfying to his author. A 5-year-old can be frightened, and accept such help, and the writer could accept it on the character's behalf.

He was always definite about his stories. I made an error once in typing because I couldn't read the writing. He very politely told me he must have said it wrong before, but what he *meant* was: and then repeated exactly what he'd written. Yet despite this clarity and certainty, he often used the provisional tense: maybe the character did certain things. Does he live his life in maybe? The pop star is the wise person who knows Ben inside, and can offer wise advice. The pop star knowing about Ben's sleeping problem came quite out of the blue; the story shifted emphasis and importance from then. This young fiction writer was using his story to hear the strong wise authority figure in his own head: the pop star is his own wise strong self.

My patient had no idea how Ben and the pop star helped him cope, though he was thrilled with writing. He invented a pair of wise mentors in his characters little Ben and the pop star. Ben, too young to have to be macho, and the *authority figure* pop star character, were teaching their author. A sensitive, aware teacher or parent can endorse such elements in children's story writing, in the way I suggested my patient tell himself stories, and write them next morning.

Other stories were written about simple things like washing hair with friends by a girl from Africa, who'd left friends and family, for treatment involving total hair-loss (see Chapter 5). These children were on chemotherapy, recovering from amputations, and other medical cancer treatments.

Ways I encouraged story-writing are described in Chapter 2 and in Bolton *et al.* (2006, pp. 208–211). Many other approaches can be used. People of any age, including children, respond to being asked to write from the beginning *Once upon a time...*

Personal writing to unblock the unwilling student

Personal writing can help with more than trauma or serious illness. A Canadian personal tutor describes a teenage student struggling with English school work.

> I wondered if personal writing could help Sarah. Since she was obstinate about reading, perhaps there were other ways to facilitate her writing? While reading *Writing Works* (Bolton *et al.* 2006) I came across many exercises. I decided to try some on Sarah. If this was to be our last class, why not try something different?
>
> I asked her to write about a place from her past, a place that was special to her somehow, whether it made her happy, or sad, or angry, or safe, or whatever. I asked her to write about it with as much detail as possible. At first, she did her usual hemming and hawing. She said she couldn't think of any places. I told her this was not to be marked, and there were no right or wrong answers. I continued reading *Writing Works*. Out of the corner of my eye, I could see her brainstorming ideas. I smiled inwardly and felt a tinge of pride. This was one of the things I had taught her. When first faced with a writing assignment, do some brainstorming and generate some ideas. See where it takes you and try to come up with something worth spending your time on. I saw her jot down some options, and then apparently deciding on one, she began to write.
>
> She had never been able to write or read for longer than twenty minutes, before checking her cellphone for the time or messages, or asking me irrelevant questions. Being prepared for that, I had come armed with three other exercises to fill out the two hours of our tutoring session. But, to my surprise, as thirty minutes rolled by, she was still writing. After an hour, I began to worry about her. After an hour and a half, I myself was tired of reading *Writing Works* and wished she would stop. But, not wanting to break the beauty of her concentration, I willed myself to read more.
>
> Finally, with just ten minutes left in our two hour session, she stopped. She unclenched her writing hand. 'Ow!'
>
>> 'That was amazing!' I said.
>> 'You haven't even read it!'
>> 'I mean that you wrote nonstop for almost two hours!'
>> 'Well, it's probably not that good.'
>> 'Do you mind if I read it out loud for the both of us?'

It was her description of a small Native reserve up north, called Wikwemikong. She had gone there with other members of her church on a youth mission for a week to teach the children. She described the beauty of the place and the angelic children, which belied the suffering many of them endured. One boy had just lost his father the week before to a drug overdose. Another girl, barely twelve, was responsible for looking after her two younger siblings after their mother had died from alcoholism. Sarah described how humbled she had been that these children managed to struggle through their grief. Since Sarah knew how to play the flute, she had taught the children music. After the week was up, she had fallen in love with them. It was then that she had realised how much she enjoyed helping others.

'It's bad, isn't it?' she asked.
'No, no. It's good. Really good. It's the best thing you've written for me. Thank you.'

Our session was over. I wished it wasn't our last. I wished we could continue.

'I hope you continue to write,' I said.
'Maybe.'
'I guess hoping you'll read is out of the question?'
'Totally,' she smiled.

I smiled back. It occurred to me that she wasn't a lost cause, or a basket case, or whatever I had thought about her. Rather, she was a bright girl with spirit who only needed to be approached in the right way. (Massimo Park)

Drama writing

In the Language Fantasy Approach, young children create fantasy or mythical drama. Therapists work with three children, each inventing and developing mythical characters, who meet challenges with each other's characters (Pehrsson and Pehrsson 2007). The children write their adventures, later recorded with dramatic sound effects. Therapists support and encourage the children's characters in encountering adversities, and keep boundaries (e.g. one character is not allowed to hurt another child's character; whatever a child says their character does or says must be written down). Pehrsson and Pehrsson perceived significant development in the children's narrative and co-operative ability, as well as creative powers and willingness to face difficulty and even adversity.

Poetry and image – with child cancer patients

Images can powerfully facilitate insight. A foreign girl alone in London with only a sister, for chemotherapy for a year, wrote simple stories with secure themes. But when asked in January to describe 2003 as an animal, she wrote *a turtle*. She explained that turtles are slow and lonely. The written image facilitated her to express her deeper feelings simply and graphically.

Traumatic memories are buried in non-speech parts of our minds. Unavailable for normal thought or discussion, they can be expressed in graphic or pictorial images: poetic, short, sharp, concrete images. Poetry writing can be deeply therapeutic and self-developing for anyone.

The pop star writer wrote this image-laden poem, with a story just beginning at the end. Note how it moves from the outside cold and dreary images to the hopeful joyful inside. He might have been attached to a drip and awaiting amputation, but he imagined a joyful light and colour-filled scene:

> Darkness, cold weather, damp and dreary
> Sleet and rain
> Cold toes and feet
> Brown and green trees in thick deep and white snow
> Owls deer and foxes
> Christmas carols and bells
> The colour of tinsel
> The smell and taste of Christmas cooking
> Drinks of all sorts
>
> Tommy wears a red Christmas hat
> with a white bobble on the end
> a shirt, a jumper, brown trousers and trainers
> His job is to set up the Christmas tree
> Putting up the actual tree, the lights
> Putting presents under the tree. (TCTU patient)

Other children wrote winter fantasy stories. Although I gave them open suggestions, several wrote horror situations, for example lost in snow and fog and pursued by someone wanting their blood; it seemed they were exploring the terrors of their life situation. Some ended in a cheerful place like Christmas at home.

Life-lines

Writing life events is useful. One project asked children to write on wallpaper unrolled across the floor. They wrote significant events as fully as they liked, starting with birth. Another class wrote 100-word autobiographies when challenged to make choices and be concise.

Writers in residence

Many schools employ writers for *residencies* or sessions using their special skills, which teachers can develop and adapt afterwards. Aware, skilled teachers and writers will perceive when pupils write therapeutically, and support them appropriately. River Wolton, above, is one such teacher.

Victoria Field helped children through the attainment dip associated with moving from being the eldest and top in small schools to the youngest and junior in huge schools a long way from home. She helped them use the explorative and expressive power of poetry in their last year at primary school and the first term of secondary school. The response was positive, particularly from boys enabled to express and share vital experiences.

Katharine Gallagher worked with Haringey *Arts Council England*-funded *Poetry in Schools* project. Children's day-to-day experience was valued, locating and connecting them to their own heritage and other cultures in writing about food. Katrina Porteus worked with primary school children writing non-fiction poetry about history, geography and so on with a 'local' approach, locating them in their own local environment and culture.

Roselle Angwyn works with children to help them learn to perceive and therefore appreciate their environments more fully. In a workshop on an English Cornish beach, children related to the place with all their senses, found an object, described it and imagined what might have happened to it, or something else about it, writing as if they were the object: using I. One of the 'special needs' children, aged nine, who normally does not concentrate write well or produce anything, wrote this, having found a piece of 'ragged knotted rope':

I was tied up, washed up, lost
I was disowned.
I am trying to break free
Owning the thunder
And the rain. (Angwyn 2010, p. 24)

Conclusion

For children, writing can be rather 'like a magician pulling ropes of silk scarves from deep within themselves' (Appelfeld 2005, p. 15). It can be somewhere they can find their mother and father, or whatever comfort and security they need, as well as inspiration and the insight and strength which comes with intense creation. We now turn to how writing can help the very sick.

Write!

After your six-minute freewrite (see Chapter 2), reread silently to yourself with care (or store, or even destroy, it). Then share it with a carefully chosen other or group, if appropriate.

1. Make lists (as long as you can) of things which:

   ○ I find tickly

   ○ are difficult to understand

   ○ make me sad

   ○ I think are secret.

   Think of other things you could make a list about.

   The lists might be poems.

   ○ You could develop what you feel about one element in one list by writing it at the top of a page and seeing how much you could write about it.

2. Think of things which are important to you, such as your teddy, the moon, your hamster, the tree outside your window, a character on a TV programme.

   ○ Ask them questions (e.g. clock: what do you feel about the time?).

- Give your questions to a friend for them to answer, and you answer theirs.

3. A new baby is going to be born. You want to give it a present.

   - What might you give? (think widely and imaginatively)
   - Write about how you might give this gift.

CHAPTER 5

'Writing is a Way of Saying Things I Can't Say': Writing with the Very Sick

I don't like to talk about the cancer even though I feel like I should. Writing helps get the feelings out of me.

Cancer patient (Morgan 2009, p. 29)

If we believe that facing that pain benefits us, if we go some way to absorbing it and make it a positive part of who we are, if we can expand our view of the world so that pain exists within it, then our appreciation of the beauty of life becomes more profound.

Teenage cancer survivor

Now having been stretched mentally to the outer limits, I've realised because of my terminal position, how we worry, too much, about the future... We can only live, and should become more aware of, the moment, now! That doesn't mean reckless and irresponsible behaviour. It means consider the value and quality of whatever you're doing now.

Palliative care cancer patient

'Grief only grows on a branch strong enough to bear it.'
Victor Hugo

Writing seems to help very sick people understand themselves better; think through issues, memories, feelings and thoughts more clearly; accommodate more appropriately; communicate more effectively with significant others; and offer the focused satisfaction of creative involvement. Appreciation of life can be enhanced, giving a sense of achievement and authority in a valued sphere: *it made it less traumatic than it might have been otherwise.* Writing can help grief take its natural course. This chapter discusses how people in palliative (end-of-life) and cancer care found writing to be *quite purgatorial, therapeutic.* These very sick writers were asked how writing had helped them; some of their responses are in italics.

Art gives no answers. The experience of therapeutic writing does however present personally intriguing questions, the answering of which is an endless quest. More questions are thrown up: in this context the fundamental ones of life: 'what happens when I die?'; 'what might my bereaved relatives feel?'; 'what is wonderful in this world I am about to leave?'; 'in which way was my life meaningful?' This life quest looks inward and, involving only paper and pen, takes patient-writers no further than bed or chair, according with the words of the ancient sage:

> Without going outside, you may know the whole world.
> Without looking through the window, you may see the ways
> of heaven.
> The further you go the less you know.

> *Lao Tsu 1973, p. 47*

A hospital therapist wrote of her patients' experience of writing:

> For some it was a pleasant hour but for others it went much deeper. Some found a new talent for story writing, which gave them creative release and improved their self-confidence and esteem. Others discovered the value of diary writing and continued to express their feelings in writing long after the sessions. Others used the time to really tackle some of the harder issues they were facing.

This chapter examines how Teenage Cancer Trust Unit (TCTU) patients, and community palliative care cancer patients (aged 40 and older), wrote stories (fictional and semi-fictional), poetry, personal journal entries, autobiographical accounts and descriptions of their homes, wards and experiences of cancer and treatment, as part of a research study (Arts Council England funded). We worked in groups (up to eight teenagers in the Cancer Unit) and individually at the bedside. Much writing was undertaken alone and read to me later. I gave four staff writing workshops, to give experiential knowledge and understanding. Two healthcare staff wrote pieces entitled 'What this writing meant to my patients and colleagues', offering insight.

I used narrative analysis (Hillman 1986, 1997) on all writings and interview transcripts (of the patients who wrote three or more pieces, most agreed to be interviewed), an 'empowering' social science methodology, paying attention to subjects' articulation of their own viewpoints and evaluative standards. It focuses upon how the past shapes perceptions of the present, how the present shapes perceptions of the past, and how both shape perceptions of the future (McAdams 1993; Riesman 1993). Steering and management groups supported, advised and oversaw the project.

Each sick person reported finding writing beneficial, in interview and in pieces called 'What writing meant to me'. They found writing helped reflection upon internal issues (e.g. what they thought, felt, remembered) and external issues (e.g. relationships, events, nature). It helped them communicate with significant others such as medical and healthcare staff and relatives. And the very process of creation gave a sense of pride or achievement.

Everyone read and discussed their writing with me. The focus was always what was helpful to them, with no judgment about appropriateness of subject or mode of expression, and no psychological analysis. The personal and developmental impact of the writing were what mattered.

The World Health Organization in 1948 defined health as: 'a state of complete physical, mental, and social well-being and not merely the absence of disease'. This would seem to be enhanced by: exploring and examining personal material privately (alone rather than talking); expressing and communicating things which *can't be spoken*; using writing to help communicate with others; and experiencing pleasure and intense involvement in creative activity. Writing can ease symptoms because the psychological and the physical are intertwined (Bolton 1999a; Bolton, Gelipter and Nelson 2000; Cresswell *et al.* 2007). *The 'placebo effect' is another way of describing the 'creative power of imagination'.* People feel better when they make things; creative expression and exploration is fulfilling and satisfying: *I'm proud and stimulated by some of the things I've written;* writing makes *something concrete.*

Seriously ill people are often distressed, anxious and fearful, find it hard to understand what they are told, and of course they are in pain. Pain is 'somato-psychic…the perception of the discomfort is always modified by the person's cognitive and emotional reaction…[and] people feel threatened by the pain when they feel out of control' (Twycross 2005, p. 5). Illness can lead to confusing and psychologically daunting life changes, to people feeling out of control of their life story (see Frank 2009). Twycross further adds that 'the ultimate tragedy is not death but depersonalisation' (2005, p. 5).

Illness and dying bring many physical and social problems. People's sense of their life story has been disrupted or even broken, and they struggle to develop a new, appropriate and yet satisfying story, instead of sinking into depression or denial (Brody 2003; Frank 1995, 2009). They seek a sense of life's trajectory, even if much shortened. A redrafted satisfying life story can enhance their experiences of living with dying, and also ease loved ones' distress and anxiety. Writing to help prepare for death has good precedence: 'Montaigne wr[o]te to heal himself, and those who attend to his Essays, of the pain and fear of dying' (Heitsch 2000, p. 105).

Writing, using image, description, characterisation and plot, can aid reflection upon memories, hopes, fears, anxieties, fears and angers, without tackling these head on, and can even be enjoyable, life-affirming and confidence-enhancing. It can enable deep emotional, spiritual and psychological work, especially when supported by experienced professionals, and create records for loved ones. Damian Hirst said, 'Art is the closest you can get to immortality' (2006, p. 47).

Some personal writings of illness or distress have been redrafted, edited and published, offering invaluable insight: 'by attending to the cry of another we articulate our own cries, frame them, contain them, and feel less stranded' (Morrison 2008a, p. 6). John Diamond, for example, makes the helpfulness of writing through terminal cancer quite clear (1998), as did Dannie Abse (2007) and Christopher Reid (2009) in their poetry about their wives' deaths.

Use of narrative and metaphor

Narrative

Narrative is a basic form of human expression and understanding (see Charon 2006); people construct stories, narrating them to each other to help make sense of the world and their role in it. For example, Colin Ludlow wrote a brief memoir about his mother having developed the same illness as himself, which had raised his level of anxiety about the possibility of his own cancer returning (see below). Both written life events and fiction seem to give comfort or insight; experiment has found that writing about fictional or recollected trauma offers equal therapeutic value (Pennebaker 2000).

Writing narratives involves an altered relationship with time. We normally perceive our lives along a road of chronology, moving inexorably from past, through present, to future, while at the same time always being in the present. Narrating a story releases the writer into a simultaneous exploration of past events, present thoughts and hopes, ideas, and fears for the future. This can enable awareness of the self as continuous (e.g. Colin Ludlow was the same person who'd pedalled happily through a student autumn).

Narrative writing involves detailed description which can clarify and act as aide memoire, pushing away assumptions, habitual perspectives and modes of understanding. 'God is in the details' (Verghese 2001, p. 1013). Something closely observed, however small, that is written about and shared, can offer insight.

Writing about positive experiences has been shown to improve mood and illness-related health-centre visits (Burton and King 2004). A teenage cancer patient with chemotherapeutically induced baldness, far from home in a different continent, wrote a happy story about washing her hair with a friend: 'She loves washing her hair, and she always wants people to be pleased about her hair.'

A staff member wrote:

> Writing highlighted issues that they perhaps were not aware were as important as they were i.e., when describing characters in a story one patient always seemed to concentrate on the girls' hair. The patient had thought she herself was fine about her own hair loss [from chemotherapy] and the stories raised it as an issue for her that she was then able to talk about and accept better.

Metaphor and imagery

Metaphor and other images are also a basic human form of making sense and connection; for example, pain as barbed wire (Padfield 2003). These patient-writers developed their own effective metaphors to enhance understanding.

Colin Ludlow explored the word 'fall'. Reflecting on a fall from his hospital bed led to realising this small event held significance for him worth exploring.

> ...Autumn, 'Fall' used to be my favourite season when I was a student. One of my happier memories is cycling...in the fresh morning air admiring the beauty of the trees blending seamlessly with the glorious stone and architecture of the college buildings. I also recollect reciting Keats' 'Ode to Autumn' with [my wife] coming home one Sunday morning after a party when our relationship was first beginning. I still love the colours of autumn, but these days prefer the fresh colours of spring and summer mornings to autumn ones. A sign of ageing I fear, although I look back with some gentle amusement at my romantic late-teenage self.
>
> Am I scared of 'falling' now? And by that do I mean, dying? I think the answer is probably 'yes' to both. Too much to hold on for. Keep pedalling... It's been a long time since I fell off my bed. (Colin Ludlow)

This starts with a narrated reminiscence, enjoyable to read and probably so to write, moving seamlessly into reflecting upon another meaning of *falling*. Colin admonishes himself to *keep pedalling*: not give up his struggle to continue his journey of life; after all the *fall* from the hospital bed was a long time ago and he's come some way since. Colin used writing to come glancingly at painful and difficult issues, moving away again, then returning via a different route.

Patients' experience of writing

These very sick people felt their writing initially *has to be written for myself*, giving space and time for private reflection upon seemingly new thoughts, ideas and memories. Even when destroyed unread, writings still communicated vital thoughts. Then they shared it with me, family and healthcare or medical staff. Sharing significant writing with another can be a form of therapeutic disclosure (sometimes cathartic), enabling vital issues to be discussed and fruitfully developed; sometimes readers perceive previously unnoticed elements. Time and again patients would cry when reading out their writing, sometimes when they'd written and privately read dry-eyed. Reading out (or to a lesser extent, having writings read) helps writers take responsibility for and ownership of the memories, thoughts and feelings expressed therein. Many patients wrote explicitly for others, whether Mum or blog readers. Their writing seemed to enable communication of issues which could not be uttered. We also developed new directions for further writings: *post-writing discussions were key.*

Personal writing is private and can be tentative, malleable: *if it's written only for the self, then it can be un-said,* or deleted and the opposite tried instead. Literary products were not a goal, though artifacts-in-progress were extremely important to writers.

Expression of the otherwise inexpressible seems to be enabled. The quietness of writing, and there being no immediate listener unlike with speech, seems to be conducive. *Writing is a way of saying things I can't say. I do it when I'm on my own, and as a way of coping with being down. I know I mustn't give in to being down and give in to the cancer and writing helps.*

Content is generally spontaneous and written *in a fairly haphazard, unstructured kind of way. I write without pre-censoring what I will say,* with *recklessness, in a moment of madness.*

These very sick or terminally ill people said they had *a mass of jumbled thoughts and feelings.* Writing in this way can help *put it in some sort of order.* It gets these *things which swirl around my head 'outside'* where *it will be easier to deal with, instead of just keeping them like bottled up.*

Many people felt the process 'unburdened' them; *what's within me is externalised, is deposited outside myself; words on a page are one of the dustbin men.* All these expressions give a sense of service rendered by the writing: dustbin men remove unwanted waste; an un-carryable load is taken away. *It took me some way towards purging it and integrating it into my life.* 'Purging' and 'integrating it into my life' might seem to be opposite, but I think he meant similar to the one who said: *once it's outside it's easier to deal with.* Purging and integrating are stages: such material cannot be integrated until it has been satisfactorily purged. It seems that writing can purge (*unburden, release from being bottled, empty from the dustbin*) personal material from an inaccessible internal lodging, to where it can be dealt with, talked about and reflected upon. Then it could be repositioned *in some sort of order*. Patients did not read each other's *essays* or interview transcripts so this similarity of metaphors is interesting.

This writing was an emotional journey for each writer. Such thoughts, feelings and memories were not lightly given to the 'dustbin men': *the writing process allowed me to discover the things that were still problems and unresolved issues in my mind…[it] brought a lot of simmering and difficult emotions to the surface*. Yet these writers felt it was worth it, the same person finishing his essay with *so it's been a good experience for me*, and another *writing is a safe vehicle for recklessness*. Aristotle speaks of watching a poetic tragedy 'producing through the pity and fear caused, a catharsis of those emotions' (Aristotle 1996, p. 10). One patient spoke of writing as cathartic, and two others as purgative (the literal translation of cathartic). The cathartic stage of experiencing these extremely painful feelings, and ensuing reflection upon emotions, memories and thoughts, and facing the situation, was disturbing and painful. People need support and help to work towards greater acceptance.

A staff member wrote:

> As for the work with patients I thought it was fantastic on so many levels. Having someone new, who was so confident in what they were doing, became a feature of the week that many patients looked forward to. The writing sessions were a welcome addition to the routine of activities and were offered in a very approachable way that many patients felt able to try. In at least one instance a patient had not been able to verbalise his feelings but found he could express them in writing and went on to use art as well. It was deeply personal and private for him and I believe he was much more at peace for it… The writing definitely affected other activities such as the patient group, [and] patients who had written together talked much more easily together than they had previously.
>
> The great thing about the writing is that the writer is in control every step of the way. It was presented in a non-threatening and non-pushy way, which helped everyone to feel safe.
>
> I found the whole experience enriching and enormously positive. The writing is a hugely powerful tool, which enables people to get in touch with themselves at a level that is much deeper than many were expecting. (TCTU staff member)

Ways of writing with the very sick

These forms of writing can be used with anyone, but methods and examples are given here specific to those at the end of their lives.

Web logging (blogging)

A patient emailed me after I'd visited:

> *A few ideas came into my head the moment you walked out the door last week. I finished up writing something. It just all came out as one fat lump. First-draft. Finished. I put it straight onto my website.*

TERMINAL 11/3/04

Have I been abandoned,
Or in the scheme of things, just set free,
Like cherry tree blossom on the air,
Or a leaf dropped upon
The turbulent surface of a stream.

Its not that my doctors don't care.
What more can they do.
I could turn, stretch out my arms
And say 'don't leave me on my own,
I'm ill and feel secure with you there'.

But I'm the one going to die.
The one bringing tears to the eyes of children.

So in an effort to understand
Why we finish up alone,
I must rationalise my fears
And become strong. (Palliative care patient)

Blogs go to an audience of anyone, as this writer made clear: 'After starting to tell you about the problems of my early teens, I feel a great relief. Some of the pressure, the need to spill more of the beans has gone, but there is more that needs to be said. Those events had a negative effect on me and the way I've lived my life.' By 'tell' he means post on the web. 'You' is strangers as well as family, friends and me. The web might be public, but can also be impermanent. Such personal writing is open to being rewritten, rethought. This plastic quality is an essential therapeutic element: *there's always an option to un-write.*

Poetry

'One fat lump. First-draft. Finished' writing was poetry. It often is. 'First-draft. Finished' poetry seems to be conducive to exploring vital existential thoughts, feelings and experiences. Quick and succinct, poetry does not have bulky prose structures of sentences, paragraphs and reaching the right-hand page margin; and it can leap from one idea or image to another. This speed of first-draft composition, which can enable a grasping of psychologically elusive but vital images, thoughts, feelings and experiences, is not specific to therapeutic writers. Listen to Seamus Heaney:

> ...Czeslaw Milosz's frequent claim that his poems were dictated by a daimon, that he was merely a 'secretary'. Which was another way of saying that he had learned to write fast, to allow the associative jumps to be taken at a hurdler's pace. (2004, p. 6)

Poetry is not always the right medium for experiences such as bereavement. Poet Mark Doty explains why he wrote *Heaven's Coast* (1996) in prose. 'Poetry was too tight, too contained for the amount of emotion I had to express when Wally died. I wallowed in sentences, they were deeply satisfying' (Doty 2003).

Poetry furthermore importantly uses image as a medium of expression and mode of exploration (Modell 1997). Are blossom or autumn leaves abandoned when they fall, or a free beautiful gift from nature? 'Like cherry tree blossom on the air, / Or a leaf dropped upon / The turbulent surface of a stream.' Without these lines, the poem would lose significance and memorability: 'Have I been abandoned / Or in the scheme of things, just set free.' The single word *turbulent* in the right place affects the whole poem (See Chapters 1 and 4 for TCTU patients' poems).

Story and fiction

Writing seems to enable the creation and telling of valuable stories, to the self and possibly also to others. Stories are our human filing system: we don't store data as in a computer, we story it. Once storied, complex and even disjointed events can take on an appearance of greater coherence and comprehensibility (Sartre 1963 [1938]).

Everyone has some sort of life story; we know to some extent who we are, where we came from, and where we're going. Illness, terminal diagnosis or bereavement disrupts or even breaks this previously workable story (Frank 1995). 'I'll never see my grandchildren', perhaps. Previous hopes, fears, plans and aspirations can become irrelevant (Brody 2003; Frank 1995). Considering their life story, including illness, bereavement or possibility of death or disablement, can enable people to make greater sense of new lives (Bolton 2005; Charon 2001; 2006, Charon and Montello 2002).

Some write fiction. See Chapters 1 and 4 for TCTU patients' stories, and their value to them.

Autobiography, reminiscence and fiction

Many wrote about life events, seeking to make some sort of sense. A very young teenage cancer patient, an asylum seeker who lost all her family except her sister, started writing about her home and family memories. Tears flooded her eyes at the subject she chose, but she was called away for treatment after a paragraph. Subsequently her eyes followed me round the ward until I hesitatingly asked if she'd like to try again. Her eyes brightened. Despite poor English and desperate tears, she started again with the same words and wrote this with enormous care.

> In Angola I lived in a small house near to the beach and next to my school. We had a lot of beautiful flowers because my mum said the flowers bring peace at home, and she liked that so much I had lots of friends and I was very happy.
>
> When we came to England we were afraid because we didn't know anything about this Country, and we didn't understand the language. We went to the Home Office and they helped us with some money and gave us a hotel where we were living about nine months. The first hotel was very good, but the second one was dangerous, and they gave us a flat in Holloway Road, where we are at the moment. My sister, Violante, looks after me, we do some cooking together, and she is very important to me. (TCTU patient)

Colin Ludlow wrote about the death of his mother, comparing it with his own cancer experience, and trying to work out the significance of her dying of the same disease. Here is an extract from my field-notes:

Colin said he used writing to help him regain a hold on reality. He felt he was identifying too closely and muddlingly with other people he knew with cancer. He found it very useful when I suggested that the illness has made him lose the plot of his life, by disrupting it so thoroughly. I suggested he's writing to 'heal his story' (Brody 2003; Frank 1995). He found this metaphor very useful.

Dialogues

Writing dialogues seemed to offer a route to making contact with self-comfort and -support (see Bolton 2008); Colin Ludlow wrote dialogues with his 'internal adviser and comforter' (see also Chapter 2). *Dialogue* is our natural form of communication with each other. Patients wrote fictional or remembered dialogues (see Chapters 1 and 4 for stories with dialogues by TCTU patients).

Conclusion

These very sick children and adults, offered appropriate assistance, found they were helped to explore and express deeply personal thoughts, feelings and experiences, reflect upon relationships, events and the natural world, communicate painful or personally vital elements with significant others, and gain a sense of pride and achievement in creation. Writing and talking about it provided essential reflection at a significant stage of living and dying. Penelope Shuttle tells us: 'When you're so tired / you can't bear the world, / that's when you really begin to live, / when you're closest to the world' (2006, p. 93). Despite pain, distress and immense weariness, people can and do realise how alive they are, and closer to the world than ever before. For this they only need basic literacy, pen and paper. We now turn to how writing can help with depression, anxiety and other problems.

Write!

After your six-minute freewrite (see Chapter 2), reread silently to yourself with care (or store, or even destroy, it). Then share it with a carefully chosen other or group, if appropriate.

1. 'Once upon a time there was a...'
   Write these words and continue, seeing what comes. If it's no good the first try, leave it and try again, perhaps during the night or early morning, by a lake or the sea, or in a crowded art gallery.

2. Choose something everyday (plant, creature, weather, element, building, person) to describe fully. Listen to Hopkins' evocation of spring:

   Nothing is so beautiful as Spring –
   When weeds, in wheels, shoot long and lovely and lush;
   Thrush's eggs look little low heavens, and thrush
   Through the echoing timber does so rinse and wring
   The ear, it strikes like lightnings to hear him sing;
   The glassy peartree leaves and blooms, they brush
   The descending blue; that blue is all in a rush
   With richness; the racing lambs too have fair their fling.

   Gerard Manley Hopkins 1953, p. 28

3. What makes a home a home?

   ○ Make a list as long as possible (at least 20 items) of what you would NOT like to change about your home.

   ○ Now make a list of things you MIGHT like to change.

   List things someone else who shares your home (could be a creature such as a cat or spider) finds unchangeable, or would like to change. These lists might become poems.

———◆•◆———

CHAPTER 6

'Keep Taking the Words': Writing to Help with Anxiety, Depression and Mental Health

Poetry is not a healing lotion, an emotional massage, a kind of linguistic aromatherapy. Neither is it a blueprint, an instruction manual nor a billboard... When poetry lays its hand on our shoulder we are, to an almost physical degree, touched and moved. The imagination's roads open before us, giving the lie to that brute dictum, *there is no alternative*... Poetry has the capacity to remind us of something we are forbidden to see... All over the world its paths are being rediscovered and reinvented.

Adrienne Rich 2006, p. 2

The composing of poetry – not just the initial effusion, but the tireless reworking and revising – was a means of drowning out [Ivor] Gurney's auditory hallucinations. The British Journal of Medical Psychology suggests that 'the poetic function of language is less impaired than other functions' in certain psychotic individuals.

Adam Thorpe 2007, p. 21

Writing, particularly poetry, can be of significant benefit to those who are anxious, depressed, suffer from poor mental health, or are struggling with major life issues such as loss due to bereavement, illness, war or becoming a refugee. David Hart describes a long-running poetry workshop with mental health users, exploring 'the simultaneously ordinary and extraordinary' (Furman 2007, p. 165). David's language makes clear his respect both for writing processes and the people with whom he worked. Jackie Brown then tells part of the story of writing her award-winning (Arvon/Observer International) poem sequence about childlessness. This is followed by a description of writing in family health, written by a patient, his general practitioner (GP) and myself, the researcher.

'Poetry' can 'remind us of something we are forbidden to see' (Rich 2006); and people with severe mental health problems can create poetry even if they can't communicate otherwise (Thorpe 2007). Poetry is 'nothing more than a facility for expressing that complicated process in which we locate, and attempt to heal, affliction – whether our own or that of others whose feeling we can share' (Hughes 1995, p. 6). Robert Frost said 'a poem begins as a lump in the throat, a sense of wrong, a homesickness, a lovesickness… It finds the thought and the thought finds the words' (Untermeyer 1963, p. 22).

People often don't know what troubles them, but are unsettled anxious, or experience physical symptoms. Our minds inaccessibly store our most distressing memories or thoughts, enabling relatively unhindered everyday living. But anxiety is still there causing sleeplessness, headaches, worsened symptoms, unexplained background anxiety, and worse. Such unexamined troubles can also lead to substance abuse, anorexia and other compulsive self-harmful chronic behaviours. Poetry can sometimes help such people find the thought and then the words (Untermeyer 1963).

Some do know what troubles them, but have difficulty sharing it helpfully, or have more significant symptoms. The biggest problems are the most difficult to express; conversely some need to express repetitively, yet friends and relatives can only listen so much, and psychotherapeutic time is limited and costly. Writing can be done at any time, for any length of time, alone in silence with only paper and pen. The beneficial effects of the *talking cure* (Freud's name for psychoanalysis) are undoubted, but it is time-limited, and as the proverb tells us, speech is silver, silence is golden. Writing is a powerful *cure* in its own right (Bolton *et al.* 2000, 2004), useful as part of psychotherapy (see Chapter 5). It can take writers very quickly to the heart of what they need to reflect upon: 'some things are easier to write and read on the page than to say' (Peterkin and Prettyman 2009, p. 85).

Writing can help anxious and depressed people face and begin to tackle their problems' source and symptoms while retaining responsibility. 'A wise man ought to realise that health is his most valuable possession and learn how to treat his own illnesses by his own judgment' (Hippocrates [father of medicine] 1950, p. 276).

Occupational therapy (OT) clients have reported feeling therapeutically absorbed or 'calm elation' in a poetry workshop (Hilse, Griffiths and Corr 2007, p. 436), helping them towards better control of actions, promoting well-being, easing of stress symptoms, and enhanced awareness of personal meaning and connection with others. Writing workshops helped mental health OT clients in struggles with low self-esteem, poor self-confidence and lack of identity and motivation: 'In these difficult times where funding is an issue and clients' narratives and stories direct the way of service provision, the use of writing as an activity that aids collaboration and helps identify needs and goals is an important innovation for OTs to use as a tool in their practice' (Cooper 2009, p. 42). 'Writing has done me more good than years of therapy: I'm even dreaming better…somehow being able to get it down on paper has helped' (Whelan 2009, p. 14).

Poetry writing helping women suffering emotional distress and problematic relationships caused by infertility has been shown to 'synthesise and release intense emotions including loss, betrayal, frustration, and anger' (Tufford 2009, p. 1). Carrie Etter (2009) explored the corollary in poetry and prose poetry: 'A Birthmother's Catechism' charts her emotional reaction to the twentieth birthday of her son given up for adoption at birth.

Many poets cathartically and insightfully unburden themselves of shocking events, thoughts or images; then sharing helps them feel less alone. 'Poetry is an attempt to explore, and create, meaning in existence'; since existence is mostly ordinary, then poetry needs to illuminate the mundane: 'poetry captures the deep emotion of lived experience in a highly compressed form' (Furman 2007, pp. 163–164). Putting images next to each other can illuminate and even clarify complex human relationships and experiences. Becoming aware of the sublime nature of the ordinary, finding meaning in the meaningless can be transformative: 'the product is a poem which is simultaneously ordinary and extraordinary' (p. 165).

'I think I'll survive', by David Hart

The Main Street Poets was a group in which people very much supported each other and were responsive to each other's writings. We had never seen each other as people with problems, only as people who make poems. This and the ready willingness to dive into new poetry adventures made the group a pleasure to work with. I call it a group, in fact every week was a new start, with sometimes different people. Someone new coming in is very helpful: a new voice, a new point of view. Made us all take stock again. And as we sat in a small room in the Day Centre, we experimented with writing in a great variety of ways. I understood these sessions to be a kind of negotiation between us. Poetry is not one thing; it is all sorts of things. Each week we discovered something new by means of it. Some of the discoveries were easy to share, some were more private and personal, and a good poem always takes you further than you know.

One day I brought a metronome and we made up, if not poems, at least some rhythmical lines to it. Another time I brought in a mixed bag of small objects and we wrote starting from those. We wrote songs and sang them; we made poems in response to pictures and during many sessions we read poems by other people as a starting point. We played with rhyme, repetition, giving each other words to use, making up lines by adding a word each around the room, giving each other in pairs a first line and writing then the rest of the poem; we made 2-line poems, 3-line poems, etc. We wrote a poem, each of us adding a line, to send to Glanville when he was in hospital. During the summer we spent one session writing in the museum and art gallery, and another in the park on the day of the eclipse. And we did much else besides.

One day I said 'write a sensible poem', then 'write a crazy poem', and when we'd done that I said 'write a serious poem', then 'write a pretty poem'. We work fast sometimes. It was interesting to discover which kinds of poems we found easy and which hard, and what those notions mean: 'sensible', 'crazy', and so forth. A poem might take five minutes to write or it might take five days or you might keep coming back to it over a period of months. I've still been working on my own poems sometimes after years. So the sessions meant either working fast or continuing to work on a long-term project. We wrote an epic poem, which meant reading some of the great long poems of the world. And we worked parallel to this on our own life-story poems. You can write your life poem straight – telling it as you would recount it, while selectively finding the right form for it. Or you can make a fictional/legendary story in which you are the main character. Or you can write episodes as they occur to you. Not at all an easy thing to do, but we built up to it.

The sound of a poem is important, which is why trusting your own voice is part of it. Your voice may come out differently in a poem from your everyday speaking voice, or when you write you might discover a variety of voices. One day we read poems in Italian and French just to hear what they sounded like, and we listened to poets reading on tape and looked at dialects. It is sometimes hard to discover the distinctiveness of your own voice, or to believe it has any. But it does, and variety of voices in the world is precious.

Sound, look, form: each person arrives at the form they need for their own poems, so it is never a matter of trying to impose this or that way of writing. But it has been interesting to try possibilities. We worked on concrete poetry, on using the space on the page imaginatively, on line breaks, on traditional forms and on finding your own. Strong individual ways of writing developed and we weren't afraid of learning from and even imitating them. Anyway it happens unconsciously. It's one of the ways in which we grow as writers.

We experimented with writing as if we were someone else: whether someone we know, or someone imagined. The trickiest part was to write a poem as if we were our own psychiatrist or key worker or someone in some such relationship with us.

And to write them a poem as a gift. Gift poems have featured in their own right. If you're not sure what to give someone, or you want to give them something really special, or you have something to say and don't quite know how to say it, write them a poem.

The members of the group were all psychiatric patients of a Mental Health NHS Trust. External, not in-patients, though occasionally someone would find themselves in a ward for a while. Their ancestries are in Britain, Ireland, the Caribbean, Africa, S. Asia, which gave us a richness of voices. It means poetry is always being re-invented. We can learn from our British past, we can value its poems, but the rhythm of language is in the spoken voice. Multicultural Birmingham has had the chance to make new poetries out of respect for, and the chance to learn from, each other.

I Came Looking for You

This poem came out of a dream and was virtually complete at first writing.
I frequently feel I want/need to regress and this was illustrated in the
dream.

I came looking for you
between a multitude of wrappings
inside that great womb
where you were protected.
I came to you in search of succour
half-expecting to find you sleeping
as they had said,
but there you were awake
and waiting for me
available and simple. (Dianne Aslett)

Thank You David

You brought the light into my life
Suffering is too painful
Poems and medicines are proper ingredients
An end of poem session has come
I am leaving behind the reasonable people
I hope one day they would stand on the peak
Of the highest level in the poems.
I have listened – I have spoken – I have written.
They gave me the real enjoyment
The poems are the real enjoyment.
The people with the sufferings of mind and heart
Goodbye – Mike says goodbye again.
God Bless. (Mike Dhanji)

What is poetry?

Poems are as much as anything about telling the truth, but it's a certain
kind of truth that doesn't appear in the same way in conversation or
in any other form of writing. And poems don't want to be negative,
they're not interested in 'problems'; they can be dark, of course, very
many poems through history have been, so have some of ours, but
there is a paradoxical beauty about a good poem, whatever light or

shade or dark it's come from. Poems have a way of coming up, also, with a humour you didn't know was there. Perhaps there is a chuckle at the heart of things.

It would not be strange to find in poetry the Moody Blues, the bedroom cupboard, St Agatha, toothache, Sisyphus, a boat on the Severn, a woman on dialysis, 'my aunt Madeleine's box of treasures': that is to say anything at all. Perhaps there is a language of roses, of the dark night, of the aching heart, of the grief that seems to be 'lost for words', for the desire beyond words for which words must be attempted. But it all begins where we are, world-bound, in a room, walking alone, working together. Of course the language of being here, of ups and downs, of memory, of dreams and daydreams, of secret sadness and uncertainty loitering at the edge of our daily assurances is common to all of us. Which is almost to say we live poetry, mostly short of articulation.

Saying 'we live poetry', all of us, might be another way of saying we are all mortal. We can't switch on playing the piano if we've never learned, we can't make a beautiful clay pot or design a cathedral or even a garden shed. But we can say 'I love you' or 'I feel terrible about what happened last week', or 'the lake is like mayonnaise in the moonlight', so we are all but poets, all of us. As long as we retain our ability to play: hopping and skipping and pretend adventures and boo, and dance and think laterally and put one word with another that doesn't usually belong together just to find out what the result sounds like. Normally you'll be pandered to if you say you want to 'cry like a rabbit in a spaceship', or 'the room is an apple and we are the pips'. But I'm a poet and will relish this kind of language whatever age or condition you are in. Like healthy.

Writing is not a risk-free area though. And if we imagine it is we are deluding ourselves. What do we do of anything worthwhile without risk? And if it matters to us, then that's what we'll expect, and we live with it (and it can hurt). For my own work, I don't believe in a sanitised, risk-free, neutralised making of art, it won't get me or anyone anywhere, whether personally or for the commonality. Poetry cannot be tamed.

Here follows a description by poet Jackie Brown about her process of writing a healing poem sequence about childlessness. Her creative journey, which led to an award-winning publication, is a process similar to therapeutic writers in a workshop or counselling setting.

Thinking Egg, by Jackie Brown (1993)

The spring of 1990 I wrote the first version of this poem in longhand as I always do, in approximately ten minutes. What prompted it, I don't exactly remember: probably I'd been intrigued by the feel of an egg. I noticed the comment about eggs in Delia Smith's cookery book; and as sometimes happens when you're in that state of hyper awareness that means you can feel a poem coming on, though you've as yet no idea what poem or what it'll be about, I'd been intrigued by her mention of the tiny pocket of air. Why? I can only guess: a void to be filled by a poem, perhaps. A writer doesn't anyway ask why: she just snatches whatever's been offered.

It's been very important for me to belong to a group of poets who I can rely on to give me honest and often terrifying criticism of any poem. As I remember, there was complete silence after I'd read this and then the verdict: intriguing but mystifying. The truth was, I think, that I didn't really know at that point: something about memory and its function in our life. The relationship of memory to truth has always intrigued me, of course it's a relative to truth and not its twin, and the relationship of fiction or story to fact, too. I put the poem away in my 'maybe worth looking at again sometime' file and forgot all about it. Then, at Arvon (www.arvonfoundation.org), I asked the tutor Catherine Byron what she thought. Of course I was hoping that she'd say it was clear as a window-pane and wonderful and the members of my workshop must be daft not to understand it. She didn't; but what she did say set me off on a journey I'd never booked to go on and which was to last for almost two years. She said But this is not one poem: it's a number of poems...

Well, very late – Eureka – I finally knew what the sequence was about. For I'd finally realised this was not just a bundle of separate poems, but fragments of one story. I was telling the life story of a woman who could not conceive children. Once you know, of course, you wonder how you could ever have missed it: the metaphor of the egg is so obviously related to birth and fertility, to motherhood.

From then on the whole writing process became far more conscious. I knew the story I had to tell. It was after all partly my own story though I wanted it to speak for all women caught in the social and personal predicament of being involuntarily childless. I found myself using word-echoes and parallel images, checking each poem with others in an attempt to ensure there was continuity, a choreography, a design in the whole. I wanted the next poem to be much quieter, more sparse, more horrible:

Poaching
...Don't attempt to poach more than two, unless you're a really experienced hand.

Delia Smith's Cookery Course Part 1

...

she's walked further to a flurried place
where infants lie flat under glass, taped
to tubes.

Sleepwalking, she has understood theft,
the urge to prise open, steal and hide,
not care

that another woman is crying somewhere
just so long as her own boat of arms
is full. (1993, p. 25)

Now what I needed for the sequence was a hinge poem which would lead backwards and forwards. I knew it had to be about the cuckoo mother who has given her gift of eggs to the childless woman. I dreaded writing it – my own feelings about my adopted children's mother were such a mishmash of thankfulness and pity and anger and heaven knows what. When I thought about her at all. There was no resolution at all and I actually didn't actually want to explore them. I've never counted up all the different attempts at this poem I drafted, typed up, rejected, binned. Probably between twenty and twenty-five. Some attempted to get into the skin of the cuckoo mother – tragically deprived of the joy of motherhood, sometimes a feckless slut who didn't give a damn for social conventions of motherhood, sometimes an admirable free spirit, at others a fairy godmother gift bringer.

Nothing rang true. Not one of them fitted in the sequence or even found a form as a discrete poem outside the sequence. I was too involved. I think we all acknowledge that extremities of emotion, pain, is what fuels the poetry but and it's a very big but, which all beginning writers need to learn, raw emotion defies shaping. When someone dies or when we lose a lover, we ululate, we don't articulate.

We may write down what we feel but it's highly unlikely that what we write will be a poem. It will be a description of a personal set of feelings, usually fairly incoherent, almost always shapeless, almost always plangent. I'm not a scholar so I may be wrong, but I'd be willing to bet my hat that Dylan Thomas didn't write 'Do not go gentle into that good night' (2003, p. 46) as he watched his father dying, but later much later when the anger had modified and was recollected, re-experienced at a distance as it were.

I was about ready to give up at this point. I couldn't wait twenty years to write my hinge poem, but I couldn't write it now, it seemed. I spent hours researching the appearance of European cuckoos, their habits, their migratory routes – I got to know more about cuckoos than anyone would want to know. Nothing worked. To save my sanity, I went on writing more poems with an eggy theme – geese that laid golden ones, Humpty Dumpty, a grandma who wouldn't learn how to suck them the right way – I can't remember them all. In the end none were used. They were just diversionary tactics, ways of continuing to write something while waiting to write what was necessary.

I'd been working at the sequence for seventeen months. I couldn't end it. I couldn't abandon it. Then a friend gave me an obsidian egg: beautiful like a night sky. I held it in one hand and a hen's egg in the other. Probably I was slightly drunk. This is the sort of serendipity that most writers have experienced. Something clicked. The mad woman in the 'Scrambled' poem had seen her own ova as stone eggs, dead-ends, genetic cul-de-sacs. What if someone knocked her stone eggs from the nest and replaced them with living fertilised ones. I couldn't wait for our guests to leave. I refused all offers of washing up and bade everyone good-night. As soon as the loo stopped flushing and I could hear the silence that meant nobody needed me in their dreams I sat down and wrote 'Cuckoo calling'. It's the shortest poem in the collection, a mere nine lines long. There's nothing clever or witty or even inventive about it, apart from a play on the words egg and spoon race ('egg-and-sperm race'). But this was it. I was just so sure. My workshop group said No it's a copout. I paid no attention. I'd cracked it.

And that was it. I wrote the last poem which brought everything full circle and sent the reader back to the beginning.

Thinking Egg

In the warm kitchen
two women are sitting
confiding failings, fears.
One woman is me.

...like an egg I'm saying
one minute tough enough
to withstand anything, next
a fingertip could crack me...

The other woman is literal –
she'll have no truck with metaphor
No she's saying *No you are not*
an egg You are a woman

and yes, my literal friend,
I guess you are right,
but I'm a woman thinking egg
and staggering under the weight. (1993, p. 41)

By chance or not, the sequence took eighteen months to complete from start to finish: the period, someone pointed out to me, of two pregnancies. I like that. After it I didn't write a poem for over two years. After such a journey, I suppose you don't unpack, do your laundry, have a night's sleep and book yourself onto the next plane for nowhere on standby.

We now turn to a description of GP David Gelipter and myself helping a depressed and anxious patient, Peter Nelson, use writing in a research study (Royal College of General Practitioners funded [Hannay and Bolton 2000; Bolton, Gelipter and Nelson 2000]).

Keep taking the words: Therapeutic writing in general practice, by Gillie Bolton, David Gelipter and Peter Nelson

David, The GP

Sometimes, a patient can have a profound effect on you. He [Peter] was such a one.

He came in despair. Not that you could tell. Quiet, gentle, articulate, just chatting. And then you could see and feel the hopelessness. We had met before and talked of his work. Residential headmaster: children with challenging behaviour. He loved it – his life – dedicated. Then, allegations of financial misdeeds: suspension from duty.

Help me, he was saying, not speaking.

Of course, that's my job. But how?

Have you thought about writing?

Why did I ask that? Discussions with Gillie, yes, but why then? He had so much to say, no time to say it, yet I thought he would burst if he did not. Might this give him time and space?

No, I haven't, he said, but I like the idea. And so he wrote. Copiously. A journal that he shared with me, and I was privileged. Activities; thoughts; desires; focusing on priorities; trying to find a new route: incidentally helping my medical model approach to him. Physical symptoms. Mental state. Almost as if I could see inside his head.

Guilty, said a committee, when he had hoped for vindication. Appeal. Guilty, said another committee. More despair. Appeal tribunal. Delay. But by the time of the hearing he'd ridden through on his words. Cathartic, he said. New jobs, new life, new focus, new worries. Then, his name cleared. Yet he felt no spite. It didn't matter anymore. He'd won anyway.

Still he writes. Keep taking the words. Perhaps I should prescribe them for myself. But I haven't the time. And anyway I'm a doctor, so I don't need them. Do I?

Peter, The Patient

I could not see. Twenty-eight years meeting other people's needs. Advice, education, counsel, time, energy and self: how draining that tap labelled 'self' can be. Blindly I ran into that wall: a solid, very high wall of emotional bricks.

Others, clients and professional alike I had helped over the wall. My own wall was impenetrable. David gave me the route. Gillie gave me the permission.

It had been a long time since I sought permission. People came to me for routes. Professionals with human needs wrapped in erudite language. Client parents with little language but anguished pleas. Client children with no language just screaming affirmation and aggression that they needed help.

David is correct, my mind would have burst. My brain hurt and needed a release. Writing gave me the route. With the counsel of David and Gillie came the affirmed permission. The writing allowed me to unpack my mind and relieve that pressure.

No deep psychotherapy, no chemical therapy. My pencil, my pad were the tools to navigate that emotional wall.

With the permission for the time to myself, my pen explored deep avenues, clearing the brain, providing some interesting excursions. As Wordsworth would have said 'transport of delight'.

As a professional working with disturbed clients I could not see the route or give myself the permission to navigate that wall. Why are professionals so blind?

I am reassured by my new work that I can still offer something to damaged children. This reassurance was discovered through writing and is still supported through writing.

GILLIE, RESEARCH FELLOW

If I give my student one corner of a subject and he cannot find the other three corners for himself, I do not repeat the lesson (Confucius). David and I offered Peter one corner of the solution to his distress. He eagerly groped for the others as part of a pilot study assessing *Therapeutic Writing in Primary Care* (Royal College of General Practitioners funded). Six GPs suggested therapeutic writing to depressed or anxious patients over two months, giving them a simple explanatory leaflet (Hannay and Bolton 2000). A training session with me included: the need to be sensitive to issues such as literacy, disability, lack of confidence; the privacy of the writing; writers' ownership of it and right to choose with whom to share, if anyone. The doctors selected patients they had a good, trusting relationship with, and continued any other treatment already begun.

Peter presented initially with depression and stress, having been unfairly dismissed from work as the live-in head teacher of a special school for severely disturbed and damaged adolescents. He began journal writing at David's suggestion, writing over 200 closely typed pages about symptoms, the distress of leaving work. He wrote angry letters (not to be sent) and fictional replies to ex-colleagues, and a questioning one to his late father.

Writing is free, available to anyone with basic skills, and can enable a high degree of control and responsibility for the management of anxiety and depression at the patient's pace. Normally symptoms would be treated with costly psychotropic drugs or time-consuming counselling. Therapeutic writing can be a partnership between doctor and patient; Peter shared writings with David, offering him greater insight than a normal consultation could allow. Peter could spend as long as he needed, exploring his difficulties and anxieties in writing, longer than he could have in a consultation. Because writing is private until a decision to share it, it also encouraged Peter to explore areas he found too painful, embarrassing or possibly inappropriate to speak of in consultation: *I doubt that I would have let anybody near enough to me to get a sensible understanding let alone make an accurate diagnosis. Writing allowed me to be more open and honest with myself.*

Other GPs commented: 'patients can write *all* the things they want to say, whereas in talking they have to choose'; 'you can't mishear what's written' (Bolton 1998). Though many patients shared writing with close friends or relatives.

Patients wrote 'not much', or 'lots, it all came flooding out', mostly about the past, some about dreams, and several letters, most not to be sent like Peter's. A young girl, however, sent her letter to her parents, the first drafts being very angry, but in the final version she found she could say things she could not say in speech, such as 'I love you' (Bolton 1998). One GP asked patients to list problems and bring them back next time as a basis for writing. Many wrote about family relationships and bereavement, three patients about dreams concerning dead close relatives. Six shared writing with no one, five with their doctor, eleven with partner, mother, or son.

Patients reported writing as helpful, relaxing, clarifying: *it helps people understand themselves better.* A common theme was outlet for anger and bottled up feelings. A depressed teenager living with his grandmother following his parents' separation reported: 'I wrote about my feelings for Gran, and about Dad leaving Mum…it got it out of me.' He was no longer clinically depressed at the end of the study.

Peter spent time and money choosing writing materials. After an initial period he took his new folder, pad and pen several miles from home; all were encouraged to approach writing in this thoughtful way. Peter found he wrote completely differently by a lake, away from the computer in his home 'work den': lyrical deeply satisfying autobiographical pieces connecting him to the carefree pre-schoolteacher-Peter.

Another GP who appreciated writing discouraged patients from bringing physical symptoms perhaps because embarrassed to present with psychological distress. 'Dis-ease is when a patient is not at ease with their body. Patients present with many psychological problems, which should not be medicalised. But they feel they need to present with medical symptoms, and feel embarrassed to show emotions. This is a way of opening this area out.' Another added: 'it is a bridge for people who find it difficult to get in touch with their feelings'.

David said 'perhaps I should prescribe the words for myself. But I haven't the time. And anyway I am a doctor so I don't need them. Do I?' He did then join a GP reflective writing group (Bolton 1999b, 2009), having realised the importance not only of treating the whole patient, but also of bringing his whole person to the practice of medicine (Dixon, Sweeney and Periera Gray 1999). Twenty years later he's still an active writing group member. Therapeutic writing, when offered by such a practitioner, can help patients take a central role in diagnosing and treating some of their own psychological problems.

Conclusion

Depression and anxiety can make people unreflectively close in upon themselves, making a bad situation worse. Writing can seem such a simple thing to agree to try, yet it can help them, little by little, perceive outwards to their environment and reflect inwards towards good memories and towards beginning to examine the sources of their unhappiness. It also creates a tangible object which can help communication with others; depressed and anxious people often don't find talking easy: Peter shared his writing with his wife and physician. Chapter 7 examines and offers advice and strategies for using writing within therapy and counselling.

Write!

After your six-minute freewrite (see Chapter 2), reread silently to yourself with care (or store, or even destroy, it). Then share it with a carefully chosen other or group, if appropriate.

1. Think of a recent or recurring dream.

   ○ Write the dream including as many details as possible.

   ○ Write a dialogue with different dream characters or things; ask them questions.

   ○ Write their replies (e.g. 'Caravan, why are you trapping me in, why is the door blocked up?' 'Look behind you. See, there's another door. Just like you: to think you're trapped when you're not').

   ○ Write your reflections following this description and dialogues.

2. Imagine you have something in your hand from your past – any time:

   ○ Describe it briefly and carefully.

   ○ Tell a story from your memory about you and it.

   ○ This might become a poem.

3. Describe yourself simply and briefly.

   ○ Rewrite this hyperbolically, praising yourself to the skies.

   ○ Rewrite it in the opposite way, negatively.

   ○ Now describe yourself realistically. Tell yourself no one else is going to read this, to enable you to be as honest as possible, remembering what Williamson (1996) says (see Chapter 3).

   ○ When you've read it through carefully, highlight all the good things you've said about yourself. These are all true. Copy them out on a fresh piece of paper, put it where you can read it again, and add to your list of excellent qualities.

———◆◆◆———

CHAPTER 7

'Follow the Wings of the Imagination': Writing and Therapy or Counselling

Jesus is reported to have riddled, 'if you bring forth what is within you, what you bring forth will save you. If you do not bring forth what is within you, what you do not bring forth will destroy you.'

Dannie Abse 2007, p. 224

'If you don't write these stories down, your heart will be filled up and broken by them.' It was as if a pen had grown in my heart.

Xinran 2003, p. 229

Books that make us imagine the other (imagine myself in their place), may turn us more immune to the ploys of the devil, including the inner devil, the Mephisto of the heart. Imagining the other is not only an aesthetic tool. It is, in my view, also a major moral imperative. And finally imagining the other is also a deep and very subtle human pleasure.

Amos Oz 2005, p. 4

Writing can readily be a vital element of any practitioner's magic bag of therapeutic strategies, needing no specialist equipment, unlike art for example. A 'pen in the heart' can indeed help prevent it from being 'broken' (Xinran 2003, p. 229) and 'bring forth that which will save you' (Abse 2007, p. 224). Writing is increasingly used within therapy and counselling, and in internet and email services. The Samaritans' email service is popular (www.samaritans.org) for example (see Bolton *et al.* 2004). Writing uses our ordinary everyday words, giving them enhanced value and more flexible use. Practitioners and their clients may have a natural but unnecessary anxiety that writing requires specialist gifts and knowledge, and much time and energy. Valuable insight can be gained with no experience or knowledge and little time.

Writing is often undertaken alone, extending the therapeutic hour, and giving clients stimulating and therapeutic activities at home. Clients can decide whether, or at what stage, to share writing with a practitioner, friend or relative.

Writing is essentially private, and qualitatively different from thinking or any communication with another person, verbal or physical. Communication is with the *self*, but delayed until writers choose to reread. This is sometimes never; destroying writing unread can be a therapeutic action. This delay of dialogue can prevent panic at the intensity of what the writing reveals, and help enable therapeutic catharsis.

The self is an appropriate and powerful interlocutor, but our culture gives little space to private dialogue. Interlocution, verbal or bodily communication with another, is at the heart of the therapeutic relationship. But we have few channels which privilege private, individual reflection, perhaps because it is readily viewed as self-indulgent.

Writing can enable this self-communication. It can feel dangerous, just as any effective therapeutic process is experienced as teetering between the destructive and the healing. Writers enter a liminal state where they move out of habitual known psychological states into unknown unboundaried states of uncertainty ('limen' meaning threshold [*Oxford English Dictionary*]). The old and cramping can be let go of, and the new and enlightening embraced. We need to move out of the known to perceive the unknown as exciting and possible.

Practitioners have sometimes said: *what if it opens clients' cans of worms which can't be dealt with solitarily?* Such liminal distress and anxiety is temporary by nature, because individuals move out of threshold states into new life mansions or gardens. In the short term writing can always be stopped and soothing activities such as digging, or a trusted friend or relative, sought. Writings do not need to be reread, but can be torn up, thrown down the lavatory, or even burnt.

Another characteristic of expressive and explorative writing is its physicality, seeming to come from the body, sometimes bypassing usual mental awareness. Writers trust their bodies, through their writing hand, not only to tell them vital things about themselves, but also to offer connections between parts of themselves or with others and society. A holistic process, this goes some way to healing the Cartesian body/mind split. It can be exhilarating and use much energy, as a group of therapists on a day course commented with surprise.

Therapists and counsellors have commented after workshops in which I have taken them into the shallows of this deep sea: 'I found it really surprising what came up', and 'it felt like forbidden luxury to let myself write anything at all'. The forbidden luxury is allowing oneself to dwell and play in the imagination, like we used to as children. The art of writing provides a container for what is found there, a container which can be brought back, just as the shaman brings healing wisdom back from other worlds. And then it can be listened to with more everyday ears. Images and metaphors can be reflected upon slowly and gently at the writer's own pace.

Writing can be useful with many symptoms and problems, such as post-traumatic stress disorder. Trauma can interfere with the way memories are laid down, so they become fragmentary and poorly integrated into the memory and therefore into the person's life story. They also become more emotionally and sensorially vivid. Writing narrative accounts, which initially might be fragmentary and even incoherent, can help people revisit and integrate stressful experiences, by working on developing their narrative nature, and the way they key into the overall story of their lives (Peterkin and Prettyman 2009; see also Frank 2009).

Some people find writing naturally. The author J. G. Ballard had a traumatic childhood in prewar and wartime Shanghai. Much of his early fiction was fragmented, with little or no normal narrative plotline, *The Atrocity Exhibition* (1970) being a published example. Italo Calvino also survived traumatic war experiences, and wrote fragmented narratives (e.g. *If On a Winter's Night a Traveller*). Ballard later in life wrote the acclaimed *Empire of the Sun* (1984), an autobiographically based fiction with a sequential narrative, and later a chronological autobiography from birth to terminal illness (2008). He wrote: 'In many ways my entire fiction is the dissection of a deep pathology that I had witnessed in Shanghai and later in the post-war world' (Ballard 2008, p. 145).

In the next description Jeannie Wright, university lecturer in therapy and counselling, with a passionate interest in writing, contributes her wisdom. It is followed by a piece by Kate Anthony, an experienced online therapist.

Creative and expressive writing in therapy, by Jeannie Wright

Writing can be magical for clients and therapists alike, like other expressive and creative arts. Results cannot be anticipated nor prescribed. A habitual writer, I have used diaries, a reflective journal, unsent letters, poems, since I was old enough to read and write. For two years, I lived and worked at the University of the South Pacific, Fiji, with people whose languages and cultures were as different from mine as could be imagined. Sometimes I asked people who consulted me therapeutically to write about distressing situations in their first language, and then talk to me about their thoughts and feelings. I've found from Sheffield to Aotearoa New Zealand, the therapeutic potential of writing can range from, 'Really helped clear my mind – as soon as I wrote it down I knew what I thought,' to, 'I had no idea I felt like that before I wrote it.'

As part of a regular workplace counselling contract of generally six sessions with very literate clients, I suggested various forms of writing therapy and evaluated that use of writing (2003a, 2005a, 2005b). Some clients, prescribed anti-depressants by GPs, initiated writing themselves: 'My diary was always my Sad Book but not now it's more a true picture of my life.' The therapeutic relationship gave this client 'permission' to continue a diary which had stopped midsentence fourteen years before.

Others were more sceptical. A woman with elderly parents, fulltime job, children still living at home, and grandchildren, had very little time for 'indulgences' like counselling or keeping an 'emotional diary'. Lyn laughed at her 'stiff upper lip' northern English preference and was quite open about 'not believing in counselling'. Our first few sessions focused upon complex, traumatic events and family relationships in which Lyn was 'the rock', supporting everyone else but not feeling 'allowed' to express her own anxieties, anger and hurt. I suggested keeping a journal might be helpful as a way of 'saying on paper' some of the things there might not be time to say or that Lyn found it difficult to say to me. Although never a diary writer, Lyn agreed to give it a try. She also found a form of 'unsent letter' extremely useful, afterwards tearing them to shreds.

For Lyn, writing became 'a salvation'. She was worried, however, about privacy. By going early to work to use the password protected computer, she found a private and accessible way to offload residual feelings. She said: 'it puts a lot of things in perspective and it's better to get it down on paper than say it sometimes. Plus it helps you put things in perspective. Instead of jumping in and having a go at somebody probably, you can put it a bit more delicately.'

Creative and expressive writing in therapy challenges some approaches to the talking therapies. There are limitations of course, some choose not to read or write as part of their counselling or psychotherapy relationship. There is also continuing debate about whether writing can lead to too much rumination on past events and difficulties. The most powerful results I have observed can include a sense of agency for clients, finding a way to write what they cannot say.

The best way to start is to try writing strategies yourself. These could include:

- Keeping a reflective journal for self exploration, used by most practitioners in training. New workbooks about how to keep a journal come out all the time (Pennebaker), so if one doesn't suit, another will (Wright and Bolton 2012).

- Writing a letter to part of yourself you feel in conflict with or have neglected. Use the 'I' voice. Then reply as if from that part, again writing as 'I'.

- Written dialogues are a form of the 'two chair' or 'empty chair' techniques originally from Gestalt; they offer imaginative leaps in switching points of view.

If you have not explored writing as a therapeutic possibility, give yourself the gift of five minutes now to pause and reflect on paper or on screen. Trust whatever comes to the end of your pen/pencil or to your typing fingers. Writing spaces, however short, are like a form of meditation. Writing is not an established complementary therapy like art or music therapy, not widely recognised in British counselling and therapy circles and seriously under researched in practice. So if you are using writing in therapeutic relationships, please consider writing up and publishing a case study, sharing your experience with the professional community.

Writing is also a vital part of reflective practice for me and a way of protecting myself from the emotional, spiritual and physical effects of listening to other people's stories, which can stick to the skin like wet sand. An important benefit of writing for me is that I write what I like, when I like, and how I like. Sometimes, talking about difficult therapeutic experiences, even in clinical supervision, can feel too exposing and raw, like rubbing sand off wet skin. Writing gives me that time and space to compose myself (Wright and Ranby 2009) and is particularly useful when I feel silenced. Finally, writing provides a testimony, a record which can be reread and reflected on. Try it.

Email and blog therapy, by Kate Anthony

This section explains the recent development of technology for therapy, including communicating by typed text with an audience of one (private email), or potentially billions through the internet. Other forms of remote or distance communication include chat rooms, instant messaging (synchronous online discussions), and forums (asynchronous online discussions). Mobile phone texting (a blend of synchronous and asynchronous discussion) is used between professionals for appointment arrangements and crisis intervention (Anthony and Nagel 2010, pp. 143–145; Goss and Ferns 2010).

Email

Email communication involves no physical presence. Therapeutic professionals can be introduced visually or aurally with website photographs, podcasts and videos. Therapists' websites are generally static however, with simply text and generic images to help with trust and relationship building. Clients seeking online therapy often want personal reflections facilitated in text, without the 'extraneous noise' of physical presence that Suler (1997) suggests 'clogs the pure expression of mind and soul'. Sometimes, however, it's the purely practical, such as geographical location or disability, which prevents face-to-face therapy. Training in online therapy and communication (available from e.g. Online Therapy Institute, www.onlinetherapyinstitute.com) is considered essential by UK organisations such as the British Association for Counselling and Psychotherapy (BACP, www.bacp.co.uk) (Anthony and Goss 2009), and the Association for Counselling and Therapy Online (www.acto-uk.org).

Clients choose their tone of writing and use of enhanced text, with *netiquette* ('internet' + 'etiquette') underpinning appropriate communication. Understanding its importance, as well as care of the nuances of cyberspace communication, often makes or breaks an online relationship, particularly the therapeutic. Shea (1994) lists ten general rules of netiquette to help therapists form successful online relationships. I paraphrase:

- Remember the human: don't assume because you know what you mean, the client will

- Adhere to the same standards of behaviour online as offline

- Know where you are in cyberspace; different communities follow different norms of behaviour

- Respect other people's time and internet connection speeds; you are not the centre of cyberspace: timing of other people's communications are not within your power

- Make yourself look good online; you will be judged by the quality of your appearance in text

- Share expert knowledge; pass on your own and others' knowledge of the field to the client

- Help control online arguments and disagreements ('flame wars'). Misunderstandings via text are rife, and speedy clarifications avoid fanning injustice and anger

- Respect other people's privacy; even if your client is shown as online through software features, it is not your right to communicate unless contracted to do so

- Don't abuse power; particularly applicable when hosting forums where you have administrative command

- Be forgiving of other people's mistakes; and educate where necessary, such as pointing out that capital letters are equivalent to shouting

Creative keyboard skills can also facilitate successful online relationships. Enhancing email text gives new ways of conveying emotion and feeling, often making for a richer experience than even face-to-face. Written communication skills form part of an online therapy model (Anthony 2000), including perceived anonymity having freeing-up power (Suler 2004), fantasy, and the concept of 'presence' where computer apparatus is no longer noticed and both parties are focused, meeting in cyberspace.

Necessary written communication skills include:

- Emoticons, such as
  - smiles: ☺, :o)
  - frowns: ☹, :o(
  - wink: ;) (denotes irony, or wanting not to be taken seriously)
- Acronyms and abbreviations, such as
  - Be Right Back: BRB
  - Laughing Out Loud: LOL
  - By The Way: BTW
- Use of capitalisation
  - THIS IS SHOUTING
  - lower case can seem disrespectful by its apparent laziness
  - alternatively, lower case can replicate a softer tone of voice
- Use of emphasis
  - I have *never* seen my mother smile
  - I have never seen my mother smile
  - I have NEVER seen my mother smile
- Use of exclamation marks
  - This is generally acceptable!!
  - This can make text seem flippant!!!!!!!!!!!!!!!!!!!!!!!!!!!!!!!!!

- Emotional bracketing
  - ((((Kate)))) is an online hug
  - And then he left me anyway <<sigh>>

New forms of keyboard expression are not only dynamic and creative but often stimulating, however distressing the issues. Using text for therapeutic communication, particularly email, allows reflective sharing and creativity of expression of thoughts and feelings. This can create a rich, vibrant environment in the shared space of the online world.

Blogs

Blogging has changed the therapeutic possibilities of therapeutic journalling both positively and negatively, for both therapist and client. Part of the phenomenon of 'Web 2.0' (see http://en.wikipedia.org/wiki/Web_2.0), it includes communal facets of cyberspace such as gaming and social networking. Blogging can improve self-reflection, provide symptomatic relief, and the opportunity to develop one's own voice (Tan 2008). Blogs can include more than text: a client who is also an illustrator of emotions regularly blogs cartoons about therapy (www.talesoftherapy.wordpress.com).

Therapist issues include:

- contracting from the start with clients about the use of blogs
- ethical protocols for public client blogs which discuss state of mind
- protocol for client blogs which discuss the therapy and/or the therapist, or cut and paste directly from verbatim text
- managing clients' emotions aroused by journal blogging, such as vulnerability concerning private thoughts in the public domain (Nagel and Anthony 2009)
- managing clients' emotions aroused by friends, family or strangers' comments on blog, particularly if these are negative or abusive
- keeping up with appropriate research.

Therapists may wish to educate clients about blogging's potential emotional dangers. More important blogging can provide an indirect route for clients to educate their therapists about their emotions. Here is a rich field of research into the effect of blogging and other technologies in therapeutic relationships upon society and mental health.

Technologically mediated written communication is now accepted despite being initially controversial. BACP's revised Ethical Framework (2010), and those of other professional organisations worldwide, specifically mention electronically mediated communication as being pertinent to practice. An edited volume by international experts introduces in many of its thirty chapters the art of technologically driven text-based writing therapies (Anthony, Nagel and Goss 2010). Client and therapist's experience of technology in everyday life has affected therapy immeasurably and irreversibly.

Now we turn to a description by me of a workshop I ran for a group of therapists and counsellors.

A therapeutic writing training workshop for counsellors and therapists

Everyone had a handful of shells picked up from the beach: wave tumbled cockles, mussels and limpets, and at least one special shell: pearled, iridescent, sounding of the sea. Seventeen people had sat with hands open waiting (one wrote: 'as if for communion') to receive their shells. Then we wrote whatever came into our heads about receiving, feeling, smelling, looking at, and hearing the dry rattle of this motley collection.

This three-hour workshop was with University Counselling Service therapists: a taster of doing it, and time for discussing it for clients. I introduced writing in the way I always do (see Chapters 1 and 2).

They found it surprising, enjoyable, unsettling, exposing even, that they wrote things they did not know were in their heads. One commented stopping writing was like waking up from a deep sleep: writing is a bit like visiting a dream life (a doctor once likened it to a long deep swim). The silence as we wrote was spiritual, with a deep wholeness. Few are used to sitting in silence with seventeen others, some strangers, for twenty-five minutes; few are used to allowing their innermost experiences, thoughts and feelings to spill out privately while with others. Yet writing with permission in an almost silent space, which feels safe enough and set apart enough, can allow this.

Jeannie Wright moved to Sheffield from Fiji six months previously:

Hold the curved, cold cone shell to my ear
It's irresistible
I can hear the Pacific
No, it's the rush-hour roar on Western Road
Glimpse the shell-white waves exploding on the reef
No, it's bits of crisps on the carpet
Is that the salt, the coconut oil, frangipani?
No, it's yesterday's oven chips and stale beer.
When fine, white sand falls onto my paper
I'm lost,
Stop the sob.
Can't cry here.
Outside a wailing siren. (Jeannie Wright)

She later wrote:

After six months, I had thought I'd reached a different sort of acceptance of place and felt shocked when I wrote this by the depth of the grieving and the immediacy of the list of 'I miss…' (Jeannie Wright)

Ideas for clients

A wide range of ways to write are possible. Lists can be unthreatening; anyone can write a list; anyone can extend it: items can be humdrum-seeming or demanding, such as Jeannie's 'I miss'. Writing 100 things which make me angry, for example, by its very length, pushes writers towards that which really creates anger. Letters, usually unsendable (like to a dead father) and then their replies, dialogues with dream people or objects, or even parts of the body can be eye-opening. Specific titles such as 'a time when I learned something vital', 'a time of joy', or rewriting fairy story, nursery rhyme or myth with the self as one of the characters can be facilitative. Narratives can be written of remembered incidents from the perspective of the writer, and then rewritten from the point of view of someone else; for example a family argument might be written by the mother, and then she might write a parallel account in the voice of her daughter. In family therapy, family members could each write, and then share with careful facilitation, an account of the same incident from their own perspective, bringing clarity and understanding.

People like to choose writing materials carefully. Some spend time and money, increasing self-respect as well as pleasure. Deciding when and where to write also makes a difference.

Therapy clients also write blogs, sometimes informing their therapist, perhaps hoping they will have time to read and respond. Nagel and Anthony (2009) discuss boundary and ethical issues around this, feeling its place in writing therapy 'is an exciting one' (p. 44).

The group's reflections

The group discussed this slowly and reflectively with silent pauses, saying how it's private: a conversation between writer and paper, and the decision to share and with whom must be the writer's. In writing's dynamic silence, broken only by the scratch of pen or pencil, an indrawn breath, rustle of paper, things can be fairly safely shared with oneself. And writing is slow, gently and gratefully slow: people commented how their minds flew ahead of their writing hands. No written words can afford to be wasted: writing like this is invariably concise and to the point.

Writing within a group is conducive for many. At home or office, would-be writers find procrastinations. Many find an alarm clock useful: they must stop by the time it pings and so cannot waste time. I use creative constraints: these words are written on a train; I must have finished by the time we pull into Abergavenny.

The group expressed the importance of the stages of (a) writing, (b) reading silently to the self and altering, expanding, and adapting, and (c) reading to others and discussing their comments carefully. The order of (b) and (c) is important: writers often don't really know what they have written until reading it to themselves. These three stages can be followed by redrafting to bring what is in the mind into focus, followed by further discussion. A sensitive reader helps writers understand their own images, see what their writing is telling them.

John McAuley wrote his disappointment. Having waited patiently, he found the shells 'dull, tired, worn, lifeless, soulless'. Yet these are his final paragraphs:

The writing – there is nothing here except all that nothingness – that lack – the promise of what might have been – a dark dank emptyness – empty shell! Even your insides do not hold or enrapture – you disappoint you are not what I wanted you to be you are poor – depleted and empty

And yet –

I don't know but there is something. The one – that I'm holding – it gets warmer, softer as I hold it clasped in my fingers – despite all that clanking hollow scraping emptyness – I can feel a little

– it is hard to see what is inside – something once lived here – there is space to crawl (I know this – I am not looking –) Inside – to be held inside and holding the outside – roundness and warmth. (John McAuley)

The shells spoke differently to art therapist John Henzell:

Shell like an ear. It's a half shell, a bivalve, its other half with which it once closed around the inner living flesh is missing. Then it smelled of the sea, of marine life – and of sex too. Now the shell is beautiful in the sense that bones can be. Shells like bones on the beach, beaches made of them, like the Australian bush after a great fire, the jet black charred ground showing off the gleaming white skeletal structures, skulls, vertebrae, ribs, femurs, tibias, joints and knuckles of all the animals who couldn't get away. If we just look at them fresh, like children look at sea shells – not realising that the animal that lived in them is dead – they are really exquisite. Instead of a charnel house we see a field of beauty. (John Henzell)

John later wrote:

Rereading the writing this workshop provoked from me – only possible because it was *written* – I'm astonished and pleasantly embarrassed at how such apparently simple things, shells, caused images, thoughts and emotions to fan out in so many directions concerning, amongst other things, life, death, beauty and sacrifice. (John Henzell)

Below is a description of another therapeutic writing training course I ran, by participant Angela Stoner. Practitioners were introduced to some processes, practices and background theory. This extract is explorative and expressive; raw and unredrafted; an example of places the pen can take you, if you let it.

The Memory Project, by Angela Stoner

This project was 'birthed' during the course of Gillie's postcard workshop. Gillie had dozens of postcards with pictures of people. She asked us to look at them and select one. There were all kinds of people abstract and real, doing all kinds of things in all kinds of emotions. Yet right from the start one drew me. It was a fairly normal picture of a girl in her early teens with rather long and wild hair who seemed to be screaming (to me at least). I rooted through all the pictures looking carefully at all of them, but when it came to choosing, even though by then the girl was a long way from me and buried among others, I still 'chose' her (it was quite the other way round of course).

Gillie then asked us to choose a picture we didn't like, and that we didn't feel comfortable with. I didn't feel comfortable with the one I'd chosen, but the one which most disturbed and repulsed me was a picture of the 'bodies' at Pompei. Gillie then asked me to imagine a dialogue between the person(s) on one picture and the person(s) on another. I found this difficult as the people on the Pompei picture weren't alive. We then described the landscape in which the conversation was taking place: smells, tastes, sounds and sights. This evoked an eerie sort of nightmare after-life desert in which these dead souls were trying to inhabit the life of the young girl. These are her thoughts, and one of the dead people:

> Girl: I am too young to see such sights. I feel alone. It is as if only I know how pointless everything is – how desolate. I don't believe in heaven or hell. We simply stop. Stop dreaming. Stop thinking. So don't you dare tell me to stop dreaming. My time for dreaming is too short and brutal as it is. I am too young to know this, but too old to swallow your lies and fairystories. Don't tell me what to think. We all end in the cold emptiness of death. Let me fill the time between how I want.

> Dead body: Now is cold nothing, but she has dreamed me again. Perhaps I can take her over – taste her again, even to taste disgust

again – oh to have nerves, skin, to touch, smell, see and hear again. Keep her preoccupied, tense, fretful, free of wonder. Then I can creep into the back stairs of her brain.

If she dared follow the wings of her imagination and think for herself I am lost. But I'm confident I can sneak into her thoughts. I am her future anyhow. It isn't much more effort to steal her present.

This is the dialogue between them.

Girl: What is the point of anything if this is where it ends.

Body: I envy you that you can still feel the wind in your hair, feel pain, sense danger.

And then the message I had for each.

– to the girl: 'Stay alive. Don't dwell on death.'

– and to the body: 'Stay dead. Don't dwell on life.'

The feeling inside me, reading this, was that these dead forces were more powerful than she was and would win. I didn't read this dialogue out and felt extremely uncomfortable with it. Next Gillie asked us to imagine a room in which both pictures were hanging.

It is a dark room, furnished in oppressive Victorian style. The whole room is dispiriting.

Suddenly I notice a pram with two dead babies in it. I look closely. They are in fact two china dolls, but the mistake is making my heart thud like a hammer on an anvil. I avert my eyes from the pram, and am again haunted by the face of a young girl screaming. Why does she feel familiar?

I read this paragraph out and the whole experience shook me considerably. I didn't quite understand what I had touched on there. I had an insight when the young girl shouted 'I'm too young to see such sights' that it may have been my imagining my mother's feelings during the war. Gillie handled the situation very sensitively, bringing us all back to the present, discussing how we might handle such situations with clients.

That night Gillie had asked us all to remember our dreams. In the morning I was writing mine (which later yielded very fruitful exploration and writing) when all of a sudden the young girl was screaming at me 'When am I going to be fucking heard? When am I going to be fucking heard?' over and over at full volume.

I then began flow-writing as if I was the girl. It became obvious that it was my 'mother' speaking, as a young girl, and I began writing in the first person as if I were her at about ten years of age, when she'd been evacuated and lost her brother in the war.

I found this heart-breaking to write. Though much of the detail and emotional language was made up, the basic story was true. I had no idea why I felt so compelled to write this, but it has occurred to me that many women are unable to give their daughters the love they need, because of traumas in their own past. A route to those daughters healing themselves is precisely by opening and experiencing those traumas at some kind of ethereal level. I never did feel loved by my mother: almost as if she daren't.

And it felt as if I'd always known this story. Interestingly, in the light of my dialogue between the girl and the bodies, my mother really did try to stop me daydreaming, and I remember often wanting to die, because that way I'd be less trouble.

When reading through the piece on coming home, it occurred to me how little I knew of my mother's childhood. I wrote to her, saying I'd be grateful for any memories she had for my writing project based on second world war childhoods (true!).

She wrote back by return of post with four pages of memories. The project has been slow so far (mainly due to a reluctance on my part) but is progressing. By reading her memories and then actively writing about them creatively in the first person, I am beginning a journey of understanding and forgiveness. And I am sure that the kind of detailed memories I am asking her for must be helping my mother, and there is the safety of the written word – where she can censor and edit before she sends anything to me – and on the face of it our correspondence is neutral and non-judgemental and not to do with our own relationship. Under the surface, I am convinced, that deep healing is taking place.

One of the more interesting things that I have done is re-visit imaginatively the little girl my mother used to be. In these 'visits' I am myself, the adult daughter from the future, and in these scenes I just let my subconscious write out some dialogue between the two. Hopefully, at last, the young girl feels she is being heard and can stop hurting.

So...amazing where these apparently simple photo exercises can take you if the workshop is handled with compassion, sensitivity and experience. [For Angela's beautiful children's book, see Stoner and Wright 2005.]

Angela wrote this with only starting suggestions from me. The methods were dialogues, metaphors, use of pictures, reminiscence, shared reminiscence (mother and daughter here), dreamwork and writing in the voice of another (the little girl, the dead body). Today I asked people to finish some sentences: 'I believe...', 'I think...', 'I want...' 'If only...' All these exercises are like saying: 'Look, a keyhole!, There's a key in your hand, put it in the lock!'

Conclusion

Clients and practitioners experience similar writing processes to poets, novelists and playwrights. Apart from psychological benefits, there is also the satisfaction (excitement even) of creating a tangible, shareable thing of interest and/or beauty. 'Imagining the other' is not only possible in creative therapeutic writing, it is, as Amos Oz says, 'also a major moral imperative... And a deep and very subtle human pleasure' (2005, p. 4).

Some therapist responses after training courses were:

'The word that springs to mind is "woomph" – this process is so powerful.'

'The playfulness of being able to write is accompanied by the childlikeness of listening to stories.'

'It feels like we've come a long way from where we started; we've done so much in such a short space of time.'

'But writing is magic – it just works!'

'I feel awe at how *ordinary* people can create such *extraordinary* writings.'

This chapter described and illustrated methods to use safely and fruitfully in therapy or counselling. A pen growing in the heart can help nourish and invisibly repair us, preventing the heart from being broken, blocked by that which needs to be brought forth. The next chapter examines and exemplifies how writing can support people struggling with drug and alcohol abuse to, among other things, 'gain an understanding of who they are so they do not have to bolster what they are not' (Judy Clinton, private communication).

Write!

After your six-minute freewrite (see Chapter 2), reread silently to yourself with care (or store, or even destroy, it). Then share it with a carefully chosen other or group, if appropriate.

1. Tell the story of a mundane episode in your life.

   ○ Now rewrite it in the third person (about 'she' or 'he' rather than 'I'), sensationalising it, as if you were a person of importance about whom every detail matters (film star/royalty).

2. List habitual phrases used by anyone in your life or past, whether they irritated, amused or comforted you (e.g. my father-in-law: 'we must find the compromise').

   ○ Choose one. Write a brief account of a time when they said this.

   ○ Write reflectively about why you think they habitually said this.

   ○ Write a letter to them telling how it made you feel.

   ○ Write their reply.

3. Think of a character from history (e.g. Nelson Mandela), a film or a book who fascinates you and you admire.

   ○ What does that character have to say to you today…?

CHAPTER 8

'Writing Gives Us Wings so We Can Fly': Writing in Substance and Alcohol Abuse Treatment

The poem carries you beyond where you could have reasonably expected to go. The image I have is from the old cartoons: Donald Duck or Mickey Mouse coming hell for leather to the edge of a cliff, skidding to a stop but unable to halt, and shooting out over the edge. A good poem is the same, it goes that bit further and leaves you walking on air.

Seamus Heaney 2008, p. 3

Writing can give us a memory of when 'we were' to nourish us when 'we are not' … I believe writing nourishes our minds, invisibly repairing them…consoling, not by providing an escape particularly, but by taking us into those very dark places. When we come out of them, we're a much better person for having been there and done that.

Blake Morrison 2008b, p. 8

Writing can help people in treatment centres 'shoot out over the edge', ending up 'walking on air' with only the high of creativity to get them there. We certainly are all 'a much better person for having been there and done that'. Fiona Friend contributes her experience in a residential centre, Judy Clinton in day care.

Creative writing in addiction treatment, by Fiona Friend

It is 3.30pm on a Tuesday afternoon. I arrive at Prinsted, the residential treatment centre where I facilitate a creative writing group. Going to the office with my box of tricks (books and any objects we may be using in the session such as shells, pebbles, cards), I check in and take the creative writing books from the cupboard. Early on I suggested that it would be better to use special exercise books for creative writing to differentiate the session. So I buy hardbound books with bright covers and the clients choose their own. Next I meet one of the treatment centre directors for handover. This usually lasts ten or fifteen minutes and they tell me how all the clients are and if there are any significant issues for them.

Prinsted

Treatment is based on the twelve steps of *Alcoholics Anonymous* (AA) and is residential, tightly boundaried, and the clients attend *Anonymous* meetings on several evenings a week. In addition to therapeutic groups and individual counselling sessions there are also yoga, aerobics, art therapy and charity work. They cook their own meals as a group and do all of the house cleaning on a rota basis. Based in a large Edwardian house with an extra extension, Prinsted has a garden, dining room, lounge, group room, kitchen, offices and counselling rooms and ten bedrooms. The clients range in number from about seven to fourteen, with ten being probably the average number.

Although the emphasis in these groups is very much on process rather than product, this very bright, imaginative and creative group do often produce remarkable work. We hope soon to compile a small book of their poems and writings.

Meet the group

This week there are ten clients. I'll describe them so you can follow the story (details and names have been changed to protect confidentiality):

Emma is a 22-year-old socialite from London. She is very beautiful and arrogant, had a massive cocaine habit as well as serious alcohol problem. She comes from a very dysfunctional family.

Miguel is a 28-year-old heroin addict from Portugal. He has been here 3 months and greatly enjoys the creative writing sessions.

Jane is 36, a mother with 4 children at home with her husband. She is anorexic, complex and highly intelligent.

Carl is a 'lively lad' from South London. His cheerful exterior sometimes gives way to dark moods. Heroin, crack and a very turbulent life have led to Carl looking a lot older than his 29 years.

Will, a highly intelligent and articulate journalist, arrived 3 weeks ago. An alcoholic, Will is 45, divorced and very lost.

Sophia, a European aristocrat, has used drugs for many of her 30 years. She is a sculptor and highly talented but has poor self-esteem as well as OCD [obsessive compulsive disorder] problems and eating disorder.

Irma, an alcoholic with a fiery temper, is from Norway. When she arrived, the group nicknamed her The Ice Queen, but she is warming up now.

Daniel is from Ireland. A gifted writer, he is a solicitor by profession and has multiple addictions, especially to women.

Fatima is a gay woman from Dubai. Highly articulate, she is coming to terms with both her sexuality and drug addiction.

Alex is 18, doesn't want to be here and is struggling with acknowledging his drug problem. He's avoided jail but his parents are at their wits' ends.

I learn Daniel and Sophia have been home for the weekend and all went well. Jane is missing her children. Alex is rebelling at being there and being confronted about his behaviour in group. Irma has lost her temper with Fatima and a conflict is brewing. Carl is leaving next week: going on to a flat, and beginning to get very anxious.

I walk past the smoking area where a few of the clients are having a cigarette. They all wave and greet me except Alex who looks sullen.

I go to prepare the lounge for the group, put a CD on in readiness and check over the materials I have prepared.

The group all arrive on time except Alex who is five minutes late. He mutters 'sorry' and I ask him to be punctual next week.

I ask for a volunteer to read the Preamble and Miguel reads it out. The Preamble was written by the first group I ran at Prinsted. I believe it's important to establish boundaries because the creative writing group is more relaxed than some of the other groups or lectures but we still have to establish a 'safe place' so the clients feel confident to tackle what can be very challenging topics. They can, if they choose, do their writing in the garden if it is warm, or in the dining room. They can make tea or coffee and have a quick break but should not talk to each other while they are doing their writing. The Preamble also stresses that the client's work is confidential and will only be shown to the counsellors or used for publication (e.g. in the centre's quarterly newsletter) with their permission. It also asks them to respect each other's work and not preface reading out their work with derogatory comments.

After the Preamble we have a 10–15 minute relaxation and meditation session, with a selection of CDs I bring in with me. Today I play dolphin music, which the clients like, and talk through an exercise relaxing the whole body. I then 'bring them back' into the room and suggest they stretch as they wake up. Today I've decided to send them out for a brief walk as it's wonderful weather and arrange for the new arrivals to go out with a more experienced group member. They are to observe an object or person and write a story or poem, to read out at 4.50pm.

Gradually they disperse and I write a brief note to Annie about how I am feeling. Annie is my virtual supervisor: my co-facilitator, or, if you prefer, my imaginary friend. The technique has been invaluable: Annie is always there to support, encourage, advise and is a great source of wisdom and reassurance.

After ten minutes or so I make myself a cup of tea, chat to Jane in the kitchen and return to the group room where they are all beginning to return. They sit writing quietly in the lounge, others write outside in the garden or at the tables on the decking outside.

By 4.50 the clients have all returned to the sitting room and I ask Emma, who is sitting on my right, to start reading. They all read their work. Only occasionally someone refuses and then usually they can be encouraged to read after a week or so. Emma has written a poem about a swing, and the memories it brings. Miguel also wrote a poem about a tramp asleep in an alleyway. Fatima and Daniel have both written stories, Fatima about a wall outside a house and Daniel about a man who liked squirrels. Carl's is a short, amusing poem about a cat and Jane's a whimsical story about a toddler. Will's is a very perceptive sketch of daily life in a cul-de-sac. Sophia writes of the plane she sees; Irma a poem about a flower; Alex a very short, angry piece about suburbia. They comment – positively – on each other's writing and then it's time for the two cooks – Fatima and Alex – to leave. Alex looks relieved and Fatima thanks me.

Sometimes I read out my own writing; I don't if it is very personal or just doesn't seem appropriate. Occasionally I just sit writing notes about the group on my feedback sheet, other times I write myself.

We move onto a second, shorter exercise of fifteen minutes. For this we stay in the sitting room. I ask them to choose a topic picked by another group member in the first exercise and write something on that. After fifteen minutes they read the resulting pieces and are all surprised by how differently others interpreted the same subject.

We have a game to close the group: a group story or poem, or call my bluff. Today I ask them to think of a colour and animal they would be. Carl is a red lion, Jane a yellow cat, Sophia a blue unicorn and so on. We finish with the *Serenity Prayer* as if at an AA or NA meeting: 'God grant me the serenity to accept the things I cannot change, courage to change the things I can and the wisdom to know the difference.'

After the group

I return to the office to do handover with my impressions of the group and tell them of any concerns I have. I mention Alex's lateness and general attitude and a brief description of how the various members of the group have been.

Then I go home and write up brief notes on the group on my checklist. These are useful both for preparing for the following week and to review groups over a period of time.

Checklist

1. Place: where did the group happen?

2. How many group members were there?

3. Where did the group take place?

4. What music did we use?

5. Which props did we use?

6. What events had happened during the week/new people joining?

7. How did they take responsibility for the group and actions?

8. How did we tackle negative things positively?

9. What comments were noteworthy and what were the reactions to each other's writing?

10. What appealed to the cheeky/naughty side?

11. What was fun?

12. What was a surprise?

13. What did Annie think?

14. What do I feel I could have done better?

15. Anything else?

I always have a written plan for a group but don't invariably follow it, as the following week's group illustrates. I make notes about any individuals who have been particularly involved or affected in the group, any who did not participate much and any particular issues that have arisen in terms of their response to the topic or others' work.

The next week: 'Carl has died'

The next Tuesday I arrive at Prinsted, slightly early: just as well, as it turns out. A group of clients are sitting on the decking area, smoking and looking very subdued. I wave and they raise their hands but look sombre. I know something has happened. In the office, Tina, the business manager, looks red-eyed.

'Fiona, I don't know how to say this so I'm just going to tell you straight. We only heard an hour ago: Carl has died. The counsellors will tell you about it.' I'm stunned. 'I'm so sorry. You OK?' She nods and I leave her, and go through to the counselling office where Sheila and Bernard look shocked and numb.

'Carl was found dead in his room at his parents' home at the weekend. He went home, relapsed and overdosed we think,' Bernard explains. 'There's going to be an autopsy.'

It's so hard to accept. Carl could light up the room with his smile and sense of humour; he was always encouraging the others. We discuss how the group are and they ask what I was intending to do that day.

'I've brought in shells and pebbles but I think I'll ask them to write a letter to Carl with their memories of him.'

'That would be good: it would start the grieving process.' Sheila says.

At the start of the group I explain that because of what has happened we would dedicate it to Carl. We have a minute's silence and then, after the Preamble, there is fifteen minutes' relaxation using an instrumental CD with wave sounds. During this time, when many of the group curl up into foetal positions on the sofas, or lean against one another for support, I have a silent word with Annie who reassures me. I've never been in this situation before; clients have died at other rehabs where I've worked but not here, part of a close-knit residential group.

After the relaxation and meditation when the group has stretched and, rather reluctantly, opened their eyes and sat up, I explain what I would like them to do. 'I would like you to write a letter to Carl. It will help you remember him. Be sure to include positive incidents and memories.'

They nod and look pleased and I give them until 5pm to do the writing. They are very quiet and subdued. Most stay in the sitting room rather than going into the dining room or garden to write, except Miguel who looks very angry and marches off with his book. He was a close friend of Carl's. He returns at 5pm and reads an extraordinary letter, full of sadness, anger, wit and love. Two of the group are tearful and they all read their letters in turn.

Even now Alex, who had looked up to Carl, has taken the task seriously and written a long, sad letter. When they have all finished reading, I read out my own letter to Carl for I also have many fond thoughts and memories of him. Then the two group members who are cooking the evening meal leave, and I suggest we each remember one particular incident about Carl and tell the rest of the group. They have a few minutes to think about it and then begin to talk in turn. It is like a story telling session and there is a lot of warmth and laughter in the room. After the group I discuss the letters with the counsellors and Sheila suggests that we read them at the memorial service which will be held there the following week. There have only been two groups like this in the five years I've been at Prinsted, but on each occasion the letter-writing exercise has been very therapeutic for the group and for me.

Clients' writing

Fruit
Perfuming the earth,
A cut through an orange is
Like a dagger through the heart
Nauseous and irritably blended and blended
To a sickly sweet death
Drained and drained from
The pulp of its life, the
Empty liquid fills my cup. (Sophie)

Sophie's poem was written in response to us looking at *Ode to Tomatoes* by Pablo Neruda (1961) to encourage description and detail. That Sophie was going through a troubled phase in her treatment is vividly reflected in the poem. These next two extraordinary poems were created when we looked at writing about fathers and read *My Papa's Waltz* by Theodore Roethke (1991).

Maybe
Father and further and further
Out. Is it too far for you to know
What it was (is was) all about?
Submerged in whatness
A miraculous reflection

Gilded in whiteness
A child with an old age pension.

Only somehow barely trying
Out for a role that was not yours
Dirty old Astra
A snowy early day time
I stand by the frozen lake
And see your/my reflection
A darkened was not
Was not maybe me.
If I'm not you
Maybe be can I be
Maybe me. (Mike)

Letter to My Dad

I know you crossed a border
But can not tell you which
One person is not who wants to be,
Doesn't chose the life
That takes inside
A boat arrived and
Made from you one history of love
I ignore the fact if
We were happy
Can you understand emptiness
Dust is created by the city
Inside the head
Code nine, a velvet night
My soul is visible forever
More than the angels
With an emotional impulse in which
My body explodes on you
Doctors, lawyers or any other jobs
I pass through all of them! He said
On the bed a Japanese comic takes 3
A deep study where emotion was expelled
The progression is through
The eye of silence and pain. (Martinho; English being his second/
third language)

Conclusion

Holding a safe space for a group to explore their feelings and emotions in writing means making sure I, as facilitator, am in a safe place (see Flint 2000). So, in addition to supervision with Bernard and Sheila at the treatment centre I have an external supervisor who is a very experienced creative writing in healthcare facilitator. The advice, support, encouragement and ideas on how to tackle particular subjects and situations has been invaluable.

Creative writing has been used more extensively in other forms of healthcare such as with older people, in hospices, and with children, than in addiction, where it has been introduced over the last 10 or 15 years. Nonetheless, a small survey I did as part of the MA in *Creative Writing and Personal Development* (Sussex University, UK) revealed that at least 15 and probably more than 20 rehab facilities and day centres out of the 85 I telephoned use creative writing as part of the treatment programme. Of the 12 treatment centres who replied, there was significant agreement in what constituted a 'successful' creative writing group in addiction treatment. Establishment of close boundaries, choice for clients to read their own work, fun and play, and the style of facilitation, were all highlighted as important.

Facilitating creative writing groups in addiction recovery is an immense privilege. At a recent group I asked one of the members who had been there the longest time to explain to a new arrival the purpose of the creative writing group. He said 'Fiona gives us wings so we can fly.'

Writing the Spirit helps with recovery from alcohol and drug abuse, by Judy Clinton

Working in the addiction field is tough. It is also the most fulfilling thing that I have ever done. Despite the frustrations, challenges and disappointments, I continue to do it because of the profound experiences that can happen within our group sessions.

I had never intended to work with recovering alcoholics and addicts. When it was suggested that I might (by a participant at one of my weekend workshops), I responded with a resounding, 'No way!' This was because my elder son had brought his life to an end through drinking eight years previously. My ex-husband had also come from a line of alcoholics and I had no desire to re-enter the territory in which I had suffered so much anguish.

I had first discovered writing as a therapeutic tool through intense personal need. During a painful and complex marriage breakdown, I had stood on a beach with a friend, looked up at the sky and cried out, 'I have no tools to deal with all this'. Shortly afterwards I started writing: anything that needed to come out of me: pages and pages of it. In the doing of it I found relief and some kind of perspective on what I was going through.

Some time later I attended a group at my Quaker Meeting (Religious Society of Friends), working with Gillie Bolton's booklet *Writing the Spirit* (1994). There I learnt about not only writing spontaneously (as I had already been doing), but how to root this practice in silence and to share with others in a non-judgmental, accepting and supportive way. I learnt that meeting in this reverential manner, with a very clear structure and a subject to write about (e.g. 'What is your experience of doubt?'), was extremely powerful, both for myself and as part of a group process.

As time went on, I felt the importance of taking this method to the mental health clients with whom I was then working as a social work assistant. It proved to be powerful for them too. It gave them a way of expressing and processing the things that were locked within them, and by sharing them they knew they were not alone.

Then my son entered the hell of rampant addiction and subsequently died. Writing was my life-line, my tool for processing what had happened. It also gave me the means by which I could highlight to others how life was for a disabled young man who felt that he didn't fit into society. As I began to recover, I led workshops again in all sorts of settings, always finding the simple structure of *Writing the Spirit* worked.

This may seem a long-winded introduction to my work within the addiction field, but I think it is critical to know this background if you are fully to appreciate what is to follow. Nothing, it seems to me, works in isolation. Without my life experiences, my professional background and my many years using *Writing the Spirit* with others, I very much doubt that I would be able to work with recovering alcoholics and addicts in the way I do.

I have now worked at The Nelson Trust, a rehabilitation centre for recovering alcoholics and addicts, running a one and a half hour session each week, for over a year. During that period I have written faithfully after every session. This has been where reflective writing has come into its own. I have expressed my feelings about the session, my responses to the clients, the things that I have felt went well, the things that did not, my reflections on addiction and recovery generally, and anything else that has felt important at the time. I have sent these writings to several valued friends and family members who have the professional background and/or characters to give me honest, constructive and sometimes challenging feedback. This process is my supervision and gives me the courage to continue when I feel like giving up. I also have supervision at the treatment centre from a staff member for issues more specifically to do with the clients. Without such support I could not do this work.

I have been looking back on these reflections and what I now write is a distillation of them.

Recovering alcoholics and addicts are chaotic. Their early life experiences have been damaging and/or grossly neglectful. Most have been seriously addicted to drugs and/or alcohol for many years and have been damaged by them at all levels of their being. Many have been in prison and have witnessed, and done, appalling things. Most have already had several attempts at becoming sober/clean and have failed to maintain it. Coming off their addictive substances is only the beginning of a tough road to recovery. It is with these people that I am working.

The clients who come to my sessions are at different stages in the treatment process. Some are 'tapers' who have completed up to a six-month intensive period of residential treatment and have recently moved into supported housing with less input from staff. Others are 'day care' who have opted to take part in a treatment programme on a daily basis, whilst still living at home. And the third group are 'after care' who have completed their treatment plans but still have some support from the centre.

All the clients have multiple life-factors: physical effects of their substance abuse, emotional and mental upheavals as they come to terms with a 'clean' life, social factors such as benefit claims, debt issues and housing difficulties as well as complex family relationships. This seriously compromises their ability to turn up regularly for sessions.

On top of this, the centre itself has tight and complicated, limited funding. Clients come to the centre from all over the country and each authority has different funding strategies. Thorough assessments have to be made before a client can be accepted, by which time they may have decided that they don't want treatment. The net result is that I never know who is going to turn up from week to week, what state they will be in, what their backgrounds may be, or for how long I might be working with them.

For weeks I fought against this situation. I was used to working with closed groups for a set period of time, whether for a one-off day or weekend workshop, or for a course of several weeks. I found it most unsatisfactory not being able to plan the content of my sessions or to be able to be sequential in my way of working. I protested to staff members at the centre; I anguished in my write-ups and there was a point when I seriously considered giving up. I felt inadequate to the task and was frustrated by what I was able to achieve under such circumstances.

My supervisor told me that this was simply the way that it was at the centre. It was the nature of working with clients in addiction and that, frankly, I had two options: adapt or leave: whilst saying that she valued what I did and did not want to lose me.

That was a turning point for me. I knew I didn't want to leave because, despite the frustrating circumstances, I cared too much about the clients and could see its value to some of them. I had to adapt. I accepted that I didn't and wouldn't know who would arrive each week and that I really did have to trust to the spirit (of Love/God/Life Force) to be at work in the sessions. I had to trust my intuition.

The clients came to me on a voluntary basis, encouraged to come by counsellors as part of their treatment plan. Most decided in the first session whether to stay or not, whilst some persevered and found they did get something out of it. One client, who said he wanted to run away during the first session, became the greatest convert to the method. Some became so difficult I had to ask them to leave. Those who were emotionally open and liked writing took to the method most easily.

I found myself working with an equal gender balance and sometimes with males only. I found this quite a challenge as the issues faced by men are significantly different, and could be outside my personal experience. What surprised and touched me was how tender the men were towards each other if one of them permitted himself to be emotionally upset. To see tough and 'macho' men break down in tears, talking movingly about their life experiences and having them validated and comforted by other men, always feels a privilege. Contrary to the general media portrayal of alcoholics and drug addicts being stupid and 'bad', my experience has shown me people who are deeply sensitive, intelligent, and creative.

Working with these fundamental qualities and potentials makes this work so satisfying. The man who wanted to run away in my first session was dyslexic and had a great block about writing, stemming from years of ridicule and failure at school. Because I tell everyone they will never have to share their work unless they choose to, he felt able to write, reassured that the standard of the writing did not matter. He found writing gave a liberation which he had never experienced before, and it became a fundamental tool in his recovery process. Other dyslexics were also able to overcome their dislike of writing, one even choosing to go to literacy classes because writing without censorship gave him such pleasure.

Some clients came with an established writing history. One recited a poem in his first session that had won him a prize. Written on a receipt, it was an entertaining piece about his hatred of shopping demonstrating his sense of humour and capacity to use words well. He attended regularly for over three months, and his writing became increasingly personal, painful, revealing and healing. He produced the piece below in less than twenty minutes, in response to being asked how he was feeling. It is unedited and glories in how recovery felt. Two years earlier, he had simply wanted to die.

Requiem for Despair

Uplifted, carried away on crests of hope,
that swell and roll, and heighten feelings felt,
so long for searched.

Illuminated, saturated, basking in the rays of golden peace,
caressing the souls, so long that stumbled in the dark.

My heart, it cries with joy at wonders now held,
where once it mourned the death already passed.

Resurrected, given long reprieve,
and every moment seems a lifetime blessed,
As angels dance upon my wondered eyes,
peace surrounds me, wraps me in its fold.

How misguided and so nearly lost,
the terror and the misery so great,
I wandered ages past in shadows long,
trudging on to my untimely fate.

My pure and truly awe inspiring life,
Sweeps clean the debris scattered on my path.
The road unknown it beckons with open arms,
Horizons of gold, futures untold,
a soft embrace, hands of grace,
upon the beauty of this world, I have a place. (Billy Rubin)

My usual structure for workshops elsewhere is: about ten minutes' silence; six-minute freeflow writing; and a stimulated piece of writing for twenty minutes or longer. We end with people reading their pieces into an attentive and accepting silence, and a time for focused feedback from other members (both activities are always optional). I found that this sequence did not work at the treatment centre.

Most clients are very uncomfortable with silence. They find that their feelings float to the surface and therefore they can find the experience disturbing. It was also hopeless expecting clients to settle straight away at the beginning of the session when they are 'all over the place' with things going on in their lives. Over a period of weeks I found a way that works much better.

We start with a six-minute exercise of spontaneous writing to dump the things that are going on: confusion, excitement, emotional pain, rage…whatever. Then people are ready and willing to become still. I find that leading the group into a guided relaxation, breathing exercise and visualisation works better than silence as it gives them something to focus on and takes away the fear of being overwhelmed by nebulous feelings whilst teaching them how to become still and centred.

Our meditations start with me bringing us into awareness of our bodies firmly on our chairs, despite thoughts and feelings ranging around. I ask us to visualise our heads as helium balloons floating through the roof, up, up, up into the atmosphere. Then we see the base of our spines sinking down through the foundations of the building and deep, deep into the earth. Now we are anchored in the earth with our heads soaring into the heavens. Sometimes I ask us to visualise a ball of light above our heads pouring light down through the crown of our heads, washing out everything unwanted. I then lead us into awareness of the body, starting at the head down to the toes, quietly telling the body to relax areas of tension, discomfort or pain. We then simply watch the breath coming in and out, or say 'I am breathing in/out', or count it in and out, on our own for four or five minutes. Sometimes I then introduce a visualisation, such as asking us to feel our way into a special, loved place. This can lead straight into the writing or we stretch and come out of the meditation first.

After these two exercises it is quite remarkable how the atmosphere in the room alters. I notice how people's voices have quietened and dropped in pitch, and there is a feeling of peace that hasn't been present at the beginning. I also find that this helps to put me in a frame of mind when I can be most receptive to what arises during the rest of the session. On one occasion I was disturbed by something that had happened before we started; I forgot the meditation exercise and, as a result, the whole session was a disaster: proving the importance of the exercise.

The clients all attend, or have attended, *Alcoholics Anonymous, Narcotics Anonymous*, or similar *12-Step Programmes*. This means they are used to the idea of 'a power greater than ourselves that can return us to sanity' and 'the God of my understanding'. Most people I work with have been at the edge of death and know about pits of despair. They have been forced to call out for help from the depths of their beings and often it has been AA or NA that has begun their journey to recovery. They are therefore very receptive to, and often hungry for, the spiritual in their lives. It is here that *Writing the Spirit* meets their needs so powerfully.

The spontaneous writing often reveals the truth of who clients are to themselves. By writing freely in this way they access the deeper wisdom within themselves which can both reveal and heal. Very often clients are amazed by what they write, and often in only a few minutes. Sometimes they will find themselves crying when writing or when reading to the group. One client's writing will often 'speak' to another in powerful ways. Clients frequently identify with each other's writing and give feedback to that effect. It is an organic process and one that is full of surprises. On a couple of occasions I have found my own experience touching one of the clients, resulting in us both being in tears. At those times I wondered if I had been unprofessional to allow this, but as I was still fully aware of what was going on, and the feedback after the session by the clients to their counsellors was positive, it appeared to have been appropriate. To do this work well I need to be open myself, and that sometimes can be deeply painful. It can also be profoundly moving. It is crucial that I attend to my own needs in this work.

I finish this account with a beautiful, reassuring poem, written in response to a postcard of a pathway leading through woods in springtime, by a former heroin addict in her forties who found release, healing and recovery through nature, writing and music. She, like others, is very uncomfortable with religious language, wary of anything smacking of 'spiritual', having encountered hypocrisy in people professing religious faith. I am so grateful to have been part of her, and others', recovery.

Green

I am the green around you,
The breeze that sways even the most deep rooted trees,
I make the dappled light dance and glint,
Sparkling at you in this green place.
Listen, hear me.

I am the pebble underfoot,
To check your step from its complacency.
Pause,
Be still and look around you,
I am here.
Watch, see me.

I am the canopy above you,
To shade you and shelter many,
I am the rough bark,
The knife-edged grass blade,
The fanning fern and the sharp bowed, sweet bramble.
Reach out, touch me,

Taste me.

I take many forms,
The red-fox,
The brown hard hare
The grey squirrel,
the white tailed rabbit,
The dappled red deer,
For all could not exist without me,
The Green.
Witness me with my tracks left in soft earth.

My feather jewels are thrown up singing,
To harmonise with the sway of the branches.
So you may hear the oldest music of the world.
Lighten your step and dance with me,
Through me.

Keep hold of a piece of me,
Keep it close and when you are grey,
Or black and blue from your concrete and brick,
I shall call to you.

Listen and you will hear me.
Watch and you will see me,
Reach out because you will touch me,
Bear witness for I am still with you under every footfall. (Ellen
Niven)

Addiction treatment centres can make effective use of skilfully run
writing workshops to help people who struggle with self-harm, as we
have seen. Asylum seekers, refugees and victims of torture have suffered
much at the hands of others. Writing can be a significant support to them
also, as shown in Chapter 9.

Write!

After your six-minute freewrite (see Chapter 2), reread silently to yourself
with care (or store, or even destroy, it). Then share it with a carefully
chosen other or group, if appropriate.

1. Philip Pullman invented a parallel universe where everyone has
   an internal daemon (1995). Always with them, this supportive

ever-present mentor manifests itself as a talking creature (leopard, moth).

- ° Think of your own daemon; it needn't be an animal, it could be a human or angel.
- ° Ask it how they can help you with your life now.
- ° Write its responses.

2. Observation:

- ° Take your notebook outside, somewhere where you can be entirely alone (a park, by the sea, the moor), or where you can be lost in a crowd (shopping mall, large museum or art gallery).
- ° Leave your book and pen in your bag at first, and for at least five minutes (as long as possible) sit looking, listening, smelling and tasting the air or feeling the ground/wind/seaspray; close your eyes for part of the time if you like.
- ° When you feel ready, write and write, remembering no one, not even you, need reread this. It might be descriptions, memories, feelings…

3. Make a list of any objects in a specific area of your house (toolshed, dressing table, fridge, kitchen cupboard, your desk…).

- ° Highlight any you use habitually/which are important to you.
- ° Choose one; describe it in three simple sentences.
- ° Imagine addressing the object, asking it these kinds of questions:
  - ▸ What do you do?
  - ▸ Why do you do it?
  - ▸ For whom?
  - ▸ Where and when?
  - ▸ How does it help?
- ° Write the reply from the object (e.g. my pencil: 'I enable your words to take wing rather than being stuck in everyday mundanity like they are when you speak…').

CHAPTER 9

'Ideas Hunt Me, Catch Me, Make Me Write': Writing for Victims of Torture, Refugees and Asylum Seekers

Introduction

What can help asylum seekers, refugees and victims of torture recover? 'Often it is the ones who build something in their heads' (Bamber Quoted in Halliburton 2010, p. 10). Writing can help them do just this. River Wolton offers her experience of working with refugees and asylum seekers, with the support of Tchiyiwe Chihana and Violet Dickenson, all members of the core team involved in the 'Different Cultures, One World' book project (2010). And Sheila Hayman, director of *The Medical Foundation for the Care of Victims of Torture* writing group *Write to Life*, explains and illustrates how writing significantly changes these people's lives.

Ink, pen and trustworthy paper: Writing and asylum seekers, by Tchiyiwe Chihana, Violet Dickenson and River Wolton

I often say to people: tell your story because your story will heal you and heal someone else. Our lives are filled with stories, drama, surprises and mysteries that make a wonderful and interesting journey.

Yvonne Cass, Vice-Chair of Refugee Council (in Karimath et al. 2010)

Dear Reader,

This is the story of a book (Karimath *et al.* 2010). A book that is not just about women or about exile, but about human experience. The core organising group were volunteers with the Refugee Women's Development Project (RWDP) at the Northern Refugee Centre. Most of us come from refugee backgrounds and all of us have been advocates for other women who are refugees and asylum seekers.

Ironically, this book came about because funding for RWDP was ending. We were determined that it wouldn't just stop abruptly like so many other projects. Our initial idea was to produce a recipe booklet to fund the project's continuation, but then we started to think bigger. We invited women that we advocate for to get involved, as well as other community groups, and River Wolton to run four creative writing workshops and two workshops in editing. Twenty women from thirteen countries of origin contributed to the book.

> It was hard to explain to some women what the writing workshops might involve. Some of them had experiences of sitting in boring workshops where they don't understand what is happening. But once the women got a taste of writing for publication, the project snowballed and gathered momentum, and now that the book has been published many women are asking when the next one is coming up! (Violet Dickenson)

Our intention was to bridge different cultures in South Yorkshire and to reach out to our readers, inviting them to become part of the book and discover their own creativity. To symbolise this, we included a recipe for Yorkshire Pudding alongside recipes from Algeria, South

Africa, Afghanistan and Cameroon. We also decided to have 'Over to You' sections with prompts, guidance and blank pages for our readers to write in, and to invite them to send writing and recipes to our website. We hoped that we could raise awareness of the thousands of displaced women who live in the region, and of the rich contribution that refugees make to the UK. Some of the broader themes, however, apply to people in many different circumstances, not just to those living in exile: how do we sustain ourselves and our families in times of hardship? How do we build our confidence and encourage each other to aim high, to gain education, to become empowered?

Asylum-seeking women face severe restrictions. Some of those who took part are destitute; their asylum claims have failed and government support has ended, but they are not allowed to work, leaving them reliant on charities stretched to breaking point. What, we asked ourselves, could these creative workshops offer women who are hungry, preoccupied with legal cases, and living in fear of deportation? Feedback showed the workshops provided a chance for women to network, get therapeutic support and relieve some of the stress, if only for an hour or two. We all found the time when you are absorbed in thinking, writing and remembering helps you forget your situation.

Creative work calms me down and helps me to survive.
(T. B., from 'Eight Things About Me')

The practical aspects were important too. We needed funding to reimburse travel expenses and childcare, and to provide lunch, snacks and hot drinks. Safety and confidentiality are also issues for refugees and asylum-seekers, many of whom fear imprisonment, torture or death if they are returned to their countries of origin.

From the start of the project we knew that we were working towards a book. Many of the women were fearful about their names and stories being made public. I was anxious about being known, but at the same time I was excited that I was writing this, and that someone somewhere else (maybe even in my country) would read about it and know that this is taking place. I was excited that we were putting things down on paper for the world to read. (Violet Dickenson).

Several of the contributors wanted to remain anonymous or to use pseudonyms. One writer explained why she'd chosen the name 'Mushroom':

I have chosen a made-up name because I have problems in my country and I don't want my real name to be public. I am one of 100,000 mushrooms growing out in the countryside. I had to leave my country because the courts and justice system are no good. I came to England four years ago and I am still waiting for a decision on my asylum case.

From the beginning many emotions came to the surface:

I started to think about all the things that have happened to Africa. I've always thought there was nothing I could do about it. In the workshops we were made to feel comfortable about writing, because we were encouraged to use everyday words, not complicated language. I felt like I didn't have to think of a clever or complicated way of saying things. When I started to write the poem ('Who Am I?') it was fantastic, I couldn't stop myself, I wanted to keep going. The poem comes from feelings and thoughts I have had for a long time, especially my anger and frustration with the government officials in some African countries. They – and the history of colonisation – have made Africa into a broken continent. I hope that one day it will be possible to have a government that will put its people first.

The writing workshops made me feel like I could bring these feelings out and put them on paper. I was still thinking about them five days later: on Sunday. Normally a Sunday is a day that I keep free for doing nothing. But the workshop and the book project kept coming into my mind, I continued writing the poem, and I was coming up with so many ideas that I felt I could write a second book by myself! This feeling that I can achieve something, that I have achieved something. After writing and talking about it, I didn't feel angry any more. It felt good to be able to write out the feelings. (Violet Dickenson)

Who Am I?

I am part of mother earth, this is my story.
I am massive and beautiful.
Then came greed and robbed me of my beauty.
You raped me of my humanity, you took trinkets
of diamonds and gold, and left me
with gaping wounds that cannot heal.

I am slowly dying, I cannot breathe
because once again greed and corruption dump toxic waste on
me.
The beauty within me has been poisoned.
Greed and corruption raise their ugly heads
and continue to drain me of my minerals,
inflicting bigger wounds on me
through wars and bloodshed.

And now I am almost dead.

I leave you a legacy of disease, drought, famine
and refugees.

My name is Africa.

At the first workshop participants were invited to write about 'Arrival'. Some wrote about arriving in different cities or countries for work or holidays, and others wrote about arriving in the UK.

After we claimed asylum we were put in a room at the airport.
The lights stayed on all night, the chairs were bolted to the
floor. We slept on the floor, in a corner, and people watched
us through the windows. They took all my documents. I
felt like I had been arrested, this had never happened to me
before. I pulled a scarf over my head to sleep. (T. B., from
'Green English Lawn')

It was important to make space for positive as well as challenging experiences:

Green hills, friendly people
helping children, helping older people.
People with big stomachs…
People say 'God bless you'
when I sneeze… ('Mushroom', from 'God Bless You')

For women who have been displaced, there are often traumatic memories. Participants were encouraged to take care of themselves, and reassured that they didn't have to write about painful and upsetting memories. It was important to give guidance about describing the memories as concretely as possible (and therefore potentially separate from the writers' current reality so that there could be a sense of distance and reflection). For an exercise called 'In the Museum of Your Life' the group was asked to make a list of five (or more) objects to put in a museum, art gallery, library, or exhibition representing their life.

> As a facilitator, the challenge of this kind of exercise is to encourage writers to use the five senses, to be specific and detailed, and not to stray too much into commenting on their objects, or using general abstract terms to describe them. I brought in some of my own things as examples: a photo, one of my mother's scarves, a tuning fork. When working with women whose English may be restricted it's important to give concrete examples and to have scribes on hand to help with the writing, give encouraging prompts and clarify ideas. (River Wolton)

> When I first came here I arrived by truck. I was very tired. The police took a photo of me. I'd like that photo. (Hana Belay Kasa, from 'Backlife')

> My collection of 'Harvest' tea-sets with twelve cups. If they send me to a deportation centre I'll give them to my friends. (T. B., from 'Eight Things About Me')

> One small brown suitcase that I carried to England from Tobago (very heavy when you are only seven years old). (Juliette Polle, from 'Past, Present and Future')

As well as arriving and surviving, an important theme was the positive qualities that women develop to thrive in challenging circumstances.

For an exercise called 'A Moment of Change' I invited the group to think back to a moment when they made a decision: to do something new, to take action, to take things into their own hands. It could be a moment that you didn't realise was significant at the time. It could also be something quite small. I asked the group to picture themselves back at that moment, to describe the place and

setting, any sounds or music, anything that they said or did, or that
others said or did, and how they felt physically in their body at this
moment. As we wrote there were tears and laughter, and the pieces
that emerged were moving and inspiring. (River Wolton)

> In August 2003 I arrived in Sheffield, Page Hall. I was housed
> by social services and going through the asylum process. I
> sat in my dilapidated house on a worn-out sofa surrounded
> by poverty. I examined my life and told myself that I did not
> deserve to be reduced to this level. I applied to enter into
> higher education against the law (higher education is illegal
> for asylum seekers)… Seven years later I have been offered a
> place at university. I have also been granted leave to remain
> in the UK. (Christine Thandi Chirambo, from 'The Miracle')

> I was lying in my bed when I realised I had had enough. For
> a seven-year-old, my bedroom was quite big, often silent
> and lonely. The arguments and insistent screams pierced the
> familiar silence. She was begging him not to hurt her. My
> mother was being beaten again by my father. This was now
> happening nightly. (Tchiyiwe Chihana, from 'A Woman's
> Worth?')

Tchiyiwe's story goes on to describe the effects of witnessing
domestic abuse, and the impetus that this gave her to make different
choices in her life. It was painful to write about, and shocking to
discover that the memories were still vivid.

> Having let out a lot more than I had ever admitted to
> feeling, I learned that there was much that I had managed
> to overcome but shelved away. I was able to finally let out
> and identify various emotions that had been locked within.
> I now had a pen for a mouthpiece and paper for a good
> listener. In addition, the knowledge that somehow, someone
> out there will get to share in my experience is both exciting
> and fulfilling. (Tchiyiwe Chihana)

A theme that emerged organically was the question of what helps us
through the worst times.

> Our comprehensive list of things that give us strength or well-
> being included music, creative work, prayer, keeping busy, family,

talking, faith, singing: things that many people, not just refugees, can relate to. When writing about these qualities it's easy to fall into vague descriptions that might not communicate anything to a reader. We worked on making them concrete by finding and developing metaphors for abstract qualities. (River Wolton)

Hope is a beach, like the one I saw when I arrived in England.
Hope is warm, not too hot, not too cold.
The sky and water are the same blue, merging together.
the sun shining a little. (Hana Belay Kasa, from 'Hope')

Peace of mind is like raindrops falling. (Violet Dickenson, from 'The Taste of Rain')

Passion is like food, it takes away my hunger and comforts me. Passion is like eating boiled maize at home with family and friends. (Natalia, from 'Passion')

After generating reams of individual and group pieces, recipes and reflections, we were faced with the task of editing and ordering. In the last session we wrote inspirational messages to our readers on everyday household objects such as tea-towels, tea-bags, kitchen roll, and scraps of paper from the recycling bin; it was great fun to do but quite a challenge for the designer to incorporate these in a legible way! We learned a great deal through trial and error, there were many ideas that we had to let go of, and many last minute decisions to be debated.

Ibtisam's poem 'The Journey of the Ink' sums up the journey that we made from blank page to the finished book and its 100 colourful, inviting and inspiring pages. In only four months we accomplished something that went far beyond our initial expectations. In the book the poem appears in the original Arabic, with English translation.

The Journey of the Ink
When I write about myself
I am like the ink in an empty cartridge
trying to write on flimsy tissue paper.
The line is faint, I try my best
but it vanishes.

The ink loses its way and ends up
on wrinkled paper with the letters confused.
The letters become two-faced,

no longer friends, like the empty space around us.

Be positive, there is hope, be strong.
Try to find your ink, your pen and trustworthy paper
to express the clarity of your heart. (Ibtisam Al-Farah)

We are glad that this project has a lasting legacy – the money raised from book sales will fund a new project, Development and Empowerment for Women's Advancement (DEWA), run by the original core group. We also held a brilliant book launch at Off The Shelf Festival, with performances in front of an 80-strong audience (www.dewaproject.wordpress.com).

Write to Life, by Sheila Hayman

We always eat well! We go to Write to Life and our tummies are full. (Gloria)

Gloria's from Northern Uganda, and she loves to eat. One of her poems, the one that always gets a laugh at readings, is about her big bum and round tummy, and how different they are from the genteel delicacy she sees all around her in 'English ladies'. She has a big smile as well, and a ready laugh, and it takes a while to discover that the laugh comes out particularly when she's nervous, or fearful that somebody is about to say things she doesn't want to think about. For years after she arrived in London, she would ride the buses, anywhere, all day long, just in case her lost children had somehow escaped from the Lord's Resistance Army, and by some miracle made it here. At dusk, she always returned home, and even now she only comes to workshops in the summer months, when she can get home before dark. She doesn't like the dark.

The Medical Foundation for the Care of Victims of Torture is one of the world's largest treatment centres, advocating for the rights of torture survivors and offering legal, practical and psychological help, as well as various therapies. Not just the usual psychotherapy, but gardening, painting, even bread making. And Write to Life, the writing group.

Gloria's a member of the writing group I run at its headquarters in Finsbury Park. Our workshop sessions always begin with food. It's a pretty basic meal, having to skirt both budget and cultural constraints, but the fact that we need it at all is proof of the power of the writing our clients do here. Fear of the dark isn't the only thing they have to battle. In addition to being refugees or asylum seekers, they are all struggling to overcome the effects of torture. They all have psychological scars, some are physically disabled, and many have no cash at all, and have to beg or borrow the means to make a journey that may take them right across London and back. But they do it, every two weeks, just to sit for an hour and a half, with the peace and space to write.

We're lucky that the group's been funded to run continuously for eleven years, making it unique in the world of refugee writing. Some of our current writers have been part of it almost from the start. So it feels almost like a family, but one that welcomes new members, who can take their own time to join in the jokes, as well as share their writing. It's a family from a dozen countries, which ironically can actually make things easier; often it's the people from one's own culture who are the hardest to trust, for fear they may be government spies or members of an enemy faction.

Tonight, as usual, people drift in late, with lots of ribbing about slack time-keeping, and food being shuttled up and down to make sure they eat. Eleven clients have turned up, which is pretty much the average out of a total of twenty, who at any time might have problems with health, housing, legal status, childcare, depression or just the bloody English weather. Together with four or five writing mentors, that's about as big as the group can comfortably be, and give time for everybody to read and share who wants to.

Because we can never tell who'll turn up, we don't even try for any sort of continuity between sessions. Luckily, our half dozen volunteer facilitators, all professional writers, have varied enough skills and talents to provide something new and different every time. Sharon, an actor and screenwriter, might set us to invent two characters who'd never normally meet, then find a way they might, and write the dialogue they'd have. Our resident poet might bring in a famous poem about trees, and a lump of wood, and get us all thinking about why poems work, and what exactly makes something a poem, anyhow? (Don't ask me, I've never got an answer to this one.)

The workshops can be about form, technique, appreciation of great writing, or just a subject that everybody shares. As well as widely differing ethnic and cultural backgrounds, our clients vary hugely in their educational level and their grasp of English. It's important that we be able to offer help to anybody fluent enough to make sense of what's going on in the conversation, because it's often the fairly recent arrivals, with their trauma still raw and their stories confused, who can most benefit from the work we do.

So we have to invent workshops that can cater for this huge range, and be prepared for whatever emerges to be nothing like what we expect. None of us, apart from the facilitator, ever has any idea what we'll be asked to write about when we sit down, and in a way that's part of the magic. Everybody, mentors, survivors and visitors, has to write, though not necessarily read out and share their work. And out of that being caught unawares and unprepared, come the most amazing, wonderful and entertaining writings, in voices we often had no idea were in us.

So long as everybody can find something in the exercise to catch their imaginations, so they all write busily, it really doesn't matter what triggers it. It's that silent room full of bowed heads and busy pens that counts.

> When I write in the workshop, it's much better than in my house, because the room is full of community for me, I feel my mind relaxing, even if I don't understand everything. (Qasim)

Often, in fact, the simplest ideas work best, and many of the most productive and creatively engaging workshops start with a theme. We did one on playground games, which revealed that hopscotch exists in every country we knew. We did one on traditional stories, at panto season, starting with Cinderella and its siblings in other cultures, and accompanied with crackers and paper hats – even more bizarre when you're trying to explain them to somebody from Eritrea.

Tonight, Sharon has brought us a very simple idea, and one we can all appreciate. 'We're going to write about food,' she says. Cheers all round. 'But not just what's on your plate, what it means. Food's about all sorts of things, isn't it? Love, and power, and wealth or poverty. It's about what's familiar, and what's strange.'

'Hot cake and cold lumpy custard!' Christine mutters. 'That's what they gave me for my first meal here. That's when I knew I was really not at home any more.' 'And what is this thing, the Full

English? How can they eat that stuff so early in the day?' wonders somebody else.

'Well, we're not going to start with here. We're going to begin with the best meal you ever had. Write about that, for ten minutes.'

As soon as this first session is over, it's obvious that food has as many meanings as the people in the room. A lot of the best meals came from loving grannies, which you might expect. But here, they may be grannies who will never be seen again, whose vegetable patches have been torn up and chickens looted by roving militias. And the tastes, the wood-smoke fragrance, have to be pulled out of memories distant in space as well as time. It's painful, but there are jokes too. Not all grannies can cook, and at least one story is of a meal so delicious that its disastrous consequences convulse us all.

'Now, I'm going to ask you about the worst meal you ever had,' continues Sharon. 'Write about it, and then look at your two pieces of writing, and see how different they are, how different the language you use, and the way you describe them.'

This time we have longer to write, and it's obviously harder for some people to begin. And not because they don't know what to write about. This is where the gulf in experience between mentor/ facilitators and writing group members really opens up. The mentors, all of us white middle class Brits, write about gristly stew at boarding school, or pushing fancy food round a plate in a restaurant while our first love dumped us.

But the writers have real stories to tell. Christine, a confident, articulate lioness of a woman, now struggling to get a university degree as a single mother with a chronically sick child, expands her story of the cake and lumpy custard into a poignant but hilarious account of the enforced gratitude and serial misunderstandings that accompany even the best intentioned encounters between asylum seeker and 'befriender.' She's followed by Barbara, a Zimbabwean who's recently joined the group, too wound up to write, but desperate to share her story of the day she was arrested. 'My baby was with a neighbour. I'd left her there, like I always did. I said I'd be back by five, like always, I just had some errands for my business, I had to go to the bank. So at the bank the men were waiting for me, the men from the government, the men who wanted my money and wanted me out of the way...' The next thing she knew, she was in a prison cell, with a dozen other women, all yelling to be released. Towards midnight, frantic and ravenously hungry, she was presented with a plate of rotten fish bones and half-raw dried beans. Now she had to choose between eating it, hoping it wouldn't kill her, or refusing it, and losing the strength to fight her way back to her child.

And after Barbara, it's the turn of Qasim, a quiet, poetic Iraqi Kurd who, like many of our clients, was a writer and journalist before he came here – which was what got him into trouble. He's done better than many since his arrival: he's fallen in love, had a child and been granted his refugee status, which gives him some small sense of security and hope of a settled future. But he lost one leg to a bomb in the war, and can't work. And so, again like many others, he struggles with survivor guilt. Friends and colleagues in his situation didn't make it out, and now that he's here, what's he doing to justify that survival? This is one reason why he makes the long journey to our workshops, in his case nearly two hours each way, and despite his one leg.

His remembered meal is also prison food, but most of us wouldn't call it that. In the twenty minutes he has to write, there's only time barely to sketch a picture of an interminable wait in the near-darkness of an isolation cell, punctuated by a daily offering of 'soup' made mostly of water, and garnished with mouse droppings, ash and human hair. Just hearing about it, we're all shocked, and then almost immediately the room fills with thoughts and ideas about food as punishment, as a weapon – meanings most people in this country would never even consider.

The conversations carry on after we disperse for the evening, on the way to our various buses and trains. Everybody takes their writing with them, and Qasim and Christine both decide to develop them in their private sessions. These are offered to all Write to Life members, in between and in addition to the workshops. The workshops are obviously public, collective writing spaces, and with their great variety and mostly cheerful atmosphere are primarily about the joy and excitement of writing; writing as a tool and a gift they can take wherever the UK Border Agency chooses to send them, as a magic castle they can build for themselves, from which no housing agency or hostile landlord can evict them.

I sit with my friend the telly and I write... .(Barbara)

But they also need time and space for the personal writing, the stuff that's harder to pull out, and can't be shared with a room full of people. So every member of Write to Life is also offered one to one sessions with a mentor who's a professional writer, who can work with them to turn an idea or a sketch into a polished piece of writing, at a pace the client can dictate. Often the first thing they write about in these sessions is their own past, the events that traumatised them and brought them here. I sometimes think of this as being a bit like the yolk of the egg the baby chick consumes to give it the strength to peck its way out into the world: the 'yolk writing' is the life story, and having written it, the writer then may be strong enough, and confident enough as a writer, to turn their gaze on the outside world.

> The ideas hunt me, come to catch me, make me write them.
> (Regine)

But these recollections come at their own pace, and can be hard to deal with – which is of course part of the rehabilitation process. For this reason, as well as the writing mentor, each client has a counsellor or therapist to call on, so that these sessions can explore past traumas, and go wherever the writing wants to, knowing help is there if it's needed.

After this workshop, Qasim takes his story of the mouse dropping soup to his writing mentor, and later produces a beautiful, extremely harrowing account of one endless night in his cell. Meanwhile I have caught something in Christine's story, which is not just about cake and custard but also about her life back home, where her mother kept chickens, and a staple diet of eggs was only relieved by the arrival of visitors. I'm her writing mentor, so the next time I speak to her, I ask her to work on it and send it to me.

> 'What, the piece about eggs?'
> 'Ah, but it's not about eggs, you see.'
> 'Yes it is, it's about my mum keeping eggs and making us have them for breakfast every day. And that stupid English man who didn't believe that Africans also eat eggs for breakfast.'
> 'No, no, it's not about eggs! It's about power, and control! It's about your Dad controlling the family by only letting you have nice food when there were other people to see it.'
> 'Oh, and putting on a show for the neighbours?'

'Yes, exactly!' I feel like Michelangelo seeing David inside the lump of marble, except that in this case it's her David, and I'm just – I don't know, perhaps the stonemason helping her to chip away the stuff that's not relevant. I'm probably more bossy and interventionist than some of my colleagues, but the excitement of this collaborative process gets the better of me, and I try to be careful only to push my writers as hard as they will welcome.

It's a tricky business, needing constant sensitivity. What do you do when somebody writes an account of an event, which is vivid and detailed except for the violent death at the centre of it, which is dismissed in one blank sentence? We know that the reason may be the self-protective way memory can strip out emotion and only leave bare facts. But it's the emotion we need to get to, both for the sake of the writing, and of the writer. There are no rules for these situations; only mutual trust and knowledge, and attention to instinct, can steer us safely through. All the more reason to be glad of that support in the background.

So Christine goes away and works on the piece, and together we nudge it into a form that manages to be both about eggs, and very much about family dynamics, and control. Out of that one workshop eventually come four or five finished pieces, all quite different in style and mood, all catalysed by that one, very simple exercise. And all ready for the next publication, reading, or event.

> I always walk around with a pen and a notebook... Just to have them in my bag reassures me, and I don't feel like I am missing something. (Christine)

These public occasions are as important a part of the work we do as the most private sessions. Writing, for anybody, is at best a lonely and dispiriting business, rarely delivering from our hours of effort anything like what we hope or imagine. How much harder in a third – or fifth – language, which may not even contain the words you need, even if you've been lucky or persevering enough to get to that point. And harder yet for a writer who may dread what the imagination or the memory might bring up at any time.

Yet writing, we have to believe, is the way to lay those ghosts, imprison them in a piece of work, not leave them running wild inside the head. And by turning an experience into a coherent story, by making it make sense to others, we also make it make sense to ourselves. It's worth the effort, in the end. But the effort is huge, on top of all the other struggles of their lives.

So our programme of readings, performances and fundraisers is not just to give back to the Medical Foundation and promote its work and ours. It justifies the struggle, and gives the writers a sense of self-esteem, of their own value, that they often think they'd lost for ever. One of them said that standing in front of an audience, reading her own work, in her own words, and hearing – or rather, not hearing, in the audience's attentive silence – the writing having its effect, was like having a mirror held up to prove that, despite everything she'd been through, all the efforts of successive regimes and bureaucracies to obliterate her, she still existed.

It's not enough to write; part of the healing process, many tell us, is to be read and heard. Write to Life has just published its seventh annual anthology, with something by almost all our writers. And we have a busy programme of events coming up – including, conveniently, one all about food. There aren't that many upsides to the lives our writers lead, to pasts in distant countries, extraordinary torments survived, and, for many, a present life as that despised and misrepresented species, the asylum seeker. But one indubitable bonus, which we try to exploit to the full, is that they will always have something utterly new, unpredictable, and compelling, to tell the rest of the world.

> I used to be a journalist, writing about politics and social issues in my country. It was quite easy because I was writing about others, using my writing as a weapon to stigmatise or denounce a situation that I found intolerable. But since I have been with Write to Life, writing has helped me externalise everything that my subconscious kept away from my consciousness. I can now use words, not as a weapon, but as a healer. It is this that helps to keep me going even when I find life so unbearable. Writing helps me to reach others, to sensitise them on issues that they are not even aware of. I find it rewarding when, during my readings in front of people, I can actually see and feel that they are touched and concerned about what I am talking about. It's a home away from home for my deepest feelings and thoughts. (Christine)

Conclusion

Victims of torture, refugees and asylum seekers struggle with and overcome language and other barriers to enable writing to help them understand and come to terms with their situations, amazingly make light of them even. Sheila Hayman and River Wolton *et al.* have given glimpses into ways of introducing writing and helping people 'build something in their heads' as a route to creating a new life and sense of self following such abuse, as Helen Bamber, founder of the Medical Foundation for the Care of Victims of Torture, suggested (Halliburton 2010). Writers in prison have other, equally large, constraints upon their expression, and find writing invaluable, although struggling with totally different situations, as shown in Chapter 10.

Write!

After your six-minute freewrite (see Chapter 2), reread silently to yourself with care (or store, or even destroy, it). Then share it with a carefully chosen other or group, if appropriate.

1. You are given a magical object.

   ◦ What is it?

   ◦ How can it help you, and how not?

   ◦ Who gave it to you?

   ◦ Why?

   ◦ Where will you go with it?

2. List a few sayings you grew up with (e.g. 'remove your coat inside, or you won't feel the benefit when you return outside'). Choose one.

   ◦ Write on how you feel about it now, and how you felt then.

   ◦ List sayings you use, if you can.

   ◦ List ones you would like to use.

3. Think of a feeling you've had recently (delight, amusement, affection, shock, physical pain).

   ◦ Write a letter to it, as if it were an old friend/foe; make sure to include some questions.

   ◦ Write answers.

CHAPTER 10

'A Craft to Take You Through Storms, and Keep You Still': Writing in Prison

The ability to see and appreciate the humanity in others is very precious. And it's the *shared respect* which helps to make our group a safe place to express yourself.

George

All the while the lines flow, cleaning the mind of many things, but leaving room for further growth.

David

Writing can make significant difference to people in prison, as Lydia Fulleylove demonstrates. It can bring the outside inside prison walls. It can enable prisoners to find strength and individuality, as well as offering unique forms of expression and communication.

The story of the prison writers, by Lydia Fulleylove

The Creative Arts are the only legal way to escape.

www.writersinprison.org

The Lost Room, and looking out

To begin with I said no. I was asked by the Writers in Prison network to take over a residency which wasn't working in a high security Category B prison. I didn't like the idea of being shut in. I wasn't sure what I felt about working with vulnerable prisoners or 'sex offenders'. Curiosity won in the end and I found myself with the unfamiliar weight of belt, chain and keys round my waist in a windowless, bare room with dingy orange walls and uncomfortable wooden chairs and tables in rows which I shifted into a unit we could all sit round, while keeping myself nearest the door, as instructed. There was a skylight. I could hear the herring gulls. That was a comfort.

I had been warned in my security briefing: 'These men may be manipulative. They may try to condition you.' In that first three hour session, I was determined to stick to my principle that here were a group of writers and that I would treat them as such, while standing back and remaining reflective and aware. There were just six men, ranging from a young fisherman who had first learned to read on coming to prison, to a former psychotherapist in his sixties. They settled into a silence which I didn't know whether to interpret as hostile or uneasy.

I had prepared a close-structured workshop which for once I followed meticulously, sensing perhaps that writers in this situation are used to rules and might initially at least feel most comfortable with a very clear sense of order. I included a collaborative poem, which I hoped might begin to give us a sense of the group working together. It was also an attempt to overcome, or make something of our surroundings. We called it 'The Lost Room':

> Scuffed floor lies morose
> hunkers down
> Orange wall shouts
> at echoing emptiness
>
> …
>
> Pipe like a straight snake intrudes and escapes
> At least something got out.

Everyone was guarded but the glint of humour in the last lines was an indication of something which has characterised the group: the opportunity for shared laughter. And the last word proved significant. Perhaps instinctively we found ourselves looking out beyond the bars and the present imprisonment; and this was to inform much of the subsequent writings and projects. The collection of writings produced for that first residency was called *Scapes*: through imagination, memory, story and poem, the men ranged across the world. As one of the group said:

> Knowing I can go anywhere with my imagination, that I can visit places I've loved, helps me stay sane and keep a sense of perspective while I'm in here. (Stephen)

After these awkward beginnings, the group grew to twelve members: individuals came and went, but a core of writers remained. At any point, a prisoner might be 'shipped out' to another prison or prevented from coming by some working of the system, yet their commitment was impressive.

The power of writing

> Poetry was a lifeline in a world dominated by talk, festooned with f words. (Chris)

Looking back, unshakeable belief in the power of the arts, and unfaltering determination were both essential to keep the projects going in a prison context. I found hostility in areas where I had expected common ground, such as the education service, yet unexpected support from other members of prison staff. What sustained me as facilitator more than anything else was my gradual realisation of the extraordinary quality of that energy and ability behind bars and of the significance of writing in the prisoners' lives. Writing was powerful and central in a way which it seldom is on the outside.

This is reflected in the words of visiting poet Mimi Khalvati, who led a workshop. In her introduction to *Flows and Prose*, the inhouse book we produced in 2007, she wrote:

> Being on site for a workshop at 8am proved to be, not only in the early morning sense, an eye-opening experience. It is rare to work with an only men group. Rarer still, after working with hundreds of groups over many years, up and

down the country, to be made aware, as if for the first time, of *why* we were there: because poetry *matters.* You'd think, to a poet, this would be self evident. But in the small world of poetry, in a freelance world of scrabbling around for a living, in a market where poetry books, like Cinderellas without their princes, are being increasingly relegated to chimney corners, it seems reasonable to assume that poetry might matter to me, but does it really matter to others? The Prison Writers put me straight. I can't quite say how: it might have been their energy, their enthusiasm, knowledge, commitment – though many writers have all these; their humour, good humour; their readiness to overflow, not only with their own words but in response to others. But more, perhaps, it was the absence of something – the more usual feeling that poetry is an adjunct to life, that other things are more vital, central – that made the difference. Seeing the group in the corridor afterwards, lining up for lunch, they seemed, though replenished by the morning, more ordinary, almost lesser men, than the giant presences sitting around the workshop tables. There they seemed like Titans, each with his own vulnerabilities, obsessions, but each man a living proof that to engage in writing, reading, is to live a life in no way paler, more circumscribed, than a life lived outside. (Mimi Khalvati)

Travelling across the world

When that first ten month residency ended, I applied for and received Arts Council England (ACE) funding for the first of two combined arts projects, with writing workshops as the focus. Four years later, we are still thriving, thanks to more Arts Council and prison funding. All the original members have moved or been released but there is a significant core of writers who have been with the group for some time and pass the baton on to help to maintain the ethos of the group, to welcome new writers, while allowing it to grow and evolve. The diversity of nationality, culture and education enriches the group.

We have travelled through a series of changing landscapes, from the birds' eye view of Scapes, to the sea in *Shipshape,* through *Cities* and on to *Wild Places* without and within. Writers re-create places they have loved, for themselves and the group: George writing lyrically about Ireland, Fernando about Portugal, Joe about Lagos, and Chris bringing us to Scotland through different poetic forms and short stories.

The invitation to look outwards is not accidental. Prisoners seldom write or talk directly about their crimes and I avoid openings which might invite them to do this. Yet the power of place is one of the ways through which they are able to express directly or indirectly their own thoughts, feelings and memories. Chris, a founder member who gave much to the group through his four years' imprisonment, wrote, in support of our Arts Council England application for the project Wild Places:

> It might be thought that setting up a project that includes 'exploring wild places within ourselves' as well as the wild places of the world, in a prison where sex offenders are concentrated would be asking for trouble. But this group has evolved a strong ethos of mutual trust and support and is conducted very differently from official training groups which can evoke anxiety and defensiveness as material explored can significantly affect a prisoner's career. By contrast our writing group does not focus directly on offending behaviour, and such material rarely comes to the surface. However, many group members have asserted with enthusiasm that their writing has enabled them better to understand personal issues underlying their offences, and perhaps to deal with such issues more effectively. (Chris)

In his villanelle 'When Poetry Revealed Herself to Me', Stephen shows how poetry and especially poetic form was enabling him to discover new aspects of himself:

> She dressed in clothes that I have never seen
> And reminded me of things I've never said
> When poetry revealed herself to me.
>
> I ran and fell, she kissed my bloody knee,
> She held me in her arms and on she led
> And took me to the man I am to be. (Stephen)

And John, who had never written poetry before joining the Shipshape
project, wrote:

Imagination

It carried with it
as it sailed away
zephyrs of the mind.
A broad reach fills the sail
as if there really was
a final destination.

Close hauled halyards sing
the soulful song of the wind
entering within.

Expanding and contracting
ploughing memory's waves
searching for understanding. (John)

Casting off – and learning the craft

Our Shipshape workshops became places of exploration and
experiment as the men gained in confidence and in trust. New
members, used to the rigidity and control of prison life, were
encouraged to let go of the idea that they must know exactly where
they're going and to grasp the idea that we can write, not just to say
what we think but to explore an idea and to find out more about
ourselves and the world. Thinking, reading and writing about the
vastness and mystery of the sea helped in this process. As group
member Jon wrote during Shipshape:

> Cast off your mind and let it steer
> a course that none have gone before
> from this benighted shore
> Your craft will take you where you will
> through storms
> …and keep you still. (Jon)

His poem points to another significant feature of our workshops:
the emphasis on the craft of writing and on the shaping and editing

process. The men have shown great appetite for learning about and using different poetic forms and structures and exploring, for example, short story, flash fiction and script. They have discovered both the satisfaction of learning the craft and the way in which form can take you in new and unexpected directions in the expression of an idea or experience.

Sharing and responding to writing: The ethos of the group

The exploration of 'wild places within ourselves as a source of creativity' was an important strand of the Wild Places project. It would have been impossible had not certain safeguards already been in place, essential for novice and experienced writers alike for safe exploration of wild places. The *process of writing* itself creates a slowing down and filtering of thought, as well as the opportunity for subconscious issues to be expressed in symbolic forms. As facilitator, I, and more experienced members of the group, offer a *model of response*: friendly support and encouragement, with feedback which is sensitive yet challenging when people are ready for it. Sometimes response can help a writer discover what a piece is 'really about' and how he can shape and edit to clarify this. Occasionally material has proved too painful for a writer but the group's unobtrusive support has been remarkable. When Tom burst into tears, another member gave him a tissue, patted him on the shoulder and the group quietly carried on, giving him chance to weep and join in again when he was ready.

Perhaps one of the most therapeutic aspects of the group is as a model of awareness and understanding of each other which can eventually be taken beyond bars into lives on re-settlement.

A writing workshop

We begin as we often do with music to mark the shift from the hurly burly of prison life. This time it's *Fingal's Cave* (Mendelssohn). Shared listening of this kind is an opportunity the men don't often have. Sometimes individuals choose to write while listening, perhaps to empty their minds of whatever came before. See David's quote heading this chapter.

Afterwards we go straight into flow-writing, starting with the line, 'I can sing a true song about myself', from Kevin Crossley-Holland's translation of *The Seafarer* (1992, p. 37). I remind newer members, 'Don't stop, don't think/criticise yourself, don't rhyme. Go wherever it takes you even if it seems like rubbish. That's where the diamonds could be!'

We settle into ten minutes of writing when the only sound is the movement of pens over paper. Sometimes, though not today, I drop in words which may make them swerve in their course or bring strangely contrasting elements together to create something new. Afterwards, everyone wants to share what they've written:

> The option not to read is always maintained and it's helpful when more as well as less experienced writers choose this occasionally, showing that it can be exercised without losing respect. (Chris)

George has chosen to write the 'true song' from another point of view. Later he re-wrote it as a poem, titled *Imelda*, which begins:

> Anguish of loss
> still fresh in her mind
> grief must be hidden,
> locked inside
> like an invisible locket,
> where only she
> and the few invited in
> could share this intimacy… (George)

When I asked him to reflect on this piece later he wrote:

> Writing and re-working this made me realise for the first time that, in writing, it is possible to become another character, irrespective of whether I had a shared personal perspective. I found I could empathise with them in a way not accessible in other forms of creativity. I felt it identified a new-found maturity in myself. (George)

Afterwards we explore the original poem, identifying the bleakness, the yearning, the exhilaration of the seafarer's life and being transported, as we so often are by the sounds of a poem. Reading together like this can offer as important an opportunity for reflection and for empathy as our own writing.

We have a short break, though some of the men stay and continue to talk or write. Then I take out my box of 'sea things' and spread them on the table. There are the permanent residents such as shells, tiny stones, dried seaweed, pieces of frayed rope (fragments: this is a prison!). And there are a few things collected fresh that morning: seaweed, egg cases. The men are silent. Everyone looks, no one says anything.

'Choose one to start with,' I say. 'Look at it, feel it, smell it… listen to it! When you're ready, start to write. Write with all your senses. Stay with the thing you have chosen for five minutes, then go wherever it takes you but bring your mind back to it at the end.'

Slowly the men reach out. It is this moment that stays with me afterwards, even more than the pieces they write. Perhaps it is because these delicate, tough sea things are here with us in the harsh concrete prison environment. I write:

The Prison and the Sea

Tom reached for the oar weed which still
glistened. He pressed it to his face,
he could smell the sea. *The sea,*
he was saying, *the sea.*

David hooked his finger through
a frail cleft of driftwood, kept
cradling it, as if he wanted
never to let it go.

In the end he said, *Would you mind – could I
keep it?* And knowing how I should not
and seeing how his hands turned it
over and over, I said *Yes.*

Lydia Fulleylove 2008, p. 28

Sailing across the arts

A crucial part of the Shipshape project was the discovery of how one art form can illuminate, develop or inspire another. It became a voyage across the arts, a different art form sometimes allowing an individual to explore a part of himself in more depth. At the beginning of the project we worked with a visual artist in a workshop, which combined brainstorming and patterning of sea-words and images with collage, using a rich variety of soft materials. Towards the end of the session, some people spontaneously wrote pieces in response to their collage. It happened to be Black History week and Abz wrote the piece below, reflecting both the outward through the history of slavery and the inward, his own voyage through prison. His collage showed a stark black ship, a huddle of bright coloured figures rowing, a white flag flying from the stern, a black flag from the bows, sea birds black and white, flying overhead – and the quay – both a landing place and a black prison gate with a white key floating behind it.

The Ship of Pain
I saw her tall black flag
flying freely at full mast.
I heard the cries from the men in rags
I smelt the happiness that was its past
I felt the hunger of their fast.

From where did this boat start?
But it's sailing into the dark,
leaving behind the land that was free.

How long does it have to sail
to reach freedom's quay? (Abz)

One to one

Cut to a windowless interview room on one of the wings, eight foot by six, the same size as a cell. This is the setting for one to one sessions, an opportunity for writers to discuss their writing with me. These times are precious in giving new writers confidence to join the group or in offering opportunities to discuss in depth a poem or story, perhaps dealing with a sensitive issue like the death of a parent which the writer may not be ready to share with the group. They often begin with the writer reading his piece aloud to me, especially if a poem.

Sam, the young man opposite me today, is passionate about his writing, but after an education consisting mostly of exclusions, he is rebellious and highly resistant to co-operating with a group. Here in prison he has discovered for himself the power of writing and the excitement of that pervades all his writing and our conversations. I've been working with him for several months and for the first time he has a reader, a listener. He's thirsty for response. For the next thirty minutes we discuss my comments on his last piece and then he pushes a new story towards me. He tells me that he thinks he might be ready to join the group. He's been seeing the psychologist and she's prepared to back him. She can see the difference his writing is making to him, the outlet it offers for his energy and the tremendous satisfaction he gets from making a story.

When I leave the prison that day, I tell the story of this encounter for myself, something which I know is important for me as facilitator to do, though that's not why I do it. I do it because the story has to be told. Here it is:

Training

His head shone in the fluorescent light,
the hollow in the centre of his skull,
the neat fit of his earlobes, dusky-pink
to dark, the muscled fitness of forearms,
the red tee-shirt patched with sweat
from training in his cell. What did he want

from me? My close attention to his words;
my accurate recall of all *the stuff*
he'd given me to read; his line to
life outside; my coming when I said I would?
Sometimes I slipped up and he was cross.
I showed him tough, weighed up the toll on me.

But what price his stories, those wild drives he took me on?
The first jail. The darkest time. The slashed arms.
The closest to losing it. He drummed his fingers
on his skull. *I have to be a father for my son.*
I've trained my body and my mind. Each time I see him
I lift him off the ground… My fitness and my writing,

they can't take those from me.
He pushed the race of jostling
words towards me. *Excuse the coffee stain.*
They'd smell faintly of smoke. I'd breathe them in.
But whose stories were they? Those speeding letters?
The trails across the jail's close quartered air?

I hope that you enjoy the latest of my stories.
He pointed to the torn plastic sleeve
on the scuffed space between us. Everything
was sharp in the dull light. I was stiff with sitting.
His long fingers traced the words I'd take away.
It's called 'Seagus and Crowburn Fly South'. (Lydia Fulleylove)

Before Sam was released, he did indeed join the writers' group. It
wasn't always an easy ride, either for him or the rest of the group,
but his presence, his ability to last a session, was a huge achievement
for him.

Landscapes of the mind

Let's travel with the prison writers to another workshop. This time
we are exploring ideas and experiences of solitude. We start with a
written meditation, choosing from a collection of grasses and wild
flowers, the natural world in the midst of the manmade.

'Observation, memory, imagination. Use all three, wherever they
take you,' I say and we're off. Josiah, through a tall seed grass, takes
us back to his native Nigeria and a precious memory of freedom
when he roamed all day from dawn to dusk.

The second part of the session is structured round Jean Sprackland's
poem *Caravan* (2003, p. 6). I give the group the first four words:
'This is not about...', then, a couple of words from each stanza and
the last word 'silence'. I ask them to write for six minutes. We listen
to a few of their pieces and discuss different kinds of 'aboutness'. Is
a poem about what it seems to be on the surface?

When we come to read *Caravan*, we're particularly aware of how
it's made, of its connections to and differences from our own pieces.
I ask the group to use this structure as a model for their own writing
about their interpretations of solitude. I've found the use of shapes

and structures of free verse poems as effective as formal poetic forms, in exploring ideas, channelling feelings and discovering something new, as well as acting as a scaffold for less experienced writers. *Caravan* is in the second person and I ask them to stick with this too.

Jonathan brought copies of his first draft back for a 'close up' feedback session soon after. The poem underwent many revisions but a 'final' version is below, along with Jonathan's reflections, a year later, on writing it. The group liked his original very short lines but as one of them said: 'Like always, in the end it's your poem. You listen to the others, you take on board suggestions, and then you listen to yourself again.'

New members of the group are always gently weaned by the others from that popular form, the 'prison rant', which they saw as a stage they all went through. In one sense, Jonathan's poem is more 'about' prison than anything else written by the group during this project: yet it's very far from a rant as he stands back and reflects on his journey.

Solitude

It had been a difficult time,
years of uncertainty,
swimming in a sea of distractions,
unable to focus on what mattered,
making a mess of everything.

So you thought of a monastery;
you'd book yourself in, retreat to a cell,
pace the paths through gardens and fields,
find yourself.

Then the knock on the door...
another kind of cell,
a different monastery:
417 cubic feet of solitude.

Your iron bed forms one coast
of your 8 by 7 world
under the picture board:
postcards from the loving, favourite sayings,
memories of places, ideas for your future,
the photo of your Loved One.

You try to ignore the thinness
of a feeble fiction of foam.

A chair in which to sit up, take note,
sit down, make notes,
a table to lean on when times are hard,
a table to write at when times are better,
a blue plastic plate
for nourishment of body and soul.
There's enough on your plate now,
almost too much at times.

Enough!
It's time to change,
reform, reconstitute.
It's all about choices...

And yes,
it is your Monastery
with its times and movements,
its regularity, its order out of chaos,
its noises and quietness,
its solitude, reflectiveness,
repentance
amongst a sense of community;
the way it works on your soul, your very being,
allows you to find yourself, to start again.
Maybe these hermits of old
had something in their solitude. (Jonathan)

This piece was inspired by the idea of exploring wild places
within and outside us. My own recent journey had been
long and difficult for many people and I was by now at a
stage when I could reflect on the past, knowing the future
will be very different. Strangely, before being arrested, I
was actually going to book myself into a monastery I knew
and had visited, in order to give myself space to sort my
life out. I love poetry and different styles of writing, and
this piece more or less wrote itself straight off. The original
draft, containing all the points I wanted to make, was twice
as long, with some lines of one or two words. The group
made suggestions for re-phrasing and for cutting it down.

I've now come back to it again and adjusted it once more! I've learned a lot about economy from this exercise. Writing it felt like a kind of catharsis; it was good to have expressed it on paper, not just discussing the monastery thing with the group. This poem will stay with me. I've shown it to my partner and family. The hermit is about to hit the world again but to help it, not hinder it! (Jonathan)

Collaboration and celebration

In both ACE funded projects, Shipshape and Wild Places, teamwork and collaboration between people with different skills and talents have been crucial. Early on we set up project teams. They drew in prisoners who weren't necessarily members of the writing group, yet who wanted to contribute in a variety of ways: writers of stories and poems for the project book and exhibition; designers of 'creative arts activity packs' for prisoners to use during 'in cell' time; an editorial team for the project book; artists who designed and painted the exhibition sails; carpenters who built stands in the woodwork workshop; and musicians and performers for the final project celebrations. John, who had always been worried about his lack of education, grew in self-esteem and confidence as he discovered that not only could he write but that he was also a valued member of the editorial team. Another member of the Shipshape team and writing group commented afterwards:

> The sense of ownership of the project was extremely satisfying, the opportunity to be involved in a worthwhile endeavour at all levels – conception, planning and execution – and one which drew on personal characteristics little used in a prison environment. The whole experience has been so satisfying, one which will stay with me forever no matter what I decide to do with the rest of my life.

Both projects finished with a celebration for an audience of prisoners and outside community members, including local writers, artists, sailors, some of whom had joined us for shared workshops during the projects. This contact through writing and art with the 'outside' community is a vital part of the project, not only a chance for 'ordinary conversations with ordinary people' but an opportunity for the wider community to see another side of this socially excluded group. As one prisoner commented, 'It makes me feel human again.'

Here we are, towards the end of the performance at the celebration of the Shipshape project, in the serene space of the chapel where, to everyone's delight, we have been allowed to rehearse over the last few days. A trio of professional musicians who have worked with us and inspired us are playing their impressionistic response to poems by the men. They have already recorded these and each writer has a copy of the CD *Fleet*. When they finish, the sounds of the sea take us to three performance poems, followed by the prison band and choir leading the audience in rousing sea shanties. Behind us is the flourish of the exhibition sails (displaying writings and paintings) and masts which afterwards is taken out to the local arts centre.

> A beautiful and joyous exhibition. Something so creative done in hostile surroundings.
>
> *Comment from The Arts Centre*

Writing in prison offers a powerful opportunity for reflection and for development in self-understanding, with the potential to help prisoners deal with issues underlying their offences. Yet, as Chris concluded in his statement in support of our ACE project, writing in prison is much more than a means of helping the criminal justice system. His final words encapsulate the spirit of all our workshops:

> This project is aimed at exploring the essential humanity in everyone, male and female, and establishing a safe outlet for expressing issues in life that affect us all. (Chris)

Conclusion

Writing gave an outlet and a way of communicating feelings and experiences difficult otherwise in prison. These men were able to express their feelings and thoughts, using writing to gain a greater and more feeling sense of the outside while inside, rather than about inner problems so much, particularly about offences. Writing is also a channel for professionals, perhaps otherwise imprisoned in their roles. Chapter 11 examines how writing can support practitioners to reflect upon their work.

Write!

After your six-minute freewrite (see Chapter 2), reread silently to yourself with care (or store, or even destroy, it). Then share it with a carefully chosen other or group, if appropriate.

1. 'Every society needs a barefoot Socrates to ask childishly simple (and childishly difficult!) questions, to force its members to re-examine what they have been thoughtlessly taking for granted.' (Matthews 1990, p. 95)

   Choose an ordinary mundane thing (e.g. moon, coffee mug, daisy in the grass, pencil, cow, red double-decker bus): now describe it for a young child who has never seen it; use all your senses, bring it to life. Now describe a relationship you might have with it (e.g. 'I would like to get on the bus and let it take me…').

2. Think of a person you know well; write a list of any or all of these you associate with them:

   - a colour, type of clothing, object, natural thing (e.g. flower), tool (e.g. spanner)
   - a smell, odour, fragrance
   - music or any other sound, or something they habitually say
   - a particular taste (e.g. the apples my grandfather grew)
   - a physical sense (e.g. warmth, shivery, irritated, serene)
   - texture or other tactile sense
   - anything from your sixth sense.

   Now write about a time you remember with that person. This might become a poem.

3. Describe minutely something:

   - extremely close to you (e.g. your fingernail)
   - fairly close (e.g. the blue-tit on the bird table)
   - a long way away (e.g. the hill on the horizon).

   Combine them into either a poem or a story.

CHAPTER 11

Understanding Misunderstanding: Reflective Writing for Professional Development

On this course I gave myself therapy in the form of a cathartic release onto the paper. Safe and not distressing but creating a realisation I can move forward and develop.

It encourages you to be honest with yourself, as well as with the group.

Medical consultants

Reflection makes the difference between 20 years of experience and one year repeated 20 times. Reflection is a state of mind, an ongoing constituent of practice, not a technique or curriculum element. A way of learning from one's own and others' experience, it informs practice, widens perspectives and challenges assumptions, taken-for-granteds and damaging social and cultural biases.

Reflective writing is the professional development I have offered for over 20 years in medicine, healthcare, clinical psychology, social work, clergy, therapy, counselling, police and so on; finding it can enable enquiry into:

- what you know but do not know you know
- what you do not know and want to know

- what you think, feel, believe, value and understand about your role and boundaries
- how your actions match up with what you believe
- how to value and take into account personal feelings
- what your assumptions or even prejudices are and how to address them.

Practitioners explore and experiment with areas of experience difficult otherwise to approach, such as:

- what you can change in your context; how to work with what you cannot
- how to value the perspective of others, however different they are to you
- how others perceive you and their feelings and thoughts about events
- why you become stressed and its impact on life and practice
- how to recognise and counteract negative social, cultural and political forces.

Reflective writing is an intuitive spontaneous form, the way novelists or journalists write initial drafts. Many reflective writers fear accounts are badly written or incoherent, yet this is very rarely true as their writing is always a privilege to hear, and each responds to others' writing with respect, compassion and empathy. Practitioners write to learn, rather than learn to write. In Chapter 8 Fiona Friend and Judy Clinton both write reflectively to debrief and better understand both themselves and those with whom they work. Writing from the heart is a route to natural self-illuminatory creativity. Marion Steel (2010), a psychotherapist, wrote about her intense grief reaction to a patient's death, using poetic and prose writing to explore the personal ramifications. A reflection upon life and death and loss, her book is not only a lambent example, but offers insight to readers. Here Jonathan Knight, a family doctor, describes poetry writing about a patient.

The Magic Trick

He looks pleased.
Surprisingly so considering
One half of his mouth is smiling
And the other is drooling.
He deals a scrap of paper
On the desk, face down.
'Don't look at it,' he lisps,
'See if we agree.'
He is satisfied with the effect
Of his opening gambit.
His carefully choreographed
Magic trick. And so
We dance around his symptoms –
The sleight of hand
That cleaved his face overnight.
I make my play: 'Bell's Palsy'.
He turns the card and we smile:
There's a twinkle in his eye.
From the other slips a tear. (Jonathan Knight 2010)

> The Magic Trick concerns a consultation with a middle-aged
> man I didn't know well. That something was wrong with his
> face was immediately apparent, yet he was remarkably relaxed.
> Before he sat down he placed a piece of paper, face down.
> Neither of us then touched it until after we had gone through
> his story, I had examined him and pronounced my diagnosis.
>
> Reflecting later, I was still struck with his calmness and
> good humour. He must have had a great shock that morning,
> but had clearly researched his symptoms, come to his own
> conclusion about diagnosis, treatment and prognosis. There
> was a sense of fun about the way he took control of the
> consultation. He wanted to test, even tease, his doctor, but
> also needed confirmation and reassurance. A trick had been
> played on him, and he now wanted to trick the doctor.
>
> From that point, the poem seemed to write itself. The
> image of a conjurer demonstrating a card trick came through
> the writing from the first draft. It wasn't until the poem was
> nearly complete that the title became clear. A magic trick

seemed an appropriate metaphor for the palsy's sudden onset; the way he chose to present his symptoms; and the way GP [general practitioner] and patient come to a shared agreement.

As reflective writing, it helped me, the doctor, to understand my role in helping him. It would have been easy, but unhelpful, to downplay or ignore his efforts, and try and re-establish the doctor's authority. By taking on the role of willing assistant, we reached a far more beneficial therapeutic alliance. The poem was one of twenty Commended poems, Hippocrates Poetry Competition (NHS category). (Jonathan Knight)

We know a great deal more than we are aware, having absorbed information unwittingly. Reflective writing can give straightforward access, and enable close and accurate observation, and the skill to use the knowledge thus gained (e.g. for perceptive diagnosis). Constraining structures and metaphors can become clearer, giving power to take more responsibility for our actions.

Writing a conversation with a story to oneself can help clarify issues and increase self-understanding. 'The more I wrote about my patients and myself, the more confident I became that the act of narrative writing granted me access to knowledge…that would otherwise have remained out of reach' (Charon 2001, p. 84).

Reflective writings inform discussion in trusted, confidential forums of peers, a personally and professionally developing process: 'we get to know ourselves and each other through the writings in a way we are never normally privileged to do'. Poet Emily Wills ran staff writing workshops in a family medicine practice; GP Simon Opher reported how 'The culture in the surgery subtly changed' (Opher and Wills 2003, p. vi). Discussions in my groups range deeply and widely, yet are always rooted within the area initiated by the writing. These might relate to prescribing, to attitude, to alternative understandings of the situation, to similar occasions with totally different outcomes, or to collegial relationships. After a weekend course on writing for professional development, a physician emailed:

Knowing that there are many of us out here trying to do this job to the utmost of our ability, on levels technical and human, makes all the difference. After that 'Leiston' course (http://www.gilliebolton.com/writing/reflective-writing/

rcpg-writing-weekend) I thought a lot about a particular palliative care experience that another group member had written and talked about. I learnt a lot from her contributions, and our conversations, and I was a better clinician with my next palliative care situations. When after that I had a really hard and sad cancer diagnosis in a patient. I kept thinking 'I can email her if I get stuck with this'. I never did, but it was an enormous support nevertheless to know that it would be possible, and to feel that a vital and honest conversation was there all the time, going on in the background. The clinical stuff we are great at finding out in so many ways, and we have each other as a resource for the deeper stuff too.

Reflective practice, based on expressive and explorative writing and carefully facilitated group work, offers a sufficiently safe environment to explore professional issues, relationships with colleagues and the work/ home interface. It allows 'oscillation' (More 1996) between examination of:

1. what clients did and possibly felt and thought

2. what this made the practitioner feel and think

3. the ways in which they responded, whether appropriate or not

4. the ways the client then responded in turn to the practitioner.

We used an exercise writing from the perspective of a patient, relative or another colleague such as a nurse, as well as writing from their own point of view. The participants also imaginatively examine alternative scenarios: how it might have been different had they acted differently. Here is Antonio Munno's experience of writing alone using advice from my book (Bolton 2010), recounted in the *British Medical Journal*:

> The family asked to meet me. Their daughter had recovered from meningococcal septicaemia, and they wanted to know why I hadn't diagnosed it… My stomach wrenched with anger and frustration. Can't they see? That's the whole point: two doctors a few hours apart both made the same clinical judgment that this was a viral illness. I felt that their criticisms were unfair… I decided to…write the story of the family's complaint from the point of view of the parents… At that point my perspective on the complaint changed… By

thinking about the complaint from the family's point of view, I understood that my role in the meeting wasn't to defend but to listen.

Munno 2006, p. 1092

'Writing one's story is a moral act' (Frank 2000). 'We are digging deep in our writing. It feels like getting to the core of you. Nobody asked us to go this deep. From the titles we chose ourselves, we could have written superficially and shallowly' (reflective writing participant).

Listening to our stories

Every one of us needs and deserves an attentive audience. We need confidence that our story is of importance to others. This means listening carefully to the twists and turns and blind alleys of clients' unique stories. What is not helpful is feeling like an 'illness with a person attached' (Petrone 2001, p. 34): losing her personhood in illness did not help this patient thrive through treatment; she added that 'this rather negated the rest of my life'.

Clients offer their own particular story to professionals; it might sound like a variation on a theme, but is unique. What is less obvious is that people tell very different stories about the same event, use different metaphors or similes, and often have very different understandings of the same situation (Sweeney 1998). Each person's story tells them who they are and about their role. We are failing to thrive if our story is incoherent or unclear, if it is a weak rather than a strong one. People's life-story plots lose clarity when they become ill or are in trouble (e.g. bereavement, imprisonment). They can be supported in reformulating stories from muddled to strong, from negative and morose to positive and life-enhancing, even if dying. Beautiful deaths occur where dying people and their families, loved ones and carers are at peace with the inevitability of death (Brody 2003; Montgomery-Hunter 1991).

Listening attentively to oneself is an essential ingredient for all of us to achieve the physical, mental and emotional well-being which is our right. If I can't listen to myself then I can't know what I want to say to others, and I can't begin to hear the needs and wants of others clearly either. It's a bit like the common aphorism: 'I can't really love others unless I love myself.' If we can listen to ourselves, we can begin to work out what we want and need, what to ask for, and what to offer.

Nobody can know me like I can know myself. Yet I don't, and I make little effort to try. Who's going to do it if I don't? Yet we really do think that clinicians can tell us what's wrong with us, and what we should do to put it right.

What do patients or clients want? There's a saying in medicine: 'Listen to the patient, they are giving you the diagnosis.' Well, the method I am offering will enable hearing it more clearly. The relationship between clinician (practitioner) and client (patient) is two way. Both bring wants and needs, impatience, blocks to understandings (as well as skill and experience). Expressive, explorative, reflective creative writing is a route to listening to oneself, and then to others.

Riverside Community Health Project: Experiences told by workers

'It's called a health project…but they do a bit of all sorts there.'

The sun is shining on the hill the other side of the valley, showing up houses in serried ranks, interleaved with bright, early spring green fields after the deluge of rain. But the wind is biting. People scurry up and down the steep hill with heavy shopping bags, or into the Edwardian stone library clutching children's hands. This library is at the intersection of four dense housing areas, some so unpopular houses are mown down and replaced by industrial units, or just scarred ground: creating even more stress in an already stressed area.

The library basement is bright and welcoming, full of animated people, children, their artwork. In the words of the Bangladeshi family and community support worker, Nazrul Islam, *Riverside* is 'a locally managed, voluntary sector organisation working with many disadvantaged communities in our neighbourhood, and addresses inequities in health'. But this basement was not always so, as Marge Craig depicts:

> A huge cave of a space: dark, *filthy*, very damp with a little stream running across the dirt floor, loads of junk from the last eighty years. Most unpromising. But we thought it was *great*. We felt so much excitement about all the things we would be able to do in our own space. Especially compared to where we were before – up three flights up to a spare classroom in the school – mums struggling with buggies, trying to talk over noise of little ones playing…

Independence is the key to set all women free – it's so true, and I think it's what our work is all about – relationships, and the economic independence and confidence for women who are at THE MOST VULNERABLE STAGE OF THEIR ADULT LIFE – when they've got babies and children who are dependent on them, when they're exhausted, anxious, dependent on others' goodwill, fed up, exhausted, exhausted, exhausted.

Yesterday when Joanne set off home in the pouring rain with baby and toddler, she said 'we're better off than people in Ethiopia where they've not had rain for three years.' Made my day. 'Cos I worry about the insularity, cut-off-ness, from the wider world of some women, understandably when overwhelmed by day-to-day concerns, crying babies, exhaustion, exhaustion... (Marge Craig)

And who are these women? Two stories:

Rahima is a Bangladeshi woman. She has been brought up in a village with lots of family and friends. A small river passes near her village, with a rice field nearby covered with green rice crops... Every household has a pond, where fishes are kept. During the summer people are outside, with all doors and windows open. Everybody gets together; mothers get plenty of help from family and friends with childcare. From this hot summery, cheerful environment, Rahima emigrated to England where she had plenty of hope.

Once Rahima came to England she lost all family contact. She found it very difficult to adapt to a different culture and environment. She is indoors constantly, feeling isolated as she does not speak any English and is unfamiliar with the local area and people. She does not have anyone to talk to properly as her husband works 70 hours a week, and she does not have much support with her two small children. Rahima tends to worry a lot. Her health is deteriorating and she tends to feel depressed most of the time, and seems to be getting symptoms of mental health problems. Rahima's hopes and dreams of living a happy life in England have now become a nightmare. (Nazrul Islam)

K, M and their three year old son D are refugees from Yugoslavia. Much of my work was spent settling them and other families into our community... It was a sunny day in August when I went with a refugee worker, with K and D to visit M in the hospice. I watched as D skipped through the gardens unaware of his Daddie's fate. M's mother developed a secondary cancer and died Friday October 22nd aged 49, M died 30th October aged 29 years. (Carol Willis)

And:

I really enjoyed being a clown along with one of our creche workers at an event we held at South Benwell School a few years ago. I liked being a clown because the kids were coming up to me and you could see how happy they were laughing at my big shoes and red nose. I've just remembered my legs were killing me at the end of the day though, having to lift them so high to walk in the shoes. (Mandy Whitfield)

There is no real dividing line between the life of the community and the life of Riverside project: 'our work is about everyday lived experience'. And: 'this is not a nine-to-five job. We go home and keep seeing people. They are so helpless and I can't shut my door.' And the staff feel they 'celebrate our real contact with people. Even if it's difficult, it's rewarding.'

Although many staff live in the area, and are therefore community members, this doesn't necessarily give them insight into the best way to work at Riverside: 'we realise we are a very small part of the people's lives. There is so much we don't know, so many ways we don't know what's right and what's wrong for them.' And it's not only moral, ethical and social dilemmas which make such work difficult, but also personal ones.

Derek Snaith wrote about some feedback which gave him 'the realisation that I am doing something right within my work', and how that felt:

She said that I was a *key worker* because I had helped start a social club for adults with learning difficulties in the area. What I had never realised in all my time here at Riverside that my work was making a difference to people. I could tell from the passion in her voice that this initiative 'The Millennium Club' is something she and others have been looking for for years. And I still am shocked when positive feedback comes from those involved in helping to run the sessions and those who come along to enjoy it.

This simple statement, and the subsequent realisation of the impact of my work, has helped me in my mind to be more confident in my own abilities and my own views. I think I will be able to be myself more at work and be more assertive when it comes to dealing with people and groups who are there purely for self-interest or generally negative reasons.

Because I now know that I have made a difference to people who are in need of supporters to do things for them and alongside them. It means I can stick my neck out and say more of what I think clearly, rather than a watered down mish-mash that is often not understood. (Derek Snaith)

These accounts were created during a morning's workshop offering space apart from the everyday busyness of the Project: 'We *never* normally *talk* to each other like this about what we *feel* and *think* about our work and the lives of the people.' For example they were amazed Derek needed that feedback to assure him of the value of his work, and were able to reinforce this in good measure. When another staff member wrote about a negative encounter which knocked her confidence, the group were surprised she was not as confident as she seemed, and offered real support. Discussions were interspersed with thoughtful silences, laughter, anxieties and tensions at difficult memories, and warm supportive sharing, and keen interest and care for their community.

Children thumped about in the library overhead as we wrote and talked. And more children laughed, cried, played in other Riverside rooms. The project's everyday business ebbed and flowed around us, leaving a clear pool in the middle for us. 'We feel like an island, at times, in a storm-tossed sea of government statistics.' I hope a porthole onto this island, this vibrant health project in an inner urban community, has been opened by this occasion when, as one said, they 'stopped the speed of life to take time to reflect upon important things, and talk properly to each other'.

'I recharge myself from my experience': Reflective writing in palliative care

Reliving vital experiences, thoughts and feelings through writing, and sharing them with others, can make a big difference to practitioners. Appropriate in any professional setting it is particularly so in palliative (end-of-life) care. Clinicians help people who are often focusing upon: Who am I beyond this body, this person in a social setting? Who is it who does this thinking and feeling, and what happens to this self when my body ceases to function? Am I 'soul' with a body, or am I my body therefore to disappear at death?

Expressive explorative writing can help approach the spiritual, because it relies upon non-linear approaches to understanding. Exploring the unexplorable can happen, and attempts to express the inexpressible. If 'the spiritual dimension of palliative care…is the final piece of the holistic jigsaw completing the integrated whole' (Cobb 2001), then imaginative expressive writing can help us to fit this final piece into place.

We live in a fragmented world. Stable forces hold sway less than they did. I am no longer just me but a body over which medicine and healthcare can take control, a mind watched over by psychiatry with its DSMs (diagnostic manuals), steered by education and monitored by quality control, emotions which are played upon by the media, and a spirit which seems to belong no-where. Writing, over which 'I' can have authority and agency, can bring back a sense of a coherent self and relationship with others and my world, rooting the mental, emotional and spiritual in the physical act of writing.

A large teaching hospital's multi-disciplinary palliative team were reflecting upon whatever they needed to reflect upon. The theme on this occasion was simply *An Important Event*. Bill Noble, medical consultant, wrote:

THE PATIENT WHO GAVE ME A JOB, BY BILL NOBLE

The nights were all the same, a pattern of anxiety provoking unpredictable tasks. A teaching hospital in 1980. I still hate the smell.

Rick was a young man with a girlfriend, reggae music tapes and leukaemia. Lots of friends of all shapes and sizes visited and gave their blood, or part of it. In the day, professors, consultants, sister, registrars, and me all talking about what to do with him and his blood, his chest, his mouth infection. In the night, every six hours for five months, I gave him injections, took blood off, put up drips. He got better, went home and I saw him on the street after I had left the hospital. He looked okay, not pleased to see me. All those stabs, jabs and 'one more times'.

Then in the evening paper at home, I read that he had jumped off the top of a tower block of flats. Dead.

Did we tell him what I realised along the way? All those things, procedures, drugs would only make him well for a short while. It always comes back and kills you in the end. He seemed to know but in all those dark hours we never talked properly.

There was a registrar who worked with me then. He probably made more real contact with our patients than any of us. He was a jolly, wide faced young man who never turned up to parties, hated his father and said if he got leukaemia all he wanted was a desert island and twenty bags of blood. He killed himself when he became a consultant.

Ten years later, at the hospice, Rick's girlfriend was in a bed, dying with the same kind of leukaemia that Rick had. So pleased to see me. We talked about Rick and dying young and couldn't find reasons. Squaring a very sad circle.

Bill had had that squared circle hanging around for years. Writing it has not taken it out of his head, nor prevented him from working on it, but deepened and expanded his memory, and what it means to him: the story now has elements he hadn't thought about before. He has no wish to write the definitive account, because that would prevent continuing to work upon it, prevent it from continuing to grow. He said: 'This writing is not an emptying of me onto the paper, as I feared before I started, but an enriching.' In ten years there will be another version, representing his thinking then. This is deep and effective reflection upon practice. Writing, and receiving support and advice from colleagues about such horrors, cannot eradicate them, but channels energy more positively. A physician commented: 'This process feels like extracting the poison.' At another meeting the theme was joy:

> When you have worked with a family who are struggling separately to accept a diagnosis and are perhaps not communicating openly with each other, bringing people to a state of open awareness is a joy. It feels as if a great burden has been lifted, for me at least, and I am certain this is also experienced by the person and their family. This probably sounds dreadful but it gives me a great sense of joy to check the computer in the morning and to discover that someone who has been dying over a long period of time has finally died. The protracted dying period is a dreadful time for all involved, in most cases, especially when people have been

told that the patient is not expected to live overnight and has subsequently lived in a moribund state for two to three weeks, with the family and carers riding a roller-coaster of emotion. A sense of peace may now prevail following so much suffering.

Less morbidly I get a sense of joy from many of the people I see, those who, despite all their suffering, will say 'Well that's enough about me, how are you?' or 'Well I'm 80, I've got to die, I have had a good life', said not just stoically, but with a tremendous sense of peace. (Macmillan nurse)

He was a little disappointed, I think that he had not focused on one patient and told a story, as he had in other writings. That this was important for his palliative care team to share was reflected in the discussion.

Understanding misunderstanding in family health consultation

Many [failures] could be avoided if only the lessons of experience were properly learned.

Department of Health 2000, p. 64

Understanding must be at the heart of the professional–client relationship. If physicians can understand patients' needs and wants, and patients understand doctors' methods and intentions, then they are likely to offer appropriate intentions, and patients to respond positively. Hippocrates himself stressed this healing relationship (1950). The ability to relate to patients' needs and wants, is not solely brain work, as Pooh wisely pointed out:

'Rabbit's clever,' said Pooh thoughtfully.
'Yes,' said Piglet, 'Rabbit's clever.'
'And he has Brain.'
'Yes,' said Piglet, 'Rabbit has Brain.'
There was a long silence.
'I suppose' said Pooh, 'that that's why he never understands anything.'

A. A. Milne 1958, p. 274

For doctors, understanding their own feelings, ideas, thoughts and reactions to patients cannot be separated. This understanding, or empathy, cannot be taught, but can be developed through reflective writing and discussion, therefore increasing clinical effectiveness.

> The modern dissociation of sensibility, as TS Eliot called it, according to which reason and emotion are compartmentalised, does a disservice to doctors. To care for the sick in a morally responsible manner, the doctor must delve into the patient's experience, imagine the patient's future, integrate thought and feeling, and with the patient, co-author the next chapter in a life story whose story-line has been interrupted by illness or injury. For this, literary skills are needed, the skills of close reading – a feel for pathos, a discriminating ear, a discerning eye, an analogical imagination, a way with words… Medical education must become in this way more literate, indeed, more literary.
>
> *Ron Carson 1994, p. 236*

Patients bring lifetimes of experience, of which practitioners are probably only aware of a fraction or none at all. Patients' knowledge of clinicians is similarly limited. Willingness to appreciate that consultations are deeply affected by such unknown hinterlands is one of the foundations of a healing relationship. Patients are helped to be open and trusting by feeling doctors accept them as they are. Understanding and making sense of patients' stories is central to the physician's role, according to Kieran Sweeney (1998).

Many patients, however, make it hard to accept them as they are; and doctors respond by being scientific, seeking evidence bases for treating presenting symptoms, being clever like Rabbit. As well as awareness of patients' unknown history, clinicians need to recognise and examine their response, based upon their personal experience and philosophy. Emotions such as frustration, anger, fear, distress, horror or sexual attraction might be disabling: 'When a good looking woman walks in you can feel yourself shutting down emotionally and everything becomes clinical and removed' (Frost and King 2000).

Elements of practitioners' own experience can affect professional relationships. One GP spent much reflective time working through feelings about the accidental death of his brother when they were little.

This helped him cope better with very sick or dying children, instead of having always to refer them to a colleague (Bolton 2010).

Physician writing groups often choose their own themes, such as 'understanding' or 'misunderstanding'.

A STORY OF AN UNDERSTANDING, BY CLIVE

Anne is a lovely young woman of eighteen or so now. A clean, fresh face, long hair, a well-proportioned model-like figure and in the seven years I have known her, a seemingly uncomplicated person with the world ahead of her. But she has a small atrial septal defect. Two years ago she was put on a list to have it repaired. Earlier this year she came with some somatic symptoms again, and opened up about her low mood, instability and even suicidal feelings. We talked about her situation, the operation, her protective family, her understanding fiancé, the steady work and career. She didn't seem able to make the obvious connection. She started seeing our counsellor. I put her on antidepressants and she felt better. The cardiothoracic surgeon stopped them and she got worse. I began to doubt the wisdom of operating; she seemed so healthy physically, but so fragile emotionally.

Then I spoke to the counsellor, as on so many previous occasions, I felt a surge of excitement as we talked, and it became apparent that we had the same fears about Anne's vulnerability. Then the penny dropped. Anne always wore the same sort of fairly low cut dress to display her cleavage. We thought she had it on display because her fear was the scars from her operation would never allow her to do so again. Anne finally opened up to the counsellor about her anxiety.

I felt a tremendous urge to dissuade her from surgery until this fear had been explored. Maybe sensing this, she did not attend twice and the next time I saw her she had had the operation and was pleased with the scar, having discussed her desire for a minimal one with the surgeon.

She wore the same style of dress with a crusty red line down her middle. The understanding was between the counsellor and myself. I could try to use some psychodynamic approach to further analyse the situation, but lack the training or expertise. However this and other realisations that come from my discussions with the counsellor touch on my sense of inadequacy. The current term is 'emotional intelligence' and I don't know how much I possess but I want more. Highly perceptive intuitive people have played very formative roles in my life but still remain somehow mysterious and intriguing. If I lacked this intelligence would I be able to share an understanding with such able people? I need to find a way to open up this part of me.

Clive was determined to understand not only this particular case, but increase his future understanding potential. The writing group he belonged to unpicked clues he could possibly have followed, and possible strategies to foster clearer understanding. We assured Clive he certainly did have 'emotional intelligence' (Goleman 1995), perhaps only needing more confidence in it, and some counselling-type training. The group also suggested the practice counsellor brought specific professional skills and experience, and considerably more time.

Jan wrote about an Asian family whose daughters suddenly, it appeared, sought social services help, and were taken into care because the father 'beat' them. The elder girl had been anorexic for some time. The case was bewildering as Jan only saw the parents individually (and not the daughters once they left) and each presented as completely nonplussed, particularly the father. We became certain of incest. We discussed how often doctors receive frustratingly disjointed fragments, and the difficulty of empathy and being an advocate for a patient who has clearly harmed another. Jan felt clearer, but less happy about continuing to see the father.

Caroline's writing concerned a bundle of allied stresses. One was the anxiety of patient referral for hospital consultations: it having been pointed out she had 'the highest referral rate of all the GPs in the practice'. Caroline felt reassured by the discussion about why and when to refer, but also determined to take a proposed sabbatical.

There is no misunderstanding between doctor and patient, or between GP and hospital junior doctor, in this next story. Learning came from a consideration of how this understanding was achieved.

ROSIE'S STORY
December
'So will I be allowed to die from this? I don't want to be kept alive. I've struggled on since my wife went, and I'd rather just get on with it.'

'I'm here to advise you and give you information and so is the hospital. It's your life and your choice.'

'You think it is cancer then?'

February

'He just got up and walked out of the clinic.'

'But he'd said he wouldn't want treating. Have you spoken to your consultant?'

'He said: ring you.'

'I think I said in my letter he didn't think he wanted treatment. I just wanted him to know his options and, having decided, he didn't want pressurising.'

'Shall I send him another appointment try to sort it out?'

'I'm pretty sure he wouldn't attend; I'm quite happy to look after him. He's a straight talker and there was nothing to say. Don't worry. I'll give him a ring.'

Reflection in May

I feel the privilege of communicating, of understanding your wish to decide on your own going, even if not its manner or time. I know if I was in your shoes I'd choose going fishing too.

Rosie had the wisdom to know her patient was serious, and to support his wish for death in dignity and peace. She also supported the junior doctor to realise he didn't know better than the patient. Rosie actively listened and heard what was needed and wanted, being more than sympathetic, and yet had no pretence of knowing and feeling what the patient felt. No one can do that for another as we are all inexorably stuck in our own skins, brains and emotions. Such pretence makes the patient or client feel their individuality is unrespected. Empathy is an ability to relate to the affective, physical, cognitive and spiritual experience of another. The physician is emotionally as well as cognitively and spiritually involved, but their integrity is intact: they are not personally hurt or involved or burdened. They often become tired and distressed: which is when reflective writing can help.

A member of another group wrote of a similar occasion when 'only a pre-registration houseman, shit-scared and out of my depth. I thought I had found a situation in which I knew what to do, for a change. Hence my consternation at the patient's refusal to let me.' Realising his initial account from his own perspective was bald, and that the memory still troubled him, he rewrote in the voice of the patient, giving him insight and comfort:

Mike's Poem

Now this body warped and twisted,
Has nearly reached its end, and lets its blood
Flow freely into my drug-seared bowel.
And now returning to my bedside this tall youth
Slightly flustered, pushes an ancient drip stand.
He looks like our Ellen's youngest;
Keen, eager to do his best, but fearful he won't make the grade.
Well, fearful or not, I can't let him have his way. 'You're
not putting that thing into me, young man!'

So now I lie, this quiet Sunday afternoon,
Waiting for some psychiatrist,
To try my failing faculties.
The day you gave me Lord is ending,
Now let the darkness fall. (Mike)

Patients can be cringing, angry, appealing, flirtatious, overbearing, motherly (fatherly), all potentially throwing practitioners into automatic response, or into personal responses which can be explored reflectively, rather than denied. A better sense of who one is and has come from can bring greater empathic stability. One family doctor refused to be involved in a research study into 'the emotional demands of general practice', stating that it was a 'waste of time because emotions are not part of a doctor's professional life' (Frost and King 2000). These elements might be called *transference, countertransference* and *projection* within a psychotherapeutic relationship, where they are not only recognised but wielded as invaluable tools. Yet, as Clive pointed out, none of them had been trained in any counselling skills.

An empathic professional relationship with patients (clients) involves trust and respect, even if in a non-professional relationship with the same person the doctor would feel neither of these. One participant said how she had to refer to a colleague a patient who had abused his wife, as she could not treat him with professional trust or respect. The third element in normal good relationships is love. Rogers (1951, 1969) chose to use the expression 'unconditional positive regard' (ancient Greeks would have called it agape) in therapeutic or teaching relationships (see Chapter 14). Personal distaste, sexual attraction or protectiveness are put on one side as the physician takes on the role of professional advocate for their patient.

> My life in poetry has taught me that empathy is an affair of the heart and imagination [we must] call [the emotions] by name rather than ignoring them completely or attempting to sanitise them. By attempting to enter my patients' stories and in essence re-imagine them through words and symbols, I learned that compassion, courage, self-effacement and humour set the stage for healing... Empathy, metaphor and imagination are really at the root of the art of medicine.
>
> *Jack Coulehan 1997, p. 108*

Coulehan also said doctors need 'emotional resilience to experience the emotional dynamics of patient care as an essential part – rather than a detriment – of good medical practice' (1995, p. 30). Physicians are involved without being personally damaged or affected by these 'full emotional dynamics', yet medical schools tended to train people to be unemotional. One doctor confessed one Friday evening to being too exhausted to relate to a patient's complex issues, requesting them to return the following week. The patient responded angrily, with no human understanding of the doctor's situation.

Suppressing or repressing emotions can lead to burnout and lowered performance (Evison 2002). Reflective writing can offer insight and strategies. A body of randomised control trial evidence demonstrates writing's power to decrease stress and boost immune systems (see Chapters 1 and 14).

Clinical governance

Practitioners are increasingly under pressure to be accountable. A UK Royal College of Nursing report argues that it is 'fundamentally about developing an open learning culture that shares information, based on effective multi-professional team working' (2000, p. 24). I would insert five more factors which, as well as information, should be shared: experience, knowledge, skills, feelings and ideas.

To teach *emotional resilience* requires that we in medical education focus actively on the recognition and articulation of students' compassion and the subtle and complex language of the emotions... Teaching methods grounded in *the narrative nature of medical knowledge, the use of stories to develop the moral imagination and the use of creative writing to promote empathic understanding* all foster a commitment to tenderness and steadiness in medical learning...within a framework of emotional resilience, detachment must be viewed as a serious risk that leads to undesirable consequences in practising medicine, rather than as a goal of medical education.

Coulehan 1995, p. 34, my italics

Back in my youth, I remember the pop group *The Animals* beseeching the good lord not to allow them to be misunderstood, because their intentions were good. Good intentions and expert clinical knowledge are not sufficient in the practice of a good physician. Reflective practice writing can take them into otherwise unexplored but vital areas.

Conclusion

Medical, healthcare and social care work can be lonely, and with minimal reflective space. Practitioners often comment on our meetings breaking that silence; how writing followed by supportive critical discussion opens doors on relationships and situations. It's a method and forum which can facilitate exploration and expression of the otherwise unexplored and unexpressed, even occasionally the unexplorable and inexpressible. And the issues examined are often joyful and successful, sometimes funny. The *Voices that Care* project compiled an anthology of writings by healthcare workers 'based on feelings and encounters with natural human emotions...as a beneficial resource to staff who need the support of colleagues' (Pierce 2010, pp. 1–2). Rebecca Pierce included humour in the themes she suggested to staff. Here is a contribution from a fertility clinic:

We once asked a lady to bring the sperm in, kept warm in a jacket. She came in the next day with the sperm inside a jacket potato. (Healthcare worker, Liverpool Women's Hospital)

This examination and example of reflective writing and group work concludes Part Two. Part Three gives in-depth exemplified advice on how to run therapeutic or reflective writing groups. We start with a chapter on how to run days or part-days, and move onto the specific requirements of residential courses.

Write!

After your six-minute freewrite (see Chapter 2), reread silently to yourself with care (or store, or even destroy, it). Then share it with a carefully chosen other or group, if appropriate.

1. 'You can't understand another until you've walked a mile in their moccasins'

   ◦ Think of someone you know reasonably well and admire.

   ◦ Write a description of their environment without mentioning them personally, it might be their kitchen, study, potting shed; or office, depending on how you know them. Include as many details as you possibly can.

   ◦ Reread carefully, adding or altering as you feel you'd like to.

   ◦ Now write a description of your own close environment, wherever you spend your most valuable time (car, garden, consulting room, bedroom): write it as if it is written by this other person you admire, from their point of view.

   ◦ Reread carefully, adding or altering as you feel you'd like to.

   ◦ Compare both pieces. Note down anything they make you feel. Is there any action you'd like to take as a result of this writing?

2. Write about a time you were puzzled; describe and tell the story of the dilemma or confusion, in as much detail as possible. Now, with hindsight, give your former self advice about what he/she could have done; be gentle on that past self.

3. An odd observation

   Allow an odd experience to tell itself onto the paper. Describe it as fully as you can. Now interrogate it for what it might be saying to you. Here is one of mine:

'coming here I passed a bag-lady / dragging her little trolley towards the summit / of the Snake Pass. No houses there / nothing but rock, sheep and car headlights. / ... We too are like this other woman / we too are travelling – up.' (Bolton, in Bolton and Padfield 1996, p. 82)

PART THREE

How to Run Groups; Conclusion

CHAPTER 12

Mystery and Mastery: Running Therapeutic Creative Writing Groups

'I was surprised by me!'

Medical writing course member

'The whole object of writing is not to set foot on foreign land, it is at last to set foot on one's own self as a foreign land.'
Adapted from G. K. Chesterton

He slipped into the room: good, just in time. Everyone was sitting down chatting, except Janice, who walked in through the other doorway, hands cradled around a steaming mug. George struggled damp woolly gloves from chilled fingers and took the chair which seemed to be waiting for him at the crowded table. Silence fell as all eyes focused on Janice. Everyone else had a pile of well-thumbed papers and a hot mug in front of them; a plate of what looked like homemade shortbread sat in the middle. He'd have to arrive earlier next week and have thawed hands and his poems at the ready too, like them. Now he had to shuffle while Janice smilingly waited for him. He didn't like being noticed like that, any more than he liked being cold.

He soon warmed up, listening to others' poems: some funny, some sad, some well written, some he even felt he could have done better.

But then, after coffee, it came to his turn. He wanted to dive under the table. But he was brave and people really grasped the pain he'd poured out in his poem: they were very gentle and supportive; no one said it was rubbish. Then Janice, whom he had noticed was silent though nodding and smiling at people's comments, said she appreciated very much how he'd expressed it, and how about saying a bit more about the model aircraft. He scribbled everything down. Then it was the turn of the woman after him, who'd written about walking in Derbyshire. He'd always wanted to do that, and loved her poem. He didn't have the courage to say so of course, but he did determine to ask her afterwards about her walking group.

He wondered what they would do next, and glanced at the clock. Amazingly it was finish time. Janice was quietly asking the group to suggest writing themes for the following week: *The Gift* was one suggestion. They all got up grabbing coats and scarves. He remembered the small rain outside; and then he thought of what he might write.

Facilitating a group

Read this chapter even if you never intend to facilitate or tutor. Understanding the process can help you gain more from a group. This does not mean being *teacher's pet*; but it may mean challenging the tutor (e.g. 'Do we have ten minutes for this activity as well?'; 'Might it be useful if we introduced ourselves first?'). You might stop speaking when you know you've said enough, and draw out someone who's said nothing; set out the chairs beforehand rather than waiting for the tutor; and be brave enough to break an awkward silence, or perhaps to hold a productive silence instead of nervously and ineffectually breaking it.

Groups don't happen: they are actively nurtured and supported by both facilitator and participants. A successful group is run for its members, and as far as possible by them. The more participants feel they run the group themselves the better. Really effective group facilitation is a powerful, yet oddly powerless, function. Even when facilitators appear to be doing little, they are holding the space, patrolling the boundaries, keeping a watchful eye on confidentiality, sexism or racism and so forth. They listen, keep quiet to enable others to speak, observe body language and tone of voice, watch for underlying assumptions, deter nosiness and inquisitiveness for its own sake, encourage the quiet to talk and the talkers to listen, juggle with the joker, are quietly firm about what the group does when without straying from the task in hand, timekeep, anticipate the doorknob person (the one who spills all the beans two minutes before end-time), and keep a light hand on the reins at all times.

Groups have huge potential energy for the good of the individuals and group as a whole. People learn from their tutors and facilitators; they learn far more from each other. What they learn can be surprising: everyone brings expectations, hopes and fears which, combining with unspoken elements, create hidden curricula. What the facilitator thinks the group is doing may be very different from what participants take away with them. A poet told me he never could tell what children would ask, when he worked in schools. The questions were rarely about poetry, but about things like his shoes; one novelist friend was asked how much she weighed.

Despite leading from the rear, facilitators are always being facilitator even when seeming to collaborate, such as when sharing some of their own personal writing.

It's not what facilitators do that matters so much as how they do it, and who they are when they do it. Facilitators in metaphorical sergeant-major's hats are as appropriate and facilitative as under-scullery-maid's caps. Just as in psychotherapy each practitioner believes firmly in the power of their own particular form (cognitive behavioural/psychodynamic/systemic family therapy), yet research shows therapy can be constructive whatever the type embraced by the practitioner: what matters is the relationship between therapist and client. The same is true of the relationship between facilitator and group. It doesn't much matter what writing exercise participants engage in; what matters is the way it is given, and how they understand the process. People will write what they need to write if they are given permission and a safe, supportive, confidential, stretching environment where they are trusted and their responsibility and authority is respected.

> Writing doesn't always help. It may just reinforce obsessive thoughts and fix them. Working in the group helps me with this because I learn ideas for more imaginative ways of writing. (Participant)

What do people want from personal writing groups?

People want:

- permission and encouragement to write and enjoy it
- insight into and enhanced understanding of the self
- support through the joyful, frustrating, difficult, painful creative processes
- constructive criticism
- tuition in techniques and skills when appropriate
- fresh ideas and directions
- comradeship and fellowship with like-minded people
- a bit of fun.

Different people will have these differently ordered. Some for example really do not want criticism or development at all; they want to be supported and approved in their writing.

> I was like a tightly bound caterpillar trapped in the cocoon of my abusive past. Through the warmth, acceptance, validation and sense of peace found within my writing group, the silken threads have softened and the transformation has taken place. I now sit, newly emerged on the top of my cocoon, fragile yet free. All I now have to do is learn to fly. (Group member)

Principles

Groups function effectively within a charmed circle: everyday concerns and involvements are held at bay, so attention can confidently be focused in towards the session's work. Firm principles are the magic wand which can support groups to create such spaces.

Respect

Respect is needed by facilitators and participants for themselves (that they can do it), and from everyone for everyone despite age, gender, race, class, interests, confidence and writing experience. Inclusivity has the extra advantage of adding richness to groups. Judy Clinton (see also

Chapter 8) contributes how 'a lady with hearing difficulties thanked me for the way I asked the group to be aware of her needs, and speak clearly'.

Constructively positive response and advice in discussion facilitates learning; negative-seeming suggestions can generally be worded positively: what might be done or attempted, rather than what not. Being honest does not mean being cruel to be kind, but saying what needs to be said as kindly as possible. Care to draw out quiet participants can be done respectfully, as well as managing the over-voluble.

Boundaries are part of respect; a group creating its own rules can create a sense of confidence and relative safety. Here are some about *confidentiality* from my experience. Members taking each other as they experience them within the closed system of the group: they forget this during the magic hours of the session, even if good friends or enemies outside the group. Members supporting each other without seeking to question beyond the boundaries of writing and group: they are there to talk about writings, and not much else. What happens in the group belongs there, so permission will be needed to discuss anything outside it: one group I ran even asked we did not discuss with life partners what happened in the group. A fair share of time for everyone to read and discuss their piece: this includes clarity as to the appropriate length of the piece; it is a boundary issue, as is the session beginning and ending on time.

Responsibility

Responsibility of each for their own writing and their response to others leads to honest and carefully judged discussion and ability to learn and develop. Whatever ideas are put forward, authority over writing always resides with its writer, not tutor or opinionated participant. Joint responsibility for the group is engendered by a shared sense of working aims, objectives, patterns and relationships. People saying what they want and hope from the start, deciding to stay and do what the majority wants, with slight modifications perhaps or leave, increases everyone's sense of authority. One participant, early in my facilitating career, said he wouldn't write, only *talk about* writing, and disrupted the whole day: I now know he should either have left, or joined in fully. Some groups benefit from 15 minutes at each session end to discuss feelings or thoughts: irritation at late-comers for example, or requests for more writing and less discussion time. Such reflexivity enables participants to think about the way the group functions and how it affects its members personally, rather than about the work it does.

Silence can be wonderfully useful, when people reflect deeply. If no one in the group has anything particular they need to say, then no one need say anything until a participant does have something to communicate. Good facilitators listen for the positive silence, allow it to deepen until the right time, and support those who find it awkward.

Trust

Trust in the processes of writing and facilitation is essential for it to inspire and elucidate. Apologies by group members for their writing really aren't helpful: everyone feels hesitant. Reading the actual written words will always be more powerful than anything said or summarised about it: talking about writing is a defensive, delaying tactic.

The Alpha Poem, by Tricia McAdoo

Here is a poem from *The Cancer Care West Writing Group*, which meets weekly for two hours at the Support Centre, Galway City, Ireland. An open group, new members join from time to time, though most have attended for at least six months. Participants were asked to write the letters of the alphabet down one side of the page and then write their poem (see Adams in Bolton *et al.* 2006). This writer chose the topic of the Writer's Group itself.

Our Writing Group

A always an experience here and very entertaining
B benefits are profound and
C certainly a way to
D delve into the inner voice by
E experiencing a
F fuller and more
G generous attitude through
H highlighting the relationship between
I inner and outer
J joyous and
K kinetic energy join a

L loving
M manner
N no negatives
O only
P positives here – no
Q qualms –
R restful
S soulful and sweet in a
T truly trusting and
U ultimately a
V valued encounter
W witnessed by sometimes
X xrated
Y yet youthful
Z zen zebras (Jacqueline K)

What are groups going to do?

They:

- probably listen to group members' recent writings; discuss them sensitively and usefully; help them develop their own voice (though some groups listen without discussing)

- generate new writing; writing together with time and subject constraints can be creative, though for some it is unconducive or even threatening; themes and titles and encouragement to write at home are generally appreciated

- share advice on reading: novels, papers, poetry, etc.: good published writing is the best tutor

- do a range of other activities, such as: invite a guest speaker; discuss published poetry (two very resourceful anthologies are Astley 2002 and 2004); have one of the group facilitate; have a performance workshop; you or a group member do a teaching 'spot' on technique (e.g. poetic metre).

I have always found objects to be conducive for initiating writing, people love them. Robert Hamberger, a poet and facilitator, has a beautiful wooden box containing a strange collection: child's shoe, length of rope, empty ring box, his late mother's fake pearls, and so on. He first asks people to write what might possibly be in the full but firmly closed box: they write amazing things he says. Then he opens it and either spills the contents onto the table for people to choose one to write about, or asks them to close their eyes and he takes it round for them to pick unseeing.

I have a collection of large, rusty, old keys; each participant gets one and is asked to describe the key first, and then to think of metaphorical keys which might or have opened doors in their lives, or doors which would have been better kept shut. I also have a collection like Robert's, and use it in myriad ways, sometimes simply asking people first to describe the object (e.g. matrioshka, tuning fork), and then write about whatever it reminds them of, an event in their lives perhaps. Or I might use a specific collection such as hats (mine includes a huge variety for both genders); people first try them on, with great pleasure, choosing one (or more) for themselves and one for a partner. Then they describe one of the hats, or the process of trying on and choosing; does it bring up any memories, for example? Then they think of the metaphorical hats in their lives and how this affects them (e.g. chauffeuring children, cook's hat…); it's an extremely popular workshop.

The life of a group

A group is a dynamic organic being with a life of its own whether it meets for two hours or a week, one session or fifty, going through a life cycle of initial caution at birth; finding out what's what and learning roles as in infancy and toddlerhood; testing out and challenging authority and positions, rights and wrongs as in adolescence; settling down to doing the work in partnership as in young adulthood; getting a bit elderly, slow but wise; and finally passing away with some grief and sense of bereavement. Knowing to expect such dynamic developments can help facilitators plan, and not feel personally assaulted by an adolescent group. And to remember how toddlers can be very demanding indeed, as young performing adults can jockey aggressively for position, power and recognition, and old age can be a time of tremendous flowering of uninhibited talent. And to know seniors can suddenly become obstreperous toddlers or teenagers at a moment's notice, just when the situation seemed to have settled into calm productivity.

It can also be likened to creating a story. The beginning and end are the vital container for the dynamic and demanding middle of the session. This story-line is like a graph: a nice smooth curve bringing participants up to height in the middle, and gently down so they are ready to leave. There are therefore appropriate times for doing things. Getting-to-know-you introductions enable reasonable confidence at the beginning. Then participants need to be clear more or less what they are there for, how they want to do it, why, where and when. Stretching, demanding, exposing activities are appropriate in the middle of a session or a group's life. Then participants need to leave the enclosed protected space slowly and gently. Allowing plenty of time to finish hearing all the writing, so there's space at the end to chat about what participants are doing next, helps them make the transition to the world out there. After a full day or weekend workshop I do a *turning outwards* again exercise, helping seal raw edges exposed by writing and sharing.

A group's life story has 'plot stages'. A group will not continue to get better and better – and better; the duration and shape of the 'plot' will vary for different groups ('The Odyssey' or a boy's comic):

- At *Preparation for the journey*, members cautiously greet each other, make safe enough contact and prepare their boat.

- *Starting out*: they sail out of the harbour waving goodbye, while beginning to gain sea-legs and perceive themselves as team players rather than a collection of individuals; they might be reserved, polite, take few risks, and withhold views and feelings to avoid conflict.

- *Mutiny* is the traditional 'middle day' when the group has constituted itself and perhaps felt rather congratulatory; members now provisionally sort out roles, flex muscles and jockey for leadership or push personal objectives, becoming assertive or defensive, distrustful and suspicious and inattentive; some can be hurt. This is an important stage, even if it seems an initially harmonious course has disintegrated.

- *Mutiny resolution* is adventurers working out who's who, who does what, when, how and why; team members become supportive and receptive, working out precisely what are we doing here?, who am I in this group? and what do I want to get out of it?; group identity and rules are created.

- In *Mission*, participants have tackled each other and uncovered quite a deal of prejudices to sidestep, and strengths and skills to harness; they are open, trusting, listening well, supportive, and willing to take risks; a reasonable team focus has developed for killing the dragon and collecting the treasure, or possibly something else which has become more important.

- *Return home* is when explorers navigate confidently to waiting loved ones, bearing gifts; the group has done its work and ends regretfully and gracefully, with optimism about the future; members leave once more as individuals; a 'rite of passage' shared lunch can ease the parting.

- *Mourning and reminiscence* is hoary old sailors meeting over a pint to yarn and reinforce their learning; a period of which facilitators are not always aware.

A group's life is a story authored by all members, rather than written by one. The stages will probably get mixed up, and earlier stages, even if undergone thoroughly, may recur. For example, *conflict* may arise at any time and need to be dealt with, and *mutiny resolution* undertaken and hopefully reached all over again: the best adventurers do continue to argue over decisions and need to resolve disputes. New rules and guidelines may need discussion and organisation. Elements of the first stage might recur, as they need to get to know each other again in areas which did not seem important initially. All relationships are within the boundaries of the group: individuals meeting each other outside the group's boundaries may knife each other or go to bed together.

Roles within groups

Participant characters

Individuals take on personae within groups. Lack of confidence can lead one to play the fool; some become dependent, treating facilitators as mum or dad; some don't realise they talk too much; others turn in on themselves like dormice and have to be cajoled to communicate. It's stimulating attempting to maintain equilibrium.

Stories rely on characters as much as plot: Tigger: the talkative and exuberant; Roo: the shy and quiet; Rabbit: the dominant and bossy; Wol: the analytic reasoner; Christopher Robin: the facilitative; Pooh: the divergently creative thinker; Eeyore: the moaner; Kanga: the kindly and motherly. There are others, including: the silent but anguished, the frustrated rescuer, the frightened pupil, the babbler, the lurker, the catalyst, the logical structurer and the teacher's pet (think of names yourself for the ones A. A. Milne [1958] left out). Troubles sometimes arise when a group contains two or more Tiggers, or when too many are Roo (or even worse anguished and quiet). Helping people to take on slightly different roles can be facilitative. People play different roles in different groups, just as in life: mum one minute, teacher or lover the next.

Facilitator roles

These roles are often played unconsciously and always with discretion: a 'good-enough facilitator' takes on each character just 'enough' of the time:

- *Teacher*: explain the sonnet form.

- *Instructor*: give directions for a writing exercise.

- *Interpreter*: repeat someone's words in order to clarify, and ensure it has been heard.

- *Devil's Advocate/Confronter*: groups need to be challenged enough.

- *Compatriot/Discloser*: facilitators reveal just enough about themselves; writing and sharing alongside participants can be facilitative, as long as they always remain facilitator, NOT participant.

- *Consultant*: offer specific advice from greater skill or experience, when asked.

- *Neutral Chairman*: is not primarily involved in activity but keeps the group to the point and to time, ensures everyone has a say, that subjects are appropriately aired, that sexism and racism do not happen, and that agreed groundrules are kept.

- *Participant*: opposite role to chairman and good in very small doses (see Compatriot).

- *Manager*: see to the essential but unexciting tasks of organisation and management. The participants need to arrive at the right time and place, with the right papers and expectations.

- There are more of course; and the boundaries blur between them.

Group management

Groups don't happen; they are created and nurtured from planning stages onwards. Many issues have already been covered; here are a few more.

Varying activities to include whole group discussion, paired work, small groups of five or six and individual writing time can keep people involved, and help shy ones speak up to fewer others. Ensuring everyone knows each other's names also helps develop trust and responsiveness. A shared sense of group responsibility means participants are likely to take on looking after quiet members or chatterboxes, and other problems. Planning for a short reflexive period at the end of the session can also support participants to take authority within the group. Any issues, positive and negative, can be aired. Bored or disruptive members can be encouraged to be honest and air problems. If necessary members can write comments anonymously, spread the papers out and all read each other's, marking papers with a tick or a cross.

Groups in my experience have wanted specific groundrules; it can be useful to suggest them to a new group. Use open questions rather than closed, such as 'how did you feel about that?', rather than 'did that make you angry?' Using the simple pronoun 'I' can help people feel more involved and responsible, instead of evasions such as 'you' (e.g. 'you get tired of...': they mean 'I get tired of...'), or 'we', with the assumption the rest of the group agree with the speaker. Sometimes 'they' is even used for 'I'. Finally, irrelevant or personal issues can be discussed at coffee time, such as George asking Mary to tell him about her walking group.

A new group can be supported to develop skills specific to a writing group, and realise there are no magic answers, particularly from facilitators. These include how to discuss others' writing, and make use of comments on their own writing. And gaining confidence to be the first to break the silence to comment on another's writing: this is facilitated by the leader saying nothing until everyone else has spoken who wishes to. All participants being involved in discussion gives responsibility and authority.

Finally there are two areas of empathetic awareness useful to facilitators. One is picking up non-verbal clues such as facial expression, posture, gesture, blushing, sweating, laughter, crying; much can be communicated this way. The second is the possibility of sub-groups; these are rarely explicit, can sometimes be constructive, and occasionally very destructive.

Judy Clinton has some suggestions from her experience of courses with a wide range of people (see also Chapter 8):

'Less is more' with writing workshops. I used to try to cram in more than is appropriate, giving people a lot of additional suggestions (like variations on the six minute exercise, how to come to a place of stillness within, etc.). Giving less makes for a more spacious feeling, and more time for the experiential side of the work, and leaves more space for people to return for more. Also when planning sessions which I organise, I found that upping the fee, with a surcharge for not paying until the day, has, much to my surprise, resulted in more people coming. Someone said maybe it wasn't so much the money as my business-like determination: 'This work is important, and I'm going to charge accordingly, and expect you to take it seriously too.'

I also find Chi Gong style energy unblocking exercises useful, especially for sluggish people in the afternoon, though not too soon after eating. An exercise from the east, related to Tai Chi, its slow gentle energising movements lead to a sense of well-being.

And thinking of lunch: the sharing that goes on over the break at a day workshop can be a valuable element for participants. I am somewhat ambivalent about joining them. I feel I would miss out on an important part of the dynamic of the day if I were to extract myself, and yet it means I have no break, which possibly accounts partly for my tiredness at the end.

When participants read their writing, I usually give people permission to not share if they don't want to. However once someone cried, and said she couldn't read out. I had a strong instinct to push her. After more tears, she did, getting stronger with each sentence. Her look of triumph at the end was a joy to behold. She'd broken through something important. (Judy Clinton)

Course length

The length of a course affects enormously the work that can be done. A single afternoon can be disappointing for all, as people just begin to discover how to start when the session ends; or it might be an epiphany for some: any more might be too much. A residential weekend or week can intensively allow for a great deal to happen as energy is not lost when participants leave and return (see Chapter 13): a very dynamic exercise can be undertaken in the middle as there's plenty of time to help people feel confident before it, and time afterwards to settle them down again. A long series of regular short meetings has the advantage of the group getting to know each other constructively, coming back each time with fresh ideas, commitment, energy, confidence in responding to others' writing, and – vitally – trust. This is particularly true if the group is closed, that is the same members at each meeting (with occasional absences), but this isn't always possible. A group may not initially know how long they need; one strategy is to set a time limit, say six sessions, review the situation at sessions four and five, and decide on a further six, if appropriate. Being in a group is different at different stages: a courtly dance, then jive, quickstep, country dance, or tarantella (for experience of working with groups with changing membership, see Chapters 8, 9 and 10).

Group environment

- *Numbers*: knowing exactly who is going to hear their writing can help participants feel confident both to write and to share their writing. So if a group is any bigger than eight, I always divide it up into small groups of five or six right from the beginning. It doesn't matter if there are fifty or a hundred in a room, what matters is people knowing from the start with whom they are going to be asked to share their writing. Too small a group on the other hand (e.g. 3), unless it's only for one short session, can be less productive too.

- *Furniture* affects a group. Think about the furniture arrangement and be there early to arrange the room. If necessary be willing to rearrange again if a different number than expected turn up.

- *People must be able to see each other.*

- Having just *the right number of seats* for everyone makes the group feel complete; if fewer people arrive than expected, it is worth removing unneeded chairs.

- *Comfort*: ensure there's enough fresh air: it's no good if everyone falls asleep. Ensure the heating doesn't go off half way through so they freeze. The room needs to be neither too big nor too small. Ask people to turn off mobile phones/bleeps (unless they're on-call in which case the group need to know).

- *Whose space?* The room being neutral tends to support a strong group, rather than belonging to any one participant.

- *Necessary equipment*, such as props (button tin for example), needs to be in place beforehand.

- *Punctuality and regular attendance* can create respect for the group and its work.

- *Dates and times*: people like to know at the beginning when they will get their breaks (coffee, tea, lunch) and when they will finish. We parcel out our energy and commitment unconsciously for the allotted time: an unexpected hour on the end of a session, when the energy has been exhausted, is as unfacilitative as unexpectedly finding it is finish time: we could have invested more energy and commitment earlier, had we known.

A suggested session plan

Here is the outline of a typical first session I might run for a group of six to eight people. As an outline, it would be appropriate for a range of groups.

1. Introductions

2. Housekeeping

3. Brief introductory talk about writing

4. Initial write

5. Writing exercise

6. Reading silently to self

7. Initial response

Coffee/smoke/comfort break (brief)

8. Groundrules for readaround

9. Supportive readaround

10. Homework (give title/theme, to be discussed by, and agreed with, the whole group)

11. Liminal space.

1. Introductions

I often use a brief writing exercise for participants to share. For example: Write a couple of sentences describing yourself as a colour (e.g. 'I am silver-grey like the moonlight just now, because I would rather hide; I think I'll go behind a cloud'). Or I ask them to write a list of what they bring to the session (e.g. pen, hope, anxiety); each reading this out leads to a lovely discussion. Depending on the size of the group, this exercise should take no more than 15 minutes.

2. Housekeeping

Timings of breaks and finish, openness to questioning and so forth – see above. Allocate five minutes for this.

3. Brief introductory talk about writing

- You can't write the wrong thing: whatever you write will be right for you, even if it is totally different from what I suggest. My suggestions are only that: suggestions. You are the writer: it is your voice which is important.

- Write as far as possible with no planning or forethought; allow your pen to do the thinking.

- We will have a readaround at the end of the session when people read out their writing.

- If, when you read yours through silently to yourself, you feel it is too private to share, that's fine – or you may read a tiny part.

- We are here to enjoy writing, for you to write in your own form and style.

- Worrying about spelling, handwriting, grammar, etc. is a waste of creative impetus and time: they can so easily be corrected later, if wished.

- Write what and how you want to write. Write what comes with no planning. Thinking too much can inhibit creativity. It's useful later to craft and work on your writing; but not today.

- This will be a confidential group, I suggest; what happens here is private to us.

The talk should last ten minutes.

4. Initial write

Beginning with a brief free-intuitive six-minute writing exercise can ease the writing process (see Chapter 2). Anything can be put on the page: odd words and phrases, lists, abrupt changes of subject, random thoughts, allowing the hand to write whatever comes with no direction, and without stopping. It might seem odd at first, but only because we don't normally pay attention to our unbidden mind's meandering. These writings are NOT for reading out, giving permission for anything to be written. Fleeting inspirations or thoughts which need attention can be captured; those distracting thoughts (horrible traffic getting here/ what shall we eat tonight?) can be stored until later, if need be; and it puts something on the white space of the paper, daunting to any writer, whether seasoned or a beginner.

Freewriting can clarify ideas and help unmuddle issues: whether personal or work or study. It can prevent things from going round and round uselessly in the mind: by putting them out there in black and white on the page. I often hear people mutter: 'Goodness, I didn't know I thought/felt/remembered that!'

The exercise should be completed in six minutes.

5. Writing exercise (an example)

- Write a quick list of people who've been important to you in your life: don't try to make it exhaustive.

- Read the list and choose one to write about any event you remember with that person. Include as many details as occur to you and don't worry if you realise later your story started in the middle; add the end on when you think of it: ordering can be sorted out later, or you might find it's fine as it is.

Depending on how people are used to writing, this exercise might take anything from between 10 and 30 minutes. I generally tell a new group it'll be ten minutes and expect them to take longer.

6. Reading silently to self

When all have finished scribbling, reread ALL you have written, including the six minutes, silently to yourself. Make any additions or alterations (such as *have you included description from any senses other than sight?*). You may find some interesting relationships between the six-minute scribble and the rest of the writing. This reading needs a surprising amount of time, sometimes 15 or 20 minutes – people need to become engrossed. I watch them and only call time when the last person has nearly finished.

7. Initial response

'How did you feel about that?': very brief group feedback that lasts for five minutes.

8. Groundrules for readaround

The group need to take responsibility for ensuring everyone has a fair share of time, that confidentiality will be respected, and any other groundrule they find important. I suggest confidentiality and positiveness, and ask them if they want to suggest anything else. Allocate five minutes for this.

9. Supportive readaround

Divide the time up, and decide how long each participant has (about ten minutes). The group then reads pieces to each other, commenting on them in turn (the facilitator chipping into each discussion at the end). This discussion is about the *writing*: not the *person* nor the *subject of the writing*.

This is a time for anyone who wants to read out their writing with no pressure; though they might choose to read a fraction, or say a few words about it. Reading aloud gives a deeper experience than talking about the writing; but occasionally when a participant does not wish to read, talking briefly about their material can be better than contributing nothing. Some writings take time before being shareable at all. Some need to be read and reread in private; often the very process of writing can be beneficial without ever being shared.

Each personal writing is part of the shared journey of the group. Listening to it, if appropriate for the writer, is a privilege. Hearing it read can be more powerful than the audience reading it silently off the page. The writer will read it with their own voice, inflection, weighting: sometimes a powerful process which can lead to tears. Giving voice to writing in this way can make it seem more true and real. Tears, often of recognition (yes I do remember, think, feel this), are all part of the journey. The group being there with the writer in this vital moment can facilitate greater understanding and acceptance.

The group sensitively discussing each piece of writing can be a valuable strategy, though it might be appropriate sometimes to have no discussion at all. Reading and hearing the writings is in itself significant.

For a group of six people, an hour is about right for this activity. You can do it in less time if pushed or if you have a new group that is very nervous.

10. Homework

Suggestions for optional further writing at home in participants' own time might be appropriate towards the end of the session, as might other supportive developmental writing suggestions. They could write for six minutes as described above (this is always facilitative as it can offer deep and valuable insight into inner thoughts, ideas and inspirations) and then begin to write on the theme they decided upon: *The Turning Point*, or *Write the Next Chapter*, or whatever. Arranging this homework should take three minutes.

11. Liminal space

A few minutes to come down before going back into that world outside this enclosed magic space: a few minutes of relaxed chat before goodbyes.

As evaluation I might ask them to list what they take away with them from the session (pen, hope, anxiety), to balance the introductory exercise. Or what colour are they now, and why? They read them out to the group as before.

Juggling

A course facilitator juggles with co-ordinating these three areas: needs of the group, needs of the individual and needs of the task.

Conclusion

Group members regularly astonish themselves with what they write, and what they gain from the writing of others. Carefully facilitated writing and group work can help people perceive the previously unperceived, even if it was before their eyes. They often discover aspects of their own selves with all the wonderment of a sixteenth-century explorer in a foreign land.

What and why and when and how and where and who of running a writing group have been covered. This chapter contains my current advice; but I often change my ways of doing things as a result of feedback. You will add to my list. You will also disagree with some of mine and substitute your own. Everyone does it their own way. Discover yours. In the next chapter we turn to residential groups, or courses with a longer duration.

Write!

After your six-minute freewrite (see Chapter 2), reread silently to yourself with care (or store, or even destroy, it). Then share it with a carefully chosen other or group, if appropriate.

1. Think of a stock type of character from a story or film (wicked witch, detective, beautiful but dim heroine, tricksy younger sibling, wicked deceiver, tall dark handsome stranger, clown/ fool, mischievous child). Choose the first one who comes to mind.

    ○ give her/him a name and describe them

    ○ write a letter to her/him, and write their reply

- write a story including this character

- now replace the character's name with 'I' throughout.

2. Collect a set of pictures of people (postcards, calendar illustrations, etc.) spread them out on the table between your participants; ask them to:

   - choose three for the person on their left, and three for themselves

   - write about this experience or describe one of the pictures

   - choose one from your pile. This person reminds you of someone. Just start writing, and see where the story gets to, of who this person is, how you knew or know them, and something you did together.

3. Create two sets of small cards:

   - one with a relationship word (mother, aunt, best friend, godparent) written on it

   - the other with a place (kitchen, toolshed, garden, study).

   Each participant takes one of each, and writes about, for example, their uncle's garage. Tell people they can swap their card immediately if they like (in case someone's mother died early, or they never had a garden).

CHAPTER 13

'It Helped Me Get Involved with Myself': Running Residential Writing Groups

'There are in our existence spots of time /
…whence…our minds / Are nourished and invisibly repaired; /
… Such moments / Are scattered everywhere.'
Wordsworth 2004 (1880), p. 208

A workshop of several days is an exciting prospect, far more demanding, exciting and potentially creative than a single session. Ordinary everyday concerns and relationships are held off for a significant time. Focus, trust and confidence in writing, ourselves and our ability to share and support can develop. There's time and space to listen to the still small voices within as well as observing acutely, and 'honouring silence' (participant evaluation). Positive quieter voices are stronger than negative seemingly dominant ones; water dripping quietly onto a hard stone inevitably wears it: the Grand Canyon was cut by mere water.

More space enables safer exploration of deep waters, especially about half way through a longer workshop. The beginning stages have given opportunity to feel confident with the group, facilitator and methods, and there's time remaining for working on issues and feelings raised, together and separately. The progress of any course or retreat resembles a graph curving towards a period of heightened learning, and coming down for the end. A challenging writing theme in the middle raises the graph's curve steeply, needing careful facilitation and selection of later exercises.

This chapter describes three longer courses or retreats. Paradoxically, intense involvement is engendered by longer, looser, more relaxed time away from normal everyday concerns.

Reflections in Writing weekend, Penzance, Cornwall

Images can enable us to listen effectively. They are things in the mind, which we don't relate to as things, but for their magical store of significance. On this retreat (Bolton 2007, pp. 39–48) I put a blue-tit's nest, an egg, a tiny jewelry box, a minute lidded basket and other containers on the table between us. I asked everyone to choose, observe and describe one carefully using all their senses. Then they imagined being inside it, and wrote whatever came. Penelope Shuttle chose the nest (2008, p. 11), writing later in evaluation: 'the course helped me break through barriers, and deal with the isolation I'd experienced since my husband [Peter Redgrove]'s death'.

Angela Stoner chose a conch shell:

Breaking

Every poem breaks a silence
a silence that wraps a wound
stifles a fear
slams down the door on pain
muffles grief.

Silence is a shell
protecting and enclosing
something mollusc-like and soft
quivering and hurt

which dare not call itself a poem
although its every muscle ripples music.
Somehow it finds the strength
to break the shell

will use it as a conch
will sound a deep red song
that's wrung from fear, from pain, from grief
and every note will ring
forgiveness, healing, courage. (Angela Stone)

> *Gillie quoted Adrienne Rich 'Every poem breaks a silence...' (1995).*
> *(Angela Stoner [for Angela's poetry collection see Stoner 2010]).*

Why do images work for us? Problematic memories are not stored verbally to be remembered at will, but locked up almost inaccessibly. I say almost because there are keys: images. Our Penzance group sought many images to reflect upon. We introduced ourselves initially to each other by writing and reading out: *If I were a place, what place would I be?* We imagined finding a bottle with a letter in it, writing what it said. Dreams were one source: I suggested people recalled one dream image when they woke, to write it down and just allow writing to flow from it (see Angela Stoner, Chapter 7). Once I explored a dream image of red shoes (see Chapter 14).

For the session in the middle of the weekend, we responded to: *When did I first die?* (also Chapter 14). A session in the middle of a longer workshop is a good position for a group to undertake a personally demanding exercise. These writers were also seasoned personal writers, and members of *Lapidus*, the organisation for healing writing.

Clothes from any time in our lives were a suggested later theme. Clothing seems to be a *key* image to significant memories, thoughts, feelings, fears, hopes, happinesses. Penelope wrote a poem about the dress she bought for her husband Peter's funeral.

Buying the Dress

My friend has to guide me through the shop,
as if I'm blind

Ranks of dresses get the better of me,
all colours, including emerald,
beating their wings, touching the air.

Then mirrors put in an appearance,
wandering past me, mewing.

I see myself in them, helpless as time.

My tongue's simple silence continues

as I make a beeline for one dress,
hold it up against me,

navy-blue ghost, a formal shadow.
I buy it. After your funeral, I'll never wear it again. (Penelope Shuttle)

The weekend was one of Wordsworth's privileged 'spots of time', when events, utterances and things noticed and remembered are supercharged. A parting homework was to write about another remembered 'spot of time'.

A wonderful healer: Reflections in Writing retreat

Reflections in Writing at Lattendales was a four and a half day writing retreat I led annually for 15 years for the Religious Society of Friends (Quaker) Fellowship of Healing. We were mostly Quakers, but there were always members of other faiths or none; this year we were all women, two-thirds of whom come year after year (Bolton and Padfield 1996). Jackie Bartlett wrote in the Quaker journal *The Friend*, 'Because there was a deep sense of being held, not only by Gillie but by each other, we were able to put into words some of those areas of experience so often believed to be beyond words.' And Bronte Bedford Payne: 'we rejoiced in our freedom to fulfil our creativity in a way we would have found impossible other than during this week of purpose and mutual trust'.

Nearly everyone's lives were changing or in transition. Heather had just learned of her husband's serious illness. This tender recollection of 51 years ago touched us all, not only with its intrinsic quality, but also for the healing power of memory:

Love Poem
The rick's loose hay tickled
Our feet, breathed
Its dusty freshness into our noses.
The chill of midnight air
Felt sweet as kisses.

Was there a moon?

There were certainly stars –
All unknown and bright as forever.

By the stream's edge
Hidden beneath the bridge,
Our two bicycles lay entwined
All night long. (Heather Hawkins)

Heather had not recalled this incident for many years. Not *forgotten* (as someone said: 'how could she?'), it needed writing to bring it to mind.

> For my own clarification of what was happening when I wrote the poem, I will tell you my recent thoughts. I would say that what I wanted was to express as economically as possible the sense-experience embedded in the memory and to let the emotional intensity come through that. What it gave to me – unexpectedly – was the experience of the promise of that time having been fulfilled: sometimes one has to stand back from the muddle of every day to comprehend this. The filter of a poem can do this. What pleased me also is that it is all literally true: so often the poem makes its own demands and moves the detail away from the accuracies of memory or personal experience; words and rhythms take on a life of their own! (Heather Hawkins; personal letter)

Form of the week

Our theme was *memory*. Monday evening's introductory session, the only time we wrote together, used my usual methods (see Chapter 2). I took a closed, carved jewelry box, asking people to describe it and write reflections such as what might be in it. I then opened it to reveal emptiness, calling it a *memory box*: 'no one has ever seen a memory, smelled or touched one, they have no financial value at all, yet are worth more to us than gold or jewels, especially as we get older'. I invited each woman to pull a vital memory out of the box and write about it: in as much detail as they could possibly remember. Jill Leeming wrote in *The Friend*: 'Gillie gave us suggestions before hastily adding "of course if you don't feel like writing that, write something else". No compulsion, just a plethora of tempting carrots.'

Many had arrived feeling nervous about writing. Elaine Brunswick described her first time in *The Friend*: 'I dragged myself to the doorstep. First day at school, driving test and job interview: I anticipated all three. As I walked into the warm and friendly living room I was ready to bite the welcoming hand and growl, fierce as a terrier.' We are brought up to think writing is the prerogative of clever people *who know how*. On these retreats we write for an audience no wider than ourselves; these are not finished pieces, but works-in-progress, or personal thoughts and feelings on paper.

Thereafter people wrote in their own time and their own way. As Patricia Adelman said in *The Friend*, 'Gillie suggested we engage in "magpie work": that is, make a habit of collecting phrases or lines from different sources, such as old songs, lines of poems, to use as stimulus for our own work.' I suggested a specific theme for each day; we then all went out into the glorious Lake District, garden or village to explore and scribble. Rosemary Hogget in *The Friend* reported me as suggesting: 'visit somewhere and let its magic work on you'. Heather Hawkins, in the same journal, said: 'beside remote tarns, seated on boulders, tucked into the angles of stone walls, we sat and gathered our personal reflections. The richness of these explorations delighted us all when we shared their fruits later in the day.' Eileen Stirrup, in the Quaker magazine *Towards Wholeness*, said that 'the weather was damp and mist enveloped us in a sense of mystery and adventure'. Elaine Brunswick in *The Friend* again:

> The four days were filled with immeasurable joy, excitement and fun. Gillie made us work while we were glorying in the beauty and harmony of the autumn fells. Her homework awakened our visions as colours, textures and sounds emerged with startling imagery. Digging into the Lakeland outdoors was a way of exposing our creativity. As I related my day on the phone, Mam said 'I thought you were supposed to be writing?' Ah yes, I thought, but we need to plodge ankle-deep in mud and clamber up sopping hillsides to quicken the creative pulse don't we?
>
> Many of us were self-deprecating at the beginning. As the week went on we gradually cracked and nibbled at our protective shells, supporting each other in the warm writing nest. We created an imaginary *apology pot*; no one was allowed to apologise for our work. (Elaine Brunswick)

We met over a substantial lunch (with pudding). In the afternoon participants wrote up the morning's notes. I sat beside the French window gaining contact with each member in turn about hopes, needs, fears, disappointments, joys. Some talked about rhyme, some about life changes.

Then after tea (with cake!), we sat in a charmed circle in the gracious Georgian drawing room overlooking the lawn towards Blencathra, read to each other and discussed our writing. We could never have *told* our experimental, playful, absurd, extreme, angst-ridden accounts like that. Writing gave permission for things to tumble onto the page, exploring seemingly incomprehensible, yet utterly insightful, images.

A beginning

Pamela wrote about a clear dream from long before which brought peace, hope and the decision to visit the Lake District regularly, culminating in this gathering. I watched Pamela over the retreat, from freezing at the thought of writing, to confidently reading beautifully observed and expressed pieces, and contributing thoughtfully and facilitatively. This, in the voice of the *Spirit of Lattendales* who

> knew that guests would come seeking healing, and I wondered if I would be up to the job. Mother said I just had to be myself, loving and peaceful. In that atmosphere staff would establish a steady routine and guests would benefit. So it was, and there was nothing solemn about it, either. Always there was lots of laughter. (Pamela Russell)

And much laughter there was indeed, alongside many other emotions I think. At the end of the first day we collected together round the fire after supper. We sat in a circle on the thick-pile carpet, each holding out our hands. I pretended to hand a gift to the person on my left. I mimed tenderly passing over a fragile object. Then it changed and the next person received a wriggling mouse. It then became a heavy gold ingot, and then a butterfly which had to be chased, and so on round the room.

Day two

We went out into the autumn Lake District, in twos, threes or singly. The theme was of a path not taken, or a life we didn't have. One wrote the vivid, clear story of her adult life, concluding she had been much more contented than she'd realised, despite having to come to terms with huge life changes: a privileged sharing with the rest of us. She also described:

> The small Norman church was empty, except for us, or so I thought. The light was bright through the plain old glass of the East window, reflecting the blue of the chancel carpet over the altar, walls and monuments. The silence was all encompassing, but gave a strong impression that there was more. Strangely, strongly and certainly, we were among hundreds of those who had worshipped here before. The sense of crowdedness increased, but all was well. We all belonged, and so we prayed and left. (Anon)

Rosemary Willett wrote about the death of a cerebral-palsied social work client, bringing the situation achingly alive, as in this fragment:

> 'I should have been there. I could have saved her,' said her mother.
> Jane was thirty.
> And now they have no role.
> 'Why are you bringing me a cup of tea?' her father asks of his wife.
> He cannot speak about his daughter.
>
> Jane's mother needs to talk.
> Her bereavement course has not been much help.
> 'She taught us and so many people such a lot.
> But all I do now is ask why?' (Rosemary Willett)

Rosemary Hoggett, despite initially reacting against *memories*, having done much sifting and examining of recollections, wrote two vital episodes from her life. Despite feeling focusing upon the present was more positive, her writing fascinatingly assessed, weighed, valued, as this extract shows:

1939 – HOVE

One day I skipped down to Patsy's house to play. It was a dark house I remember with an alleyway at the back. War had just been declared. We didn't know what war was – no-one explained. Mother was just upset by it.

Patsy and I found some sticks of wood lying in her yard, for guns, and we marched up and down the alley pretending to be soldiers, trying to get ourselves into the spirit of war, feeling very important.

Then the siren went – we'd not heard it before, except I think in a trial test, so we all knew how it sounded. I dropped my gun at once, and, without saying goodbye, fled. I was terrified. Would I get home in time or be killed by a bomb as I ran through the streets? Could I run faster than a bomb?... I think it was in this first conscious moment of war that I first knew real fear and my age of anxiety began. (Rosemary Hoggett)

Day three

Today's food for thought was 'A memory which isn't yours': relative or ancestor's, or of the rocks, rivers, lakes, animals or birds. Bronte, struggling with double bereavement and ill-health, wrote about her aunt. The previous evening we had listened to her Victorian musical box, intriguingly housed inside a photo album. I had touched a photo, exclaiming 'What a beautiful girl!' Bronte was startled; writing about this aunt helped her perceive the painful struggles and disappointment of this long dead woman. Bronte was reconnecting herself with her past, reviewing it with greater love and compassion; here is a fragment:

THE WIND OF CHANGE

As your niece I found you an enigma. Your influence over my life was so profound that I find it hard to look at your photographs and to write objectively about you; my mother's only sister, with whom my life became entwined. I remember you so well, but only after the wind had changed for you, when you were a badly dressed, grossly overweight figure, with false teeth and cruelly cut, thinning hair. (Bronte Bedford Payne)

In my first draft of this chapter I said Bronte 'rather feared and disliked' this aunt. Bronte replied at length, saying:

I would say that my Aunt induced most of my major depressions and miseries. In one diary, when aged about fourteen, I have written 'I would like to kill her' – not lightly written at all, after what she had imposed upon my mother and me. No. I did not fear her. I did not even dislike her. She was simply an enigma. She also understood me, in a particularly intuitive way, for she arranged for me to enjoy music in my life at a stage when it would otherwise have been impossible. She lived in a remote farmhouse in an incredibly beautiful place, Gillie, which I could not tear myself away from. Every holiday for weeks on end, and for many years during the war, my sister and I lived with her as her daughters. The singing lessons involved a walk or cycle ride over the moors from Wharfedale to a village near Skipton: about five miles in all weathers. It was so difficult, but so precious, one would not dream of ever missing such an opportunity. (Bronte Bedford Payne; personal letter)

Elaine wrote about her friend undergoing a mastectomy that very day:

2000 – Dryburn Hospital

The nurse told Jean that when you have a mastectomy shedding the breast doesn't hurt. It's the cutting of the muscle and prodding of the lymph nodes deeper and deeper – to see if they are hard – that is painful. The body, she went on, being a wonderful healer forms scar tissue immediately. Unfortunately, this is a bad thing and Jean must stop it by lifting her arm above her head to tear open the wound. Otherwise she will lose its full extension, the nurse said.

I caught my own curves in the mirror and silently hugged their naked beauty. (Elaine Brunswick)

Dorothy, who had earlier aroused belly laughs by writing about her uncle when young testing a hypothesis that animals have a sense of humour, donkeys in particular, now wrote:

Some years ago my husband, our daughter and I set off for an autumn weekend in Buxton. We arrived at the hotel almost at the end of the dinner period. Alison and I grabbed our suitcases, but Ron left his in the boot, together with his overcoat and a new pair of handmade walking shoes. After the meal he went out to get his luggage. The car had gone. Husband was more concerned – illogically, I thought – over the loss of his shoes than the disappearance of the car.

The police came round and took all the details, including our home address, Ron said that he was very tired, and should the car be found in the night, he did not wish to be informed until at least 8 o'clock in the morning. This message, as we shall see, got garbled in transmission.

Meanwhile, back at home, my parents had walked over to attend to our cat. While they were there it began to rain heavily, so they decided to stay overnight. My mother used one of my nighties and Dad tried on Ron's pyjamas but they were too tight, so he too finished up in my night attire. The garment in question was sleeveless with really big pink flowers printed on it, and round the yoke was a flounce with a lace edge. You need to picture this.

About two o'clock in the morning, the doorbell rang. Father got up and was about to go downstairs when my mother pointed out that he could lean out of the bedroom window to see who was there. It was a policeman. 'I've come to tell you your car's been found' he said. Mystified, Dad said he hadn't got a car.

> 'Are you Mr Reynolds?' asked the policeman. 'No' said Dad, always economical with words.
> Policeman: 'Is this *Hillcote*'
> Dad: 'Yes'
> Policeman: 'Do you live here'
> Dad: 'No'
> The constable turned his torch upwards and saw…an elderly transvestite!
> Recovering somewhat, he said 'Well, then, who are *you*?'

All was eventually explained, and the next day we retrieved the car from Chesterfield. It was littered with cigarette ends, but was otherwise intact: and the precious shoes were still there. But I often wondered what the policeman told his colleagues. (Dorothy Reynolds)

Day four

Our last full day's theme was: 'A memory of today for tomorrow.' Mary (a vicar) had previously written 'a great moan' (as she called it) about her house having roads on three sides; now she wrote:

> This is silence that you can hear and feel
> shared silence and silence alone,
> silence that surrounds and permeates you

silence in which your mind freely expands
out of your bruised noise-pummelled brain,
silence bringing healing and clarity of vision.

This silence
contains the songs and warning-notes of birds –
robins, wrens, blackbirds, blue-tits.
This silence
contains the activities of the house –
laughter and greeting, cleaning and cooking,
taps and running water,
heating pipes and floorboards creaking.

This is silence that you can tune into.
It is deep with the participation of many people.
Long-standing Quaker people,
new-comers, young, enquiring and thoughtful people,
noisy, gregarious, never-stop-talking people
and laughing playing children –
all are held in the silence here. (Mary Dicker)

Day five

Today we left after breakfast, with a photocopied anthology. An editorial team, created on the middle day each year, collated this with pieces from everyone. The final theme was: 'Your most precious memory.'

This week's retreat in a Quaker house of healing was different in kind, though not in quality, from the rest of my life: a retreat for me also. Through it I learned to *walk beside* the many people who write with me, rather than lead or pull them. This group taught me to support the participants to give to each other rather than always look to me, to allow the house to work its peaceful magic, the glories of the Lake District and the caring and sharing of eating and walking together. I have learned to make suggestions for people's writing, but leave it wide open for them to write whatever they want and need to write in their own space and time and then share it in whatever way feels right to them. I always write too during the week, very little. Here is this year's poem:

Quiet candle flame
reflects twice in the window:

a pair of gold wings

Groupwork, and dreams

The *way* a group like this is run (see Chapter 12) contributes to participants' respect and care for themselves, each other and their writing.

> I personally found the group most supportive this year: the combination of the opportunity to be alone with enabling people around, was helpful and therapeutic. I think that I said to you that you must find the week very tiring, particularly because you enable the group to structure itself, rather than direct it. Group theory suggests that there are stages in the development of groups: forming, storming, norming and performing. This group did not appear to *storm*. I wonder if this was partly due to the attributes and personalities of the members, but also to your skill. I think that the use of silence was very significant in the development of the group through the week. (Rosemary Willett; personal letter)

> Gillie gave us many ideas, dialoguing, writing in different voices, fairy stories, responding to colour everywhere, including coloured paper! We looked at gifts we had received, wrote of the masks we wear and much else. We were challenged to look closely, describe precisely and in detail. We each had our own time with Gillie after lunch, which was invaluable, and in the evenings we shared the writing of the day. The range of work was staggering. We laughed, we were moved to tears, and were constantly surprised. It was a privilege to share at this level. Gillie had asked us to treat these days as a gift to ourselves. Angels and leaves surrounded us. (Rosemary Hoggett in *The Friend*)

Carol said to me during our afternoon private talk: 'I don't want to write about dreams: I don't like them. I had a terrible one once and don't want to think about it.' She wrote this:

The Knife and the Sword

In my dream I used the knife,
felt it go in.

I killed with it, I was quite clear
that that was what I'd done.

At Tai Chi class I touched the sword,
I picked it up.
I felt its weight and balance
swinging in my hand.

I strike without hitting,
I'm quick and I'm neat –
step, parry, punch.

My Yin absorbs your Yang,
balances round,
becomes my Yang.

One day I will raise the sword.
It's blunt, it won't kill anyone,
but I will see its flash. (Carol Gardiner)

This poem expresses her rising sense of power to wield her *yang*, her masculine strength, positively and not for harm: but she will see the *flash*. Carol wrote to me later: 'and I've been remembering more dreams and even writing them down. The things I wrote at Lattendales are so important that I know I have to write more.'

Further Lattendales 'Reflections in Writing' weeks

Each week had its own theme, subdivided into a writing suggestion for each day; here are some:

Senses
Those:

- with the eyes of a painter: colour, shape, form

- with the ears of a musician: the sounds around you

- with the nose of a perfumier: really pay attention to present and past smells

- with the touch of a sculptor: texture, etc.

- with the taste of a chef: this led to some visits to coffee shops

- with the sense of a film producer.

Elements

- Rock, earth and stone. A workshop with crystals and fossils to hold in the hand and then write when ready.
- Water: waterfalls, baths, puddles, rivers felt, tasted, seen, smelt, heard during the day.
- Air: as above.
- Fire: as above, including imagined.
- Metal: as above.

Ways of perceiving

- Hats: we chose from a large bag of hats to try on and share, and then thought about the different 'hats' we wear in our lives, and the way people perceive us so differently.
- Kaleidoscopes made of mirrors: fragmented, opposite perceptions.
- From the perspective of an old person, a child, a foreigner, a martian.
- Perspectives created by dreams.
- From the point of view of someone you don't like, or even hate.

Gifts

- A gift you would like. I read to the group John Burningham's picture book *Would You Rather...* (1978), which ends with: 'would you rather live with...a rabbit in a hutch, chickens in a coop or a dog in a kennel, or perhaps you would rather just go to sleep in your own bed' (pp. 31–32).
- A gift to you.
- A gift from you.
- A gift of the spirit.
- A gift of action.

- The wrong, *backhanded* or funny gift.

Animals

- We started with a heap of postcards of animals, which we looked at, shared, and then chose one, or allowed it to choose us, to start us writing.

- A creature you meet here in the house, garden, village or fells.

- A creature in your life.

- An imaginary animal (e.g. Lewis Carroll's Jabberwock).

- Your animal self.

- Using animal metaphors: e.g. if my work were an animal what animal would it be?

Place and things

- We started with a collection of small treasures I brought with me (such as a Victorian button hook). We looked at, chose for each other, talked about and wrote.

- Coming here, does it remind you of another arrival in your life?

- Write as if you are someone else arriving here.

- Contrast the inside with the outside, using metaphor.

- Think and write about a precious object in your life.

Journeys

- An initial workshop with a tin of buttons: choose a collection for a journey and pass them to someone else. Write about the experience, the buttons, the sharing.

- Items which express the journey of your life found on this morning's walk.

- List and explore what you need to take with you on your journey.

- List journey destinations in your life; choose one to write about fully.

- Companions for your journey: past or present.

Wordsworth's spot of time

- Write about an occasion in your life which was memorable and significant; you do not need to know why.

Agnes Coates described a *Button* workshop in *Towards Wholeness*. It is followed by my button fragment:

> Who but Gillie could see an unfolding plan in the emptying of a box of buttons?! Black, white, pearl and coloured buttons. Regimental, initialled, flower buttons. Leather buttons, fur buttons and buttons for baby clothes. 'Play with them' Gillie said. We did – wonderingly. 'Choose a few and hold them in your hand.' We did. 'Now write about them.' Write about a handful of buttons? There was a puzzled silence; and then we all began to write, and write and write! My own clutch produced the story of my life; others were more profound, including thoughts on animal welfare, the environment, and personal problems. We had begun a fascinating journey into our own minds, memories and spirits. (Agnes Coates)

> This Nan-coloured blue button is very tightly contained: the swirl of navy-blue leaves are tightly twined within the button disc. My Nan was held closely within her late Victorian role as a woman, mother and grandmother. She wasn't allowed to keep her own home once her husband had died, although she was no older than I am now. She spent the rest of her life shuttling between daughter and son and their families. She was sort of proud and prickly in a way: I now know because she'd been stripped of her role. She wanted to be careful all the time that people recognised her individuality: that she wasn't just her daughter or son's mother. (Gillie Bolton)

Charney Manor

Here are two descriptions of an initial write at a similar Quaker retreat at Charney Manor, from *The Friend*:

After supper we sit in a huge oval in the upper room (a Medieval Solar). The simple instruction given by Gillie is 'Write out of the silence the words that bubble from the heart, the belly, the fingers, without thought'. My pen doesn't wait for the silence. It's moving ferociously over the paper before she has finished speaking. I can't say how long it takes, but eventually one by one we sink into the pregnant silence. We are now requested to underline three phrases which we then read out as if in worship: one phrase each until all the phrases are given back to the silence where they came from. This amazingly rich and diverse patchwork of ideas is the foundation of all that will follow in the next two days. (Margaret Holman, Denise Bennett)

To be asked at the inaugural gathering to write whatever arose out of the silence normally reserved for worship [Quaker Meetings are conducted in silence]; for it to be trusted that something would come; and for that 'something' indeed *to* come, was not only new to me, but little short of amazing. At the end of the weekend we experienced a Meeting for Worship of such quality of silence and ministry as to be a poem in itself. (Patricia Adelman)

Reflection and silence

The very writing of this chapter has led to further levels of reflection. Several participants' letters, written on receipt of the first draft, are quoted above. Rosemary Hoggett also wrote: 'I thought you captured so well the spirit of the week, and it was really good to relive it all again. I'm realising that for me writing has become a vital part of my development, and I'm only just beginning to appreciate fully its power. I've always loved writing since our Meeting's *Writing the Spirit* (a course I wrote for Quaker Meetings to undertake on their own [Bolton 1994]). Heather Hawkins commented: 'reading it brings the experience back to me with great pleasure, especially as the other participants come so vividly to mind'.

Silence is a vital element in all this work. Writing's quiet is only broken by the scratch of a pen or a sigh; the quiet as a group waits for someone to read, or while they pause appreciatively thinking after hearing a piece, the silence while people decide what if anything they wish to say. On this retreat week all our work is hung around and in silence: Quaker silence before breakfast in the Quiet Room around a lit candle, and at the end of the day, the silence into which we each drop our writing as appropriate, reading aloud to each other.

Morning Light
Outside, swifts chase
and dart against a sky layered sulphurous grey
with china blue and billowy white;
near-to they are substantial, sleek
and glossy dark; at distance
like black butterflies dancing to the clouds
above trees barely touched by Autumn.

inside, we hear their cries, but,
bathed in our silence,
we are held by the flame. (Ann Jacob)

This chapter shows (rather than tells) how the longer space of several days away can intensify and yet relax writing, our response to it, and support of each other's development. This book is nearly at an end. Juhani Ihanus collaborated in the concluding chapter: a deeply perceptive Finn, he has worked in therapeutic writing even longer than me.

Write!
After your six-minute freewrite (see Chapter 2), reread silently to yourself with care (or store, or even destroy, it). Then share it with a carefully chosen other or group, if appropriate.

1. Think of a favourite picture. Write as if you are there, or about the person, or what the place or objects remind you of.

   ◦ The picture contains a message for you about your present life: what is it?

   ◦ If you are running a session: take in a pile of pictures (postcards or from a calendar) of either land-/urban-scapes, still life, food, animals…

2. Write a letter to your writer-self; write the reply. Do this especially if you are stuck in any way with your writing, or if you are in the

middle of something and have to leave it frustratingly for a while and are afraid of losing your thread and it going cold.

If you are a facilitator wishing to read more, see Hunt (2006, pp. 90–93).

3. Write a story of any memory: include as many details as possible.

New retell it: write a different version in one (or more) of these ways:

- if it is in the past tense (we drank), rewrite it in the present (we drink)

- if in the first person (I drank), retell it in the third (he drank)

- from the point of view of a significant other person (might be a child)

- from the perspective of a creature (animal, insect, fish) which was/might have been there

- from the point of view of an object (your coffee mug, a tree)

- as a fairy story or myth (once upon a time there was…); or as a romantic fiction, detective story, fantasy/sci fi or other genre.

CHAPTER 14

'Tread Softly Because You Tread on My Dreams' (Yeats 1974): Conclusion. A Conversation between Juhani Ihanus and Gillie Bolton

Writers who are not self-obsessed and wriggling through what they hope are their own labyrinthine psyches are very likely not writers at all.

Jenny Diski 1998, p. 45

When I write, no matter how hard I try to make the process a rational, cerebral one, I know that will not suffice. There is always a moment (if there isn't then I'm in trouble) when some vasty deep has to be approached, and the spirits that dwell in it summoned. It is a strange moment, akin to dreaming. It's a phantom period, tantalising, troublesome, and sometimes malign – a hint of what's to come perhaps.

Sally Beauman 2002, p. 32

Expressive and explorative writing is a process akin to dreaming: that powerhouse of insight drawn on by artists and scientists. It can help us perceive and realise our dreams if we tread with respect, willing to work at and trust their strange, metaphoric riddles. Juhani, adjunct professor of cultural psychology at the University of Helsinki, pioneered Finnish biblio-/poetry therapy and its vibrant organisation offering initial and in-service training and dialogue. He posed a series of questions to initiate discussion about some of our field's many roots and diverse shoots. My responses show how developing a practice over 25 years, studied by a process similar to action research, led to my theoretical approach. We then turned briefly to discuss the research of others.

> *JI: By way of autobiographical reminiscing: words and healing, writing and therapy, therapeutic writing and writing therapy are rich fields of expressive explorations. Writing can add personal meaning to experiences, and by writing we can reach personally meaningful experiences. When and how did your personal exploration into these areas begin?*

GB: Personal expressive and explorative writing started me on a roller coaster. Picking me up from a quagmire of silent, unacknowledged childhood abuse, it rattled, rolled and threw me through incomprehension and terror at times, to deep insight, acceptance and forgiveness. As a young mother my psychological volcano nearly blew me apart; I was on the verge of losing husband and children. Living in a village so small that my children's school had 12 other pupils, I had no idea what to do. My husband suggested I wrote my autobiography. I started this anodyne task at the kitchen table in neat round handwriting in a scarlet school notebook, detailing a charming childhood in a little house on the corner of my grandfather's dairy pasture, and later in a seventeenth-century wooden farmhouse above his meadows. Here is an extract, later turned into a poem.

Good Night

After her bath Mother lifts her to the window
to say goodnight to the stars

in summer she can see the cows
as they amble up the meadow
to chew cud and think about nothing
under the oaks where mushrooms grow;
their shadows are long
and their bags swing empty after the milking.

Cream for her porridge is rising in the dairy,
icy water rushing over the churns.

Good night cows.

What made my writing change? Perhaps the horrid frightened little girl inside me grabbed my pen and began to scrawl, and my other internal girl, a *Campaign for Nuclear Disarmament* political left winger, egged her on. My writing became wild. Round and round in blood red circles on flipchart paper; scrawled huge and felt-tipped black. Expletives, explosions, exclamations. In spider scrawl on tiny scraps with a stiletto sharpened pencil. Certainly no grammar, syntax, or much sense.

I wrote kneeling in the corner window of a 14th floor office; duvet wrapped in a house corner; hidden among tree roots; on a beach; on top of the moor, my page pegged in place. Anywhere I suppose but at desk or table. And anywhere there was no one else. And in the dead of night, or very early in the morning out with the thrush and blackbird. When the rest of the world was tucked up out of the way and didn't know what I was doing.

I reread these manic scribbles. Made what sense of them I could. Not logical sense; I opened them up to more scrawlings, allowing images full rein to gallop where they would. They reared up, and having failed to unseat me, clamped the bit between their teeth and took off. It didn't so much feel like redrafting, as working out what those images were which haunted me, listening to those voices inside which I had been unable previously to hear. I really trusted this had very real significance, that it was worth the effort and time. I had faith in my strength, however terrifying some of it was. It felt life-saving.

I read about forms of therapy: Gestalt, psychodynamic, body-work and rebirthing. I read Fritz Perls, John Rowan and Ronnie Laing. I picked and chose seemingly at random ideas I could use for myself. I intensely crafted my scrawls into poems which were real epiphanies to me, in the James Joycean sense. I played with genre, such as fairy story: a writing strategy I've used a terrific amount since. I asked those little girls within me to speak, my dream characters, the hankie my child-self chewed at night-time, the shadows on the ceiling in my childhood bedroom (one of the scariest I ever did): written dialogues, letters: raging outbursts sometimes. I wrote fictionally in many voices: one of the daughters of Lot, a little boy who died when he was nine. And I endlessly asked Why? What? How? Who? When? Where? Why?

I played endlessly with images: the seemingly safe playhouse under the drooping leaves of riverside willows, the house key I hadn't been able to fit in the lock when sent home for forgotten picnic items. I scribbled furiously to understand a tiny dream image about a pair of red shoes, eventually remembering the folk story red dancing shoes which could not be removed, but chopped off with an axe.

Red Shoes

I
'Wear these shoes,
my love,
and dance for your Daddy.'
She laughed then,
clapped her hands.

II
Later she wielded so many knives
in each hand, she became a blur
of steel, catching and sparking
blades of light
to chop out laughter, singing,
dancing
cut by mummy's voice
'Stop That – Now.
It'll End in Tears';
to ward off daddy's hand
excited
by her excitement.

III
Little-girl slippers
gnaw into woman's flesh:
'Dance to Daddy's tune, my love,
dance.'

She knows
the only way for a girl
to be safe
is to slice
her self
from her body.

Only an axe
at the ankle
can remove slippers
buckled to flesh;
even then, her butchered feet
in scarlet silk
will pirouette alone before her
every time she tries to laugh.

Now, though she's hobbled
on wooden feet
into marriage, motherhood:
the meat cleaver's still there
dancing,
ready.

IV
She watches the hammer
jig on the anvil
to beat that living glow
right out of the steel:
takes the tempered blades,

pares Daddy out of her mind,
and hurls the knives
up and away,
a blue brightness winking in the sun
so she can jive –
feel herself in heart, brain and toes;
her skirt is a bell
under outstretched hands,
her laugh a banner
of scarlet silk.

Bolton (2000a, p. 351)

Why did eggs and tomatoes (yellow and red) together nauseate me? As
I scribbled and reread I remembered my parents, brother and I saw a
rat eating something on the garden side of the French window as we
ate lunch; my father went round and shot it. The first notes for this
poem arrived in therapist training (Bolton 2003). We were asked to

write: *When did you first die?* (see also Chapter 13). A truly dangerous title starting a very long writing adventure.

I really listened to those writings with all the ears of my internal cast. The terrified little girl began to believe she was really being heard. At last. After 40 years of being sternly told: *These are things we do not speak of; in our family we pretend they did not happen.* Well they did happen. But writing, poetic imageful silent trustworthy writing, was the only way of giving voice. Writing of which the only audience was myself. No one else read those scrawls, and probably couldn't anyway. Free explorative private expressive writing was the only avenue to what I had to hear about my own experience.

Amazingly that writing was an exciting adventure. I never knew what was going to appear; excitement outweighed terror. And I began to heal. Because once I knew what had happened to me, that I wasn't just mad, that this had been done to me as an innocent trusting child: I was able to act on the knowledge my writing gave me. My actions brought healing, forgiveness; but unfortunately not forgetting.

JI: What memorable landmarks can you now associate in your journey into therapeutic writing?

GB: First, realising I didn't have *one* story, and *one* voice to tell it with. Discovering my multiple voicedness (Bakhtin 1981; Rowan 1990), and the many different narratives they could tell of my life and relationships. And helping others towards this: I perceive them discovering powerful aspects of themselves, and that they can contain and disarm inner critics and hurt children, and find powerful inner mentors. It's a privilege to see them integrating these differing selves, gaining integrity.

Dream exploration and examination (Freud's *Royal Road*) were significant. And so was solitary writing with a sense of place: our tiny house surrounded with garden, dogs, hens, goats, vegetables and fruit; Lumb Bank Writers Centre, once Ted Hughes' house in Yorkshire (www. arvonfoundation.org).

Northern College (www.northern.ac.uk), where directing the creative writing programme led me to realise writing's potential for others. One of eight British colleges, linked to the trades union movement, Northern College is dedicated to working people gaining education they couldn't when young. Near a coal mining area with pits closed just before I started, leaving unemployment and unhappiness (mining is a way of life and community), these ex-miners and others crowded into gracious palladian rooms with tall windows overlooking ornamental lawns, haha, palladian summer house, and my own office in the baroque wing. They taught me the power of writing to heal, educate, inspire, and give great shots of self-confidence. One I remember had been one of the first to enter Belsen Concentration Camp after the war.

Teaching creative writing at Sheffield Hallam University English Department, where in a Victorian house surrounded by lawns we learned together how writing gave insight, understanding, self-awareness.

JI: Something about your own organisational/academic ('attachment/affiliation') history?

GB: I'm a freewheeler at heart, and always a partial freelancer; my personal story led me to need independence. Research affiliations have been to academic medicine (Sheffield University), palliative and cancer care (hospices, University College Hospital London Teenage Cancer Trust Unit), and academic literature and medicine (King's College London).

JI: You have been active in many fields (creative writing, therapeutic writing, academic research, supervision, counselling, consultation, etc.). Is it really possible to combine all these, or have splits and fragmentation sometimes emerged?

GB: Over the years juggling has been an art. Sometimes I've dropped the balls; sometimes the best ones have stayed in the air.

JI: Can you say anything about the underlying principles (values, or foundations) of your work? What kind of mindscapes or states of consciousness have accompanied your work?

GB: Once upon a time a young seeker after the truth set off to find the wisest person in the world. Travelling over mountains and valleys, oceans and deep forests, deserts and swamps, our adventurer eventually arrived at a high lonely place. Here the wise one dwelt, but the dream of receiving wisdom seemed as distant as ever, as there was no suggestion of tuition. The only set activity was daily meditation lasting an unspecified time: 3 minutes, 3 hours, on one memorable occasion 3 days, the end being signalled by a bell. One day in furious frustration our student got up, grasped the beater, and rang the bell – hard – and then stood in fear and trembling at such audacity. The wise one, however, got up slowly and creakily bowed, speaking for the first time: 'Thank you; you have learned the first lesson: to take responsibility. We must all ring our own bells, and never give others the authority to ring them for us. Now your education can begin.'

Therapeutic and reflective writing can enable:

- exploration of narratives of experience from different perspectives
- reflexive clarification of values, principles, ethics, feelings and identity
- critical examination of metaphors in daily use
- metaphor 'games' to express the otherwise inexpressible
- imaginative acute observation and description.

In order to gain the most from writing (or any art), we knowingly and *willingly suspend our disbelief for the moment* with whatever the writing presents us (Coleridge 1992 [1817]). We enter Keats' *negative capability* (1818): willingly becoming absent-minded, or mentally absent from our habitual cognitive way of being. *Mindfulness* is being aware only of whatever presents itself to our senses, with all attention focused on present activity. This can enable non-reliance upon habitual knowledge and skills and greater openness, reducing stress.

Einstein (1973) called this consciousness 'an appreciation of the mysterious, the fundamental emotion which stands at the cradle of true art and true science' (p. 80). Socrates said 'wonder is the beginning of wisdom', because an open enquiring state of mind is when anything might be possible, when startling inspiration appears as a result of no cognitive logical thought. The sculptor Juan Munoz (2008) spoke of an aim of his art 'to make [the viewer] trust for a second that what he wishes to believe is true. And maybe you can spin that into another reality and make him wonder.'

This reality spinning often involves imaginatively entering the consciousness of others, to wonder about their experience. Terry Eagleton (2008) comments on its empathetic and ethical role in our lives:

There would seem to be a need for some special intuitive faculty which allows me to range beyond my own sense-data, transport myself into your emotional innards and empathise with what you are feeling. This is known as the imagination.

It makes up for our natural state of isolation from one another. The moral and the aesthetic lie close together, since to be moral is to be able to feel what others are feeling. (p. 19)

The activities of the culturally refined Nazis have disabused us of thinking the aesthetic necessarily helps us to act morally. Rather that if we can allow ourselves to be in a state of *mindfulness, negative capability, willing suspension of disbelief,* then our moral and ethical faculties will be brought to the creative process. The Nazis called this *degenerate;* they denigrated, expatriated or murdered those who used it.

The imagination, which enables writers to enquire into the world, their own experience, and the possible experience of others, is both wise and fundamentally trustworthy. Insight and support are gained by writing if the self is respected, the processes of writing trusted, and reliable confidential readers carefully chosen. Writing works when enquirers take full responsibility for actions, including writing and the sharing of it. It is essentially playful and straightforward; the greatest wisdom or inspiration is the simplest.

> *JI: Some significant preceding figures and/or works in the field of biblio-/ poetry therapy?*

GB: Marion Milner described how she took her cue from Klee's 'take a line for a walk…' in *On Not Being Able to Paint* (1971 [1950]). Instead of painting, I wrote, and never looked back from my walk. She also inspiringly wrote *Eternity's Sunrise: A Way of Keeping a Diary* (1987). Tristine Rainer, a student of Anaïs Nin, said 'Just write!', in *The New Diary* (1978). And I did. And so could anyone using her lovely straightforward advice. I also avidly read Virginia Woolf's diaries (1977, 1978, 1980). Other useful authors were Progoff (1975) and Elbow (1981). Colleagues writing inspiringly recently include Celia Hunt (Hunt and Sampson 1998, 2006).

> *JI: You have expressed doubt concerning such specialists as 'Writing Therapists', that they might not be 'the very best thing' (Bolton 1999a, p. 27). Specialist interpretations, from your point of view, might thus be forced power manoeuvres, estranging a writer from her/his experience. But is there not, in writing therapy, a way of co-constructing and co-interpreting meanings, making texts tremble in communicative nets, without any final words or terminal interpretations? Are we also in writing therapy*

too individualistic with our meanings (as solitary possessions), concerned
with who has the rights to right meanings?
How do you see the role and function of a therapist's own expressive
writing in relation to her/his work in writing therapy groups? Can she/
he take actively part with her/his own writing contributions?

GB: The more open and less rule-bound we are about therapeutic
or personal development writing, the more effective it'll be. And the
more people who can offer it, the more clients, patients and personal
development people we'll reach.

Writers gain dialogic relationships with their own writing, which
they own. As soon as writing therapists or anyone seen in authority
interprets the work of another, the less dominant person may lose
authority and control of their work. We need to be aware of where the
power lies, of having more impact than we intend.

Therapeutic writing is an adventure undertaken with curiosity.
Doctors, nurses, therapists, writers, counsellors, social workers,
occupational therapists and so on are potentially excellent writing
facilitators. Personal experience of writing as a living life element is the
vital training they need. I only ask people to do things I have done
myself. If we ask our patients and clients to embark on journeys fraught
with dragons and demons, and enlightened by angels, we need to have
travelled the path before them, and to write alongside them. I normally
scribble companionably alongside clients or groups; this writing usually
lacks power, though, as my primary attention is on them. I rarely read
it out, though I'm happy to (depending on its content) if the group ask.
It's good for people to see their leader involved in a similar way to them.

JI: You mention in your book (Bolton 1999a, p. 13) that there is no real
distinction between therapeutic writing and creative writing. Still, this
distinction is often maintained, especially by professional writers. And
especially many medical practitioners even seem to deny (too much!)
creativity and expression in therapy. Are these kind of attitudes old-
fashioned, dichotomising, and conservatively blocking out expressive
'transgressions'?

GB: Fiction, drama, poetry, journal writing all draw upon the self, at least
in initial explorative stages. A writer dialogues with their inner selves:
Bakhtin calls this a writer's sense of being multi-voiced or polyphonic
(1981; see also Rowan 1990). Personal memories, dreams, reflections,

hopes, fears and so on are explored and mined, sometimes courageously. Sally Beauman's 'spirits' are these inner thoughts and experiences not generally expressed and laid open to the scrutiny of others. That this process is personally illuminative and helpful, though complex and sometimes painful, is asserted by many.

Any creative or reflective writing of any worth seems to involve lifeblood coursing through the pen. 'Maybe all poetry…is a revealing of something that the writer doesn't actually want to say, but desperately needs to communicate, to be delivered of'. (Hughes 1995); 'Every poem breaks a silence that had to be overcome'. (Rich 1995, p. 84); 'The blood jet is poetry' (Plath 1981, p. 270); 'Writing *To the Lighthouse* laid [my parents] in my mind' (Woolf 1982 [1980], p. 208); 'I ceased to be obsessed by my mother. I no longer hear her voice; I do not see her. I suppose that I did for myself what psychoanalysts do for their patients. I expressed some very long felt and deeply felt emotion. And in expressing it I explained it and then laid it to rest' (Woolf 1976, pp. 80–81); 'One ought to write only when one leaves a piece of one's flesh in the inkpot each time one dips one's pen' (Tolstoy 1991, p. 18).

Published writers often begin by exploring 'vasty deeps' (Beauman 2002), surprising themselves; even Alan Bennett said, 'an author is sometimes surprised by what he or she has written' (2009, p. 17). Creative writing's initial stages are explorative, intended only for writer and trusted first reader. Personal material (memories, dreams, reflections…) is often drawn upon (sometimes in a state close to the hypnagogic) in a qualitatively different way to thinking and musing. Vital personal images emerge, allowing access into mental and feeling areas not habitually experienced. This writing might be notes, scribblings, journal entries.

In the second stages, published writers focus away from themselves and towards communicating with unknown readers. Literary readers are not primarily interested in writers personally (unlike therapeutic writing readers), but in what they have to say. In the third and final editing stages the text is worked on minutely, often with editorial aid, to make it publishable. The first two stages can be deeply personally illuminative, the initial also cathartic.

> *JI: You have regarded poems or images as 'windows' (Bolton 1999a, p.64). Could you add a bit more about this?*

GB: Ah yes: sunshine comes through spaces not walls:

Cut doors and windows for a room
It is the holes which make them useful.
Therefore profit comes from what is there;
Usefulness from what is not there.

Lao Tsu 1973, p. 11

Explorative and expressive writing, especially when playing with image, cuts spaces through social and psychological conventions and personal barriers, enabling vital communication between people and between writers and themselves. Below I suggest the metaphor of the boundaries between the auditorium and backstage of an opera house.

> *JI: You stress explorative, expressive attitudes, and the need to 'unremember writing rules', by saying the most important rule is: 'there are no rules' (Bolton 1999a, p. 16). But we are not tabula rasas; there are memories (of what we have been expected to do); there are knowledge bases and codes (formed into rules for behaviour); there are coping strategies, lifestyles, habits, resistances, etc. These cannot be simply erased, and they extend their intense influence to writing, too. Possibly, we may have strict psychic sets of rules, even when we think we are writing expressively, making a 'gift of writing' for ourselves and for others. How to expel those 'criticising ghosts' (Bolton 1999a, p. 34)? And is it really possible, since we are also beings with pasts? By rewriting both the official and personal histories?*

GB: No, we can't un-remember rules. People often, however, do find this instruction wonderfully freeing. In a workshop, people are enclosed into a safe-enough situation with a carefully built up sense of trust and confidence and empathetic listening and sharing. It's more a form of words, inviting people to write differently from how they've been taught. Proposing something brand new would be much more frightening than requesting the light-hearted seeming 'forget all those boring old rules!'

And we can't un-listen to our internal critics. Nor can we expel those 'criticising ghosts'. But we can counteract them. I help people communicate in dialogues or letters with their *internal wise counsellor/ mentor*, discovering its name. Internal mentors are greater than internal critics. Along the way writers personify these critics and dialogue with them too. Powerful stuff.

> *JI: What kind of dangers (if any) do you see in therapeutic writing? I would like to present here one candidate, not of intellectualisation but of 'emotionalisation': the overwhelming (vicious circle or 'soap opera' kind*

of) impact of empathy and emotions (from manic to depressive moods), and the making transparent of one's intimate and sensitive issues, the making public of one's emotional and private life. Maybe this tyranny of revealing the intimate, present in early psychoanalysis, has reached even humanistic 'alternative therapies'? Are we anxiously (in anguish) writing poems and efficiently utilising them (like natural resources) in order to get at once what we feel we deserve? Will therapeutic writing turn into an achievement in the therapeutic production and communication system?

GB: Therapists have said my approach is dangerous. Yet we live in a dangerous world (has it not always been thus?). We can have faith in ourselves, trust in a fantastic process which has been used for centuries, be responsible for our facilitation, generous enough to give our own writing focused time and energy, and have sufficient unconditional positive regard (let's call it love rather) to support people through their writing adventures. We need to take our terrors and anxieties, our hopes and fears seriously, and take ourselves close to our own boundaries in order for change to happen. And it certainly feels dangerously close at times (see Hart, Chapter 6). Boundaries are where power resides: being critically aware of them, and challenging them, is what being alive – really alive – is about.

Your 'candidate of emotionalisation': in the wrong hands, yes, you could well be right! That's why writing adventures need to be playful, explorative, non-definitive and infinitely varied. The only people I've met stuck with writing in the way you mention have taken advice to write a set amount of journal (3 pages say) every day with no 'games' (dialoguing, unsent letters, metaphor creation and expansion, etc.). And, yes, 'revealing the intimate' can become a tyranny of us spying on ourselves, as well as making ourselves open to others, as the writings of Foucault so powerfully show (1990 [1976], 1992 [1984]).

JI: If we think of biblio-/poetry therapy theoretical backgrounds, you seem to have relied on humanist (humanistic psychology) traditions. How about psychoanalytic, psychodynamic or cognitive traditions? Or is the field becoming theoretically more and more eclectic, and interdisciplinary or even transdisciplinary? Perhaps, for example, psychoanalysis differs from humanistic psychology in its emphasis on the unconscious (for me, particularly in language rather than in the individual unconscious). Humanistic psychology, on the other hand, assumes the priority of consciousness and choice. Freud (1893) once quoted Charcot: 'Theory is good, but it doesn't prevent things from existing.' Maybe you sign the same dictum?

GB: My theoretical background has been so eclectic as to resemble a magpie's nest; and remember I'm neither psychologist nor therapist. I started in social anthropology, being influenced by such as Lévi-Strauss' theory of the importance of myth, and how we are like *bricoleurs* creating our worlds (1966). I then went into education where influences included Dewey and his insistence on love of learning (1910, 1988 [1992]), and Bruner's theory of narrative and story, the way our specific cultures shape our minds, and that people learn if they are vividly interested and involved (1996, 2002).

Perhaps the humanistic psychology tradition was made attractive by being open, loving and non-time and -rule bounded. I've drawn on Gestalt practices and theory. I early discovered Carl Rogers' 'profound experience that human beings become increasingly trustworthy once they feel at a deep level that their subjective experience is both respected and progressively understood' (Thorne 1992, p. 26) and principles of the loving relationship between teacher and taught (1951, 1969; Mearns and Thorne 2007). Rogers' 'core conditions' for facilitative counselling and educational practice and my Quaker values helped form my teaching and writing facilitation (see Chapter 3). Humanistic psychologist John Rowan's theory that we are made up of different aspects, or 'subpersonalities' which work together more or less harmoniously, rather than there being a unitary human self (1990), is significant.

Elements of Freudian, along with Jungian, theory underlie Western psychological understanding. A central idea is that dreams, and images arising from hypnagogic states in freewriting and bodywork, give access to hidden psychological areas. I think these areas, instead of being *un-* or *sub*conscious, are like the huge backstage rehearsal spaces, offices, canteens, costume and scenery stores, of Covent Garden Royal Opera House, to which audiences have no access, only experiencing auditorium and public spaces. It takes specialist enquiry to gain admittance to the essential areas beyond the wings of the stage.

JI: Some are seeking solutions in the direction of social cognitive-affective approaches. How do you see their position? More abstraction to word processing through social cognition and metacognition?

GB: We're the quick-fix society. Cognitive-behavioural therapy can get results quickly in straightforward cases. It does use writing, but in a directive manner perhaps. Not, I think, in the open-ended way we're talking about.

> *JI: The Finnish Association for Bibliotherapy (founded 1981), the first European association in our field, followed reading groups in psychiatric hospital libraries 30 years earlier, poetry therapy groups in clinical contexts from the 1970s. Biblio-/poetry therapeutic practice has expanded into education, rehabilitation, counselling, social/community work and personal professional development across the whole life span. Therapeutic and creative writing are continuously in fruitful interaction. Finnish biblio-/poetry therapy books have been edited since 1985, 'Kirjallisuusterapia' [Bibliotherapy] journal published since 1993, continuing education programmes at the University of Helsinki with both of us taking part, you as visiting lecturer. Can you describe special characteristics of this field in the UK?*

GB: UK organisations are: *Lapidus* (www.lapidus.org.uk, founded 1996), promoting creative writing and reading for health and well-being, both personal and community for a membership of writers, medical and healthcare professionals, therapists, artists, and social care and education professionals. The *National Association for Writers in Education* (www. nawe.co.uk, founded 1987, originally *Northern Association*) furthers knowledge, understanding and enjoyment in teaching and learning of creative writing at all levels in schools and higher education, and among freelance writers in schools and community. Both organisations run educational conferences where people also network. There are no continuing education programmes on biblio-/poetry therapy, however much needed. Dynamic, practical work with diverse client groups is happening, despite this lack of specific education, showcased here and in other collections (e.g. Bolton *et al.* 2006, 2010).

> *JI: In* Writing Cures *(Bolton et al. 2004), Jeannie Wright refers to 'the passion of science, the precision of poetry'. What kind of passionate therapeutic writing research do you see in the future? Could there also be electronic futures for therapeutic writing, building networkshops? Your own future projects, plans?*

GB: Oh golly, yes, there could be some wonderfully passionate therapeutic writing research (e.g. Bolton 2008). We need dynamic qualitative methods (like narrative): there's an awful lot of bad science around out there, and technology pretending to be science. Scientific enquiry should be just that: enquiring. And yes, electronic and web-based methods are growing and will develop further (see Chapter 7).

JI: James W. Pennebaker and colleagues produced a kind of 'scientific paradigm' for research on writing therapy, well presented in Writing Cures *(Chapters 1 and 2: Bolton et al. 2004), and replicated/criticised/ re-evaluated quite extensively (e.g. Schoutrop, Lange and Hanewald 2002, pp. 151–157). Trauma writing can reduce psychic and physical symptoms, after only five sessions, and with nobody other than the writer reading and commenting on it. Reading more and more and valuing such reports, I somehow feel ambivalent as to this success: is this 'paradigm' directing writing therapy too much to cognitive control, mastery and solipsism, promising quick and easy relief, and at the same time marginalising imaginative and expressive-emotional intensive activities, and above all the* interactively *and* dialogically creative encounter *(forget the old echo of the 'encounter therapies') in a sharing and caring/'holding' and 'handling' writing therapy situation? I saw that J.K. Wright had the same kind of doubts in* Writing Cures.

Are we forgetting the basic searching that proves a sense of self, a sense of being alive (about which Winnicott [e.g., 1971] spoke): I am alive, I am searching experiences, and enriching myself in the interaction with a not-me. I become seen and read and understood as alive, my existence reflecting back to me from the other, from the not-me. (But is it really me looking there – in a screen, through glasses – or is it as though there isn't really me, as though me is not perceived as 100 per cent existing, but existing somehow 'maimed', without members to remember how to connect? This lack, this desire for what is missing, must be written, expressed in every conceivable way.)… Now I am getting off the track, and at the same time sensing that I am on the track of something missing… I trust that you can reflect on/through this as yet formless mist.

GB: YES. You're right. The kind of writing we recommend as therapeutic is rooted in the creative. Calling it a *tool*, which some do, suggests instrumentality rather than a glorious process in its own right. Associated with this is an anxiety about the potential harm or danger involved in therapeutic writing. David Hart (see Chapter 6) says writing is not 'risk-free', that it 'cannot be tamed'.

The research you refer to, Juhani, is generally instrumental; writers do not reread, nor keep, nor redraft, nor have it responded to. In many trials, completed writings are posted into an anonymous box to be read and processed into statistics by an anonymous researcher. It must be a venting process, valuable of course but only part of writing's potential power. Research is needed into not *does it work?* (because we've known this for millennia), but into what?, why?, how?, when?, where?, who? Listen to this example:

> Clinicians have noted that [cancer] patients [during their last year of life] do not discuss their dying unless they are given a context in which to do so, and that when patients are given opportunities to shift their focus to inner life concerns – existential and relational concerns – then a sense of preparedness for coping with mortality may enhance emotional well-being during this poignant period. When cancer patients focus on the medical at the exclusion of other facets of their lives, we believe that they miss critical opportunities to address the emotional and existential issues that would lead to intimacy with loved ones and closure. These issues are critical to improving quality of life at the end of life and in fact have recently been documented as being core attributes to a 'good death' experience for 81–90% of patients. In the spirit of facilitating this process, we have developed a written expression intervention that seeks to provide patients with a vehicle for processing the emotional and existential issues that arise in the face of the later stages of a terminal illness.
>
> *Schwartz and David 2002, p. 258*

Although the intervention described here was appropriately facilitative, in-depth, creative and valuable, this was a quantitative study on such a tiny sample (12 patients) that the quantitative outcomes are insignificant. Qualitative data, such as patients' personal responses, were sadly not obtained.

> *JI: *) With this asterisk, enchanted by the star- and wordlight, I thank you, Gillie, for letting me, during our moment of meeting, take part in your quest for relational knowledge by feeling, dreaming, learning and loving. I sense the danger zone but also the excitement of sharing the unknown, the potential space, and the flow of self- and co-inventive words. Yes, may the other catch that too: in other words.*

Write!

After your six-minute freewrite (see Chapter 2), reread silently to yourself with care (or store, or even destroy, it). Then share it with a carefully chosen other or group, if appropriate.

1. 'Reading the Psalms, or Hardy, or Gerard Manley Hopkins's 'terrible sonnets' (1953) can be cathartic. By attending to the cry of another we articulate our own cries, frame them, contain them, and feel less stranded' (Blake Morrison 2008a, p. 6).

   ○ Reread a loved book or poem which you appreciate. Write a letter (not for sending) to the author, telling them what you feel, and in what ways it has influenced you.

   ○ Write their reply.

2. Do something you've never done before!

   ○ If you can't think of anything, you must make yourself. If you still can't think of anything: next time you wake in the night, ask your dream self or ask other people for ideas. AND DO IT!

   ○ And of course write about the experience: what you did and what it felt like and so on.

   ○ Write about it in the third person, as if you were a character with a fictional name.

3. Write something of a type you've never written before. Go through your favourite books (biography, poetry, fiction, drama, memoir) and choose a form you've never written before (I'll write a whodunnit perhaps...).

4. Think about yourself at different times of your life. Ask these questions of your former, or future, self (e.g. the child, bold rebellious teenager, patient parent, wise senior), and write the replies:

   ○ What do you want?

   ○ What's stopping you from getting this?

   ○ What might you do to get it?

   ○ Who could help you?

   ○ What could help you?

Appendix: Writing Exercises by Theme

Note: Asterisks denote a fully explained exercise.

References

Abse, D. (2007) *The Presence*. London: Vintage.

Abse, D. (1998) 'More than a green placebo.' *The Lancet 351*, 9099.

Adams, R.K. (2011) *RKA Writing*. Available at www.rkawriting.co.uk, accessed on 12 May 2011.

Anderson, C. M. and MacCurdy, M. M. (2000) *Writing and Healing: Toward an Informed Practice*. Urbana, IL. The National Council of Teachers of English.

Angwyn, R. (2010) 'Speaking for the thunder and the rain.' *Writing in Education 51*, Summer, 21–24.

Anthony, K. (2000) 'Counselling in cyberspace.' *Counselling Journal 11*, 10, 625–627.

Anthony, K. and Goss, S. (2009) *Guidelines for Online Counselling and Psychotherapy Including Guidelines for Online Supervision* (3rd Edition). Lutterworth: BACP.

Anthony, K. and Nagel, D. M. (2010) *Therapy Online [A Practical Guide]*. London: Sage.

Anthony, K., Nagel, D. M. and Goss, S. (eds) (2010) *The Use of Technology in Mental Health: Applications, Ethics and Practice*. Springfield, IL: C. C. Thomas.

Appelfeld, A. (2005) 'One man's road to freedom: Interviewed by H Anderson.' *Observer Review*, 21 August, p. 15.

Aristotle (1996) *Poetics* (trans. M. Heath). London: Penguin.

Astley, N. (ed.) (2004) *Being Alive: The Sequel to Staying Alive*. Tarset, Northumberland: Bloodaxe.

Astley, N. (ed.) (2002) *Staying Alive: Real Poems for Unreal Times*. Tarset, Northumberland: Bloodaxe.

BACP (2010) *Ethical Framework for Good Practice in Counselling and Psychotherapy*. BACP: Rugby. http://www.bacp.co.uk/ethical_framework/ [accessed 2 February 2011].

Bakhtin, M. (1981) 'Discourse in the Novel' (trans. C. Emerson and M. Holquist). In M. Holquist (ed.) *The Dialogic Imagination: Four Essays by M. M. Bakhtin*. Austin, TX: University of Texas Press.

Ballard, J. G. (2008) *Miracles of Life: An Autobiography*. London: Fourth Estate.

Ballard, J. G. (1984) *Empire of the Sun*. London: Victor Gollancz.

Beauman, S. (2002) 'Spell it out.' *The Guardian Saturday Review*, 13 July, p. 32.

Bennett, A. (2009) 'Alan Bennett writes about his new play, 'The Habit of Art'.' *London Review Books*, 5 November, pp. 15–17.

Bolton, G. (2010) *Reflective Practice Writing and Professional Development* (3rd Edition. London: Sage Publications.

Bolton, G. (2009) 'Writing values: Reflective practice writing.' *The Lancet 374*, 20–21.

Bolton, G. (2008) "Writing is a way of saying things I can't say.' Therapeutic creative writing: A qualitative study of its value to people with cancer cared for in cancer and palliative health care.' *Journal of Medical Ethics: Medical Humanities 34*, 1, 40–46.

Bolton, G. (2007) 'Reflections in Writing.' In V. Field and Z. Ansari (eds) *Prompted to Write.* Truro, Cornwall: Fal Publications.

Bolton, G. (2006) 'My magical mystery tour.' *Lapidus Quarterly*, Summer, pp. 4–7.

Bolton, G. (2003) 'Around the Slices of Herself.' In K. Etherington (ed.) *Transformations: Healing the Wounds of Childhood Trauma.* London: Jessica Kingsley Publishers.

Bolton, G. (2001) 'Open the Box: Writing a Therapeutic Space.' In P. Miller (ed.) *BAC Counselling Reader, Vol 2.* London: Sage Publications.

Bolton, G. (2000a) 'Red Shoes (poem).' *British Journal of General Practice 50*, 453, 351.

Bolton, G. (1999a) *The Therapeutic Potential of Creative Writing: Writing Myself.* London: Jessica Kingsley Publishers.

Bolton, G. (1999b) 'Stories at work: Reflective writing for practitioners.' *The Lancet 354*, 243–245.

Bolton, G. (1998) 'Stories of Dying.' In T. Greenhalgh and B. Hurwitz (eds) *Narrative Based Medicine: Dialogue and Discourse in Clinical Practice.* London: BMJ Publications

Bolton, G. (1994) *Writing the Spirit: Material for Spiritual Exploration.* London: Quaker Resources for Learning.

Bolton, G. (1991) 'Between the Slices (poetry sequence).' *Bete Noire 10/11*, 96–108. Hull: Hull University.

Bolton, G. and Padfield, D.J. (1996) *Reflections in Writing* (poetry/prose anthology). Kelso: Curlew Press.

Bolton, G., Field, V. and Thompson, K. (2010) *Writing Routes: A Resource Handbook of Therapeutic Writing.* London: Jessica Kingsley Publishers.

Bolton, G., Field, V. and Thompson, K. (eds) (2006) *Writing Works: A Resource Handbook for Therapeutic Writing Workshops and Activities.* London: Jessica Kingsley Publishers.

Bolton, G., Gelipter, D. and Nelson, P. (2000) 'Keep taking the words: Therapeutic writing in primary care.' *British Journal of General Practice 50*, 450, 80–81.

Bolton, G., Howlett, S., Lago, C. and Wright, J. K. (eds) (2004) *Writing Cures: An Introductory Handbook of Writing in Counselling and Psychotherapy.* New York: Brunner-Routledge.

Brody, H. (2003) *Stories of Sickness* (2nd Edition). Oxford: Oxford University Press.

Brown, J. (1993) *Thinking Egg.* Todmorden, Lancashire: Littlewood Arc.

Bruner, J. (2002) *Making Stories: Law, Literature, Life.* Cambridge, MA.: Harvard University Press.

Bruner, J. (1996) *The Culture of Education.* Cambridge, MA: Harvard University Press.

Burkeman, O. (2010) 'Can worries really be sealed in an envelope?' *The Guardian Weekend*, 9 October, p. 91.

Burningham, J. (1978) *Would You Rather…* London: Jonathan Cape.

Burton, C. M. and King, L. A. (2004) 'The health benefits of writing about intensely positive experiences.' *Journal of Research in Personality 38*, 150–163.

Carroll, L. (1954 [1865]) *Alice in Wonderland.* London: J. M. Dent.

Carson, R. (1994) 'Teaching ethics in the context of the medical humanities.' *Journal of Medical Ethics 20*, 4, 235–238.

Castenada, C. (1993) *The Art of Dreaming.* London: HarperCollins.

Charon, R. (2006) *Narrative Medicine: Honouring the Stories of Sickness.* New York: Oxford University Press.

Charon, R. (2001) 'Narrative medicine: Form, function and ethics.' *Annals of Internal Medicine 134*, 1, 83–87.

Charon, R. and Montello, M. (2002) *Stories Matter: The Role of Narrative in Medical Ethics.* New York: Routledge.

Cixous, H. (1991) *Coming to Writing and Other Essays* (ed. D. Jenson). Cambridge, MA: Harvard University Press.

Cobb, M. (2001) *The Dying Soul: Spiritual Care at the End of Life.* Buckingham, UK: Open University Press.

Coleridge, S. T. ([1992] 1817) *Biographia Literaria.* London: Dent.

Cooper, P. (2009) 'Playground of the page.' *Mental Health,* p. 42.

Coulehan, J. (1997) 'Empathy, passion and imagination: A medical triptych.' *Journal of Medical Humanities 18,* 99–110.

Coulehan, J. (1995) 'Tenderness and steadiness: Emotions in medical practice.' *Literature and Medicine 14,* 222–236.

Cresswell, J. D., Lam, S., Stanton, A. L., Taylor, S. E., Bower, J. E. and Sherman, D. K. (2007) 'Does self-affirmation, cognitive processing or discovery of meaning explain cancer-related health benefits of expressive writing?' *Personality and Social Psychology Bulletin 33,* 238–250.

Crossley-Holland, K. (1992) 'The Seafarer.' In J. Raban, *The Oxford Book of the Sea.* Oxford: Oxford University Press.

Department of Health (2000) *An Organization with a Memory: Report on an Expert Group on Learning from Adverse Events in the NHS.* London: The Stationery Office.

Dewey, J. (1988 [1922]) 'Human Nature and Conduct.' In J. A. Boydstone (ed.) *John Dewey: The Middle Works 1899–1924, Vol 14.* Carbondale: S. Illinois University Press.

Dewey, J. (1910) *How We Think.* Mineola, New York: Dover Publications.

Diaghilev, S. (2010) Quoted in A. O'Hagan, 'Diaghilev: Lord of the Dance.' *Guardian Review,* 9 October, pp. 16–17.

Diamond, J. (1998) *C Because Cowards get Cancer Too.* London: Random House.

Didion, J. (1968) *Slouching towards Bethlehem.* London: Penguin.

Diski, J. (1998) *Don't.* London: Granta Books.

Dixon, D. M., Sweeney, K. G. and Periera Gray, D. J. (1999) 'The physician-healer: Ancient magic or modern science?' *British Journal of General Practice 49,* 441, 309–312.

Doty, M. (2003) Personal communication – response to question following a lecture at King's College London.

Doty, M. (1996) *Heaven's Coast: A Memoir.* New York: HarperCollins.

Duncker, P. (2002) *Writing on the Wall.* London: Pandora Press.

Eagleton, T. (2008) 'Coruscating on thin ice.' *London Review of Books,* 24 January, pp. 19–20.

Einstein, A. (2002 [1929]) 'Interview with Sylvester Viereck 1929, Berlin.' Quoted by K. Taylor, 'When fact and fantasy collide.' *Times Higher Educational Supplement,* 20/27 December, p. viii.

Einstein, A. (1973) *Ideas and Opinions.* London: Souvenir Press.

Eisner, E. (1985) *Beyond Creating: The Place for Art in America's Schools.* Los Angeles: Getty Center for Education in Art.

Elbow, P. (1981) *Writing with Power: Techniques for Mastering the Writing Process.* Oxford: Oxford University Press.

Eliot, T. S. (1936) *Collected Poems (The Four Quartets).* London: Faber.

Etter, C. (2009) 'A Birthmother's Catechism.' In *The Son.* Hunstanton, Norfolk: Oystercatcher Press.

Evison, R. (2002) 'Helping Individuals Manage Emotional Response.' In R. L. Payne and C. L. Cooper (eds) *Emotions at Work: Theory, Research and Applications in Management.* London: Wiley and Sons.

Fanthorpe, U. A. (1996) In G. Bolton and D. Padfield, *Reflections in Writing* (poetry/prose anthology). Kelso: Curlew Press.

Flint, R. (2000) 'Fragile Space – Therapeutic Writing and the Word.' In F. Sampson (ed.) *Writing in Health and Social Care*. London: Jessica Kingsley Publishers.

Flood, C. (2008) 'Women and zines' *Lapidus Journal*, Autumn, pp. 9–14.

Forster, M. (1996) *Hidden Lives: A Family Memoir*. London: Penguin.

Foucault, M. (1992 [1984]) *The History of Sexuality Vol 2: The Use of Pleasure*. Trans. R. Hurley. Harmondsworth: Penguin.

Foucault, M. (1990 [1976]) *The History of Sexuality Vol 1: An Introduction*. Trans. R. Hurley. Harmondsworth: Penguin.

Frank, A. (2009) 'The Necessity and Dangers of Illness Narratives, Especially at the End of Life.' In Y. Gunaratnam and D. Oliviere (eds) *Narrative and Stories in Health Care: Illness, Dying and Bereavement*. Oxford: Oxford University Press.

Frank, A. (2000) 'Narratives of illness and care: Why now?' Paper presented at *Narrative Matters: Personal Essays and the Making of Health Policy* seminar, March, Virginia.

Frank, A. (1995) *The Wounded Storyteller: Body, Illness and Ethics*. Chicago: University of Chicago Press.

Freud, S. (1893) 'Charcot.' *The Standard Edition of the Complete Psychological Works of Sigmund Freud, Vol. 3*. London: The Hogarth Press.

Frost, C. and King, N. (2000) 'Physician heal thyself: The emotional demands of general practice.' *Proceedings of the British Psychological Society's Occupational Psychology Conference*, January, 5–7 Brighton.

Fulleylove, L. (2008) 'The Prison and the Sea.' *Obsessed with Pipework, 44*, 28.

Furman, R. (2007) 'The mundane, the existential, and the poetic.' *Journal of Poetry Therapy 20*, 3, 163–180.

Gao, X. (2009) 'Interview by Maya Jaggi.' *The Guardian Review*, 2 October, pp. 10–11.

Goleman, D. (1995) *Emotional Intelligence: Why it can Matter more than IQ*. London: Bloomsbury.

Goss, S. and Ferns, J. (2010) 'Using Cell/Mobile Phone SMS to Enhance Client Crisis and Peer Support.' In K. Anthony, D. M. Nagel and S. Goss (eds) *The Use of Technology in Mental Health, Applications, Ethics and Practice*. Springfield, IL: C. C. Thomas.

Greer, B. (2009) 'Something of the night' *The Author*, Winter, pp. 133–134.

Gross, P. (2006) 'No art form is an island.' *Writing in Education, Journal of the National Association of Writers in Education 40*, Winter, p. 23.

Halliburton, R. (2010) 'Why the arts are needed, just as much as doctors.' *Time Out*, 30 September, pp. 10–11.

Hamberger, R. (2007) *Torso: A Poetry Collection*. Bradford: Redbeck.

Hannay, D. and Bolton, G. (2000) 'Therapeutic writing in primary care: A feasibility study.' *Primary Care Psychiatry 5*, 157–160.

Heaney, S. (2008) '"To set the darkness echoing': Interview with Dennis O'Driscoll.' *The Guardian Saturday Review*, 8 November 2008, pp. 2–4.

Heaney, S. (2004) 'In gratitude for the gifts' *Guardian Review*, 11 September, pp. 4–6.

Heaney, S. (1980a) *Selected Prose 1968–1978*. London: Faber & Faber.

Heaney, S. (1980b) *Selected Poems* ('Digging'). London: Faber and Faber.

Heitsch, D. B. (2000) 'Approaching death by writing: Montaigne's essays and the literature of consolation.' *Literature and Medicine 19*, 1, 96–106.

Help the Hospices (2005) *Guidelines for Arts Therapies and the Arts in Palliative Care Settings*. London: Hospice Information.

Hillman, J. (1997) *Archetypal Psychology*. Putnam, CT: Spring Publications.

Hillman, J. (1986) *Healing Fictions*. Putnam, CT: Spring Publications.

Hilse, C., Griffiths, S. and Corr, S. (2007) 'The impact of participating in a poetry workshop.' *British Journal of Occupational Therapy 70*, 10, 431–438.

Hippocrates (1950) (trans. J. Chadwick and W. N. I. Mann) *Hippocratic Writings*. Harmondsworth: Penguin.

Hirst, D. (2006) 'Death becomes him' *London Time Out*, 22 November, pp. 46–47.

Holmes, R. (1989) *Coleridge: Early Visions*. London: HarperCollins.

Hopkins, G. M. (1953) *Poems and Prose*, ed. W. H. Gardner. Harmondsworth: Penguin.

Hoy, M. (ed.) (undated) Cry Baby in *Hard Stuff 2*. Sheffield: Families and Friends of Drug Misusers Project (Hi RISE Publications), unpaginated.

Hughes, T. (1995) *Interview Paris Review*, http://stinfwww.informatik.uni-Leipzig. de/~beckmann/plath/thint.html [accessed 8 September 2004; no longer available]

Hughes, T. (1982) 'Foreword.' In S. Brownjohn, *What Rhymes with Secret?* London: Hodder and Stoughton.

Hughes, T. (1967) *Poetry in the Making* ('The Thought Fox'). London: Faber and Faber.

Hunt, C. (2006) 'Guided Fantasy on the Reader-in-the-Writing-Process.' In C. Hunt and F. Sampson *Writing Self and Reflexivity*. Basingstoke: Palgrave Macmillan.

Hunt, C. and Sampson, F. (2006) *Writing Self and Reflexivity*. Basingstoke: Palgrave Macmillan.

Hunt, C. and Sampson, F. (eds) (1998) *The Self on the Page: Theory and Practice of Writing in Personal Development*. London: Jessica Kingsley Publishers.

Kani, J. (2007) *Front Row* BBC Radio 4, London, 1 February.

Karimath, C., Chirambo, C., Al-Farah, I. Wilde, J., T. B., Chihana, T. and Dickenson, V. (2010) *Different Cultures. One World: Women's Voices from South Yorkshire*. Barnsley: Northern College.

Keats, J. (2000 [1817] p. 1019) Letter to George and Thomas Keats, Sunday 21st December. In 'D. Wu and D. Miall (eds)' *Romanticism: An Anthology*. Chichester: Wiley-Blackwell.

Keats, J. (1818) Letter to John Taylor, 27 February.

Knight, J. (2010) 'The Magic Trick.' In D. Abse, Prof Sir B. Keogh and J. Naughtie (eds) *The Hippocrates Prize*. Oxford: Top Edge Press.

Kotre, J. (1995) *White Gloves: How We Create Ourselves Through Memory*. New York: The Free Press.

Laitinen, I. and Ettorre, E. (2007) 'Writing of sadness and pain: Diary work with depressed women in Finland.' *Journal of Poetry Therapy 20*, 1, 3–20.

Lao Tsu (1973) (trans. Gia Fu Feng and J. English) *Tao Te Ching*. London: Wildwood House.

Lester, D. and Terry, R. (1992) 'The use of poetry therapy: Lessons from the life of Anne Sexton.' *The Arts in Psychotherapy 19*, 47–52.

Lévi-Strauss, C. (1966) *The Savage Mind*. Chicago: University of Chicago Press.

Ludlow, C. (2008) *Shadows in Wonderland: A Hospital Odyssey*. London: Hammersmith Press.

McAdams, D. P. (1993) *The Stories We Live By: Personal Myths and the Making of the Self*. New York: William C. Morrow and Co.

McCabe, A., Peterson, C. and Connors, D. (2006) 'Attachment security and narrative elaboration.' *International Journal of Behaviour Therapy 30*, 398–409.

Matthews, G. (1990) *Philosophy and the Young Child*. Cambridge, MA: Harvard University Press.

Mearns, D. and Thorne, B. (2007) *Person-Centred Counseling in Action*. (3rd Edition). London: Sage.

Middlebrook, D. W. (1992) *Anne Sexton: A Biography*. London: Virago.

Miller, A. (1987) *The Drama of Being a Child*. London: Virago.

Milne, A. A. (1958) *The World of Pooh*. London: Methuen.

Milner, M. (1987) *Eternity's Sunrise: A Way of Keeping a Diary*. London: Virago.

Milner, M. (1971 [1950]) *On Not Being Able to Paint*. London: Heinemann.

Modell, A. H. (1997) 'Reflections on metaphor and affects.' *Annals of Psychoanalysis 25*, 219–233.

Montgomery-Hunter, K. (1991) *Doctor's Stories: The Narrative Structure of Medical Knowledge.* Princeton: Princeton University Press.

More, E. S. (1996) 'Empathy as an hermeneutic practice.' *Theoretical Medicine 17*, 243–254.

Morgan, N. P. (2009) 'Writing – it's good for you.' *Coping with Cancer Magazine*, March/April, p. 29.

Morrison, B. (2008a) 'The reading cure.' *Guardian Review*, 5 January, pp. 4–6.

Morrison, B. (2008b) 'Interview with Rebecca Atherton' *Inside Out 1*, 1, 6–8.

Motion, A (2009) 'Yet once more O ye laurels' *The Guardian Saturday Review* 21 March, pp. 2–4.

Motion, A. (2006) *In the Blood: A Memoir of My Childhood.* London: Faber and Faber.

Munno, A. (2006) 'A complaint which changed my practice.' *British Medical Journal 332*, 1092.

Munoz, J. (2008) Notes from Tate Modern Gallery's Juan Munoz Retrospective Exhbition, curated by Sheena Wagstaff, 27 April.

Nagel, D. M. and Anthony, K. (2009) 'Writing therapy using new technologies – The art of blogging.' *Journal of Poetry Therapy 22*, 1, 41–45.

Neruda, P. (1961) *Elementary Odes of Pablo Neruda*, ed. G. Massa. San Francisco: Cypress Books.

NHS Estates (2002) *The Art of Good Health: Using Visual Arts in Healthcare.* London: NHS Estates.

O'Farrell, M. (2009) 'The Yellow Wallpaper' *The Guardian 2*, 9 January, pp. 18–19.

Oliver, M. (1992) 'The Summer Day.' In *New and Selected Poems.* Boston, MA: Beacon Press.

Opher, S. and Wills, E. (2004) 'Workout with words – A poetry project in a GP surgery.' *British Journal of General Practice 54*, 499, 156–157.

Opher, S. and Wills, E. (2003) *Doorways: Poems from May Lane Surgery.* Dursley, Gloucestershire, UK: May Lane Surgery.

Oz, A. (2005) 'The devil's progress.' *Guardian Saturday Review*, 3 September, pp. 4–5.

Padfield, D. (2003) *Perceptions of Pain.* Stockport: Dewi Lewis Publishing.

Paterson, D. (2010) ''Lust in action': Shakespeare's sonnets.' *The Guardian Review Section*, 16 October, pp. 2–4.

Pehrsson, D.-E. and Pehrsson, R. S. (2007) 'Language fantasy approach: A therapeutic intervention by creating myths with children.' *Journal of Poetry Therapy 20*, 1, 41–49.

Pennebaker, J. W. (2000) 'Telling stories: The health benefits of narrative.' *Literature and Medicine 19*, 1, 3–18.

Pennebaker, J. W. and Chung, C. K. (2007) 'Expressive Writing, Emotional Upheavals, and Health.' In H. Friedman and R. Silver (eds) *Handbook of Health Psychology.* New York: Oxford University Press.

Peterkin, A. D. and Prettyman, A. A. (2009) 'Finding a voice: Revisiting the history of therapeutic writing.' *Journal of Medical Ethics: Medical Humanities 35*, 2, 80–88.

Petrone, M. (2001) 'The Healing Touch.' In D. Kirklin and R. Richardson (eds) *Medical Humanities: A Practical Introduction.* London: Royal College of Physicians.

Pierce, R. (2010) *Voices that Care*, Writer at Work Project, B.A. Hons in Creative Writing, Liverpool John Moores University (Unpublished).

Plath, S. (1981) *Collected Poems.* London: Faber and Faber.

Progoff, I. (1975) *At a Journal Workshop.* New York: Dialogue House Library.

Pullman, P. (1995) *His Dark Materials.* London: Scholastic.

Rainer, T. (1978) *The New Diary: How to Use a Journal for Self-Guidance and Expanded Creativity.* London: Angus and Robertson.

Reid, C. (2009) *A Scattering.* Oxford: Areté Books.

Rich, A. (2006) 'Legislators of the world.' *The Guardian Review*, 18 November, pp. 2–4.

Rich, A. (1995) *What is Found There: Notebooks on Poetry and Politics.* London: Virago.

Riesman, C. K. (1993) *Narrative Analysis.* London: Sage Publications.

Roethke, T. (1991) Collected Poems. London: Faber.

Rogers, C. R. (1969) Freedom to Learn: A View of What Education Might Become. Columbus, OH: Charles E. Merrill.

Rogers, C. R. (1951) Client-Centered Therapy: Its Current Practice, Implications, and Theory. Boston: Houghton Mifflin.

Rowan, J. (1990) Subpersonalities: The People Inside Us. London: Routledge.

Royal College of Nursing (2000) Clinical Governance: How Can Nurses Get Involved? London: RCN.

Sartre, J.-P. (1963 [1938]) Nausea. Harmondsworth: Penguin.

Schneiderman, H. (1995) 'Editorial: Literature, humanities and the internist.' Annals of Internal Medicine 122, 8, 618–619.

Schoutrop, M. J. A., Lange, A. and Hanewald, G. (2002) 'Structured writing and processing major stressful events: A controlled trial.' Psychotherapy and Psychosomatics 71, 3, 151–157.

Schwartz, C. E. and David, E. (2002) 'To Everything There is a Season: A Written Expression Intervention for Closure at the End of Life.' In S. Lepore and J. M. Smyth (eds) The Writing Cure. Washington DC: American Psychological Association.

Shea, V. (1994) Netiquette. San Francisco: Albion Books.

Shuttle, P. (2008) 'Nest Preface Poem.' In G. Bolton (ed.) Dying, Bereavement and the Healing Arts. London: Jessica Kingsley Publishers.

Shuttle, P. (2006) Redgrove's Wife. Northumberland: Bloodaxe Books.

Smith, R. (2002) 'Spend (slightly) less on health and more on the arts.' British Medical Journal 325, 1432–1433.

Smyth, J. M. (1999) 'Written emotional expression: Effect sizes, outcome types, and moderating variables.' Journal of Consulting and Clinical Psychology 66, 174–184.

Sorrell, M. (1996) 'The Words Came Tumbling Out.' In G. Bolton and D. Padfield (eds) Reflections in Writing. Kelso, Scotland: Curlew Productions.

Spiegel, D. (1999) 'Editorial. Healing words: Emotional expression and disease outcome.' Journal of the American Medical Association 281, 14, 1328–1329.

Sprackland, J. (2003) Hard Water. London: Cape Poetry.

Staricoff, R. L. (2004) Arts in Health: A Review of the Medical Literature. London: The Arts Council of England.

Steel, M. (2010) Do You Realize? A Story of Love and Grief and the Colours of Existence. Ropley, Hampshire, UK: O Books (John Hunt Publishing).

Stone, E. (1998) Black Sheep and Kissing Cousins: How Our Family Stories Shape Us. New York: Times Books.

Stoner, A. (2010) Weight and Flight. Kingsbridge, Devon, UK: Overstep Books.

Stoner, A. and Wright, M. (2005) Once in a Blue Moon: The Mermaid's Tail. Truro UK: Fal Publications.

Stubbersfield, A. (2006) Joking Apart: A Poetry Collection. Wales: The Collective Press.

Stuckey, H. L. and Nobel, J. (2010) 'The connection between art, healing, and public health: A review of current literature.' American Journal of Public Health 100, 2, 254–263.

Suler, J. (2004) 'The online disinhibition effect.' CyberPsychology and Behavior 7, 3, 321–326.

Suler, J. (1997) 'Text-talk: Psychological dynamics of online synchronous conversations in text-driven chat environments.' In Psychology of CyberSpace, www.rider.edu/suler/psycyber/psycyber.html [accessed 15 August 2010].

Sweeney, B. (1998) 'The place of the humanities in the education of a doctor: The James Mackenzie lecture.' British Journal of General Practice 48, 998–1102.

Tan, L. (2008) 'Psychotherapy 2.0: MySpace: Blogging as self therapy.' American Journal of Psychotherapy 62, 2, 142–163.

Tasker, M. (2005) 'Something inside so strong…' *Hospice Information Bulletin 4*, 3, 1–2.

Thomas, D. (2003) 'Do Not Go Gentle.' In N. Astley (ed.) *Do Not Go Gentle: Poems for Funerals*. Tarset, Northumberland: Bloodaxe Books.

Thorne, B. (1992) *Carl Rogers*. London: Sage.

Thorpe, A. (2007) 'Strange hells.' *Guardian Saturday Review*, 10 November, p. 21.

Tolstoy, L. (1991) Qutoed in H. Exley (ed.) *A Writer's Notebook*. London: Exley.

Tufford, L. (2009) 'Healing the pain of infertility through poetry.' *Journal of Poetry Therapy 22*, 1, 1–9.

Twain, M. (2009) Quoted by Rosemary Hill in 'The past through a lens.' *The Guardian Review*, 28 November, pp. 16–17.

Twycross, R. (2005) 'Death without suffering?' *European Journal of Palliative Care 12*, 2, Supplement, 5–7.

Untermeyer, L. (1963) '*January 1, 1916*': *The Letters of Robert Frost to Louis Untermeyer*. New York: Holt, Rinehart, and Winston.

Verghese, A. (2001) 'The physician as storyteller.' *Annals of Internal Medicine 135*, 11, 1012–1017.

Whelan, B. (2009) 'Salt and vinegar: Stories from Brighton.' *Lapidus Journal*, Spring, p. 14.

White, M. (2004) 'Arts in Mental Health for Social Inclusion: Towards a Framework for Programme Evaluation.' In J. Cowling (ed.) *For Art's Sake – Society and the Arts in the 21st Century*. London: Institute of Public Policy Research.

Williams, N. (2008) 'How I write.' *Time Out*, 25 September, p. 75.

Williams, W. C. (1976 [1944]) 'A Sort of Song.' In *Selected Poems* (edited and introduction by C. Tomlinson). London: Penguin Books.

Williamson, M. (1996) *A Return to Love: Reflections on the Principles of a Course in Miracles*. London: Thorsons.

Wills, E. (2008) *Developing the Negative*. Norwich, UK: Rialto.

Winnicott, D. W. (1971) *Playing and Reality*. London: Tavistock Publications.

Woolf, V. (1982 [1980]) *The Diary of Virginia Woolf: Volume 3 1925–30*. London: Penguin (28 November 1928).

Woolf, V. (1977, 1978, 1980) *The Diary of Virginia Woolf: Volumes 1, 2 and 3*. London: Hogarth Press.

Woolf, V. (1976) (ed. J. Schulkind) *Moments of Being: A Collection of Autobiographical Writings*. San Diego, CA: Harcourt Brace and Company.

Wordsworth, W. ([2004] 1880) *The Prelude*. In D. Walford Davies (ed.) *Selected Poems* London: Dent.

Wright, J. (2009) 'Dialogical journal writing as 'self-therapy': 'I matter'.' *Counselling and Psychotherapy Research 9*, 4, 235–240.

Wright, J. K. (2005a) 'Writing therapy in brief workplace counselling.' *Counselling and Psychotherapy Research 5*, 111–119.

Wright, J. K. (2005b) 'Writing on prescription? Using writing in brief therapy.' *Healthcare Counselling and Psychotherapy Journal*, October, pp. 28–30.

Wright, J. K. (2003) 'Five women talk about work-related brief therapy and therapeutic writing.' *Counselling and Psychotherapy Research 3*, 3, 204–209.

Wright, J. and Bolton, G. (2012) *Personal Development Writing in Counselling and Psychotherapy: How to Write a Reflective Journal*. London: Sage Publications.

Wright, J. K. and Ranby, P. (2009) ''Composing myself on paper': Personal journal writing and feminist influences.' *Women's Studies Journal 23*, 2, 57–67.

Xinran (2003) *The Good Women of China* (trans. E Tyldesley). London: Vintage.

Yeats, W.B. (1899) *The Wind Among the Reeds*. London: Elkin Matthews.

Subject Index

Author Index